The Criminal Cases Review Comm[

CW00674562

The Criminal Cases Review Commission

Hope for the Innocent?

Edited by

Michael Naughton
University of Bristol, UK

Forewords by

C. Ronald Huff
University of California, Irvine, USA

Michael Mansfield, QC
Tooks Chambers, UK

and

Michael Zander
London School of Economics, UK

First published in hardback in 2009 by
PALGRAVE MACMILLAN
First published in paperback 2012

Palgrave Macmillan in the UK is an imprint of Macmillan Publishers Limited,
registered in England, company number 785998, of Houndmills, Basingstoke,
Hampshire RG21 6XS.

Palgrave Macmillan in the US is a division of St Martin's Press LLC,
175 Fifth Avenue, New York, NY 10010.

Palgrave Macmillan is the global academic imprint of the above companies
and has companies and representatives throughout the world.

Palgrave® and Macmillan® are registered trademarks in the United States,
the United Kingdom, Europe and other countries.

ISBN 978–0–230–21938–0   hardback
ISBN 978–0–230–39061–4   paperback

This book is printed on paper suitable for recycling and made from fully
managed and sustained forest sources. Logging, pulping and manufacturing
processes are expected to conform to the environmental regulations of the
country of origin.

A catalogue record for this book is available from the British Library.

A catalog record for this book is available from the Library of Congress.

10   9   8   7   6   5   4   3   2   1
18   17   16   15   14   13   12   11   10   09

Printed and bound in Great Britain by
CPI Antony Rowe, Chippenham and Eastbourne

Dedicated to innocent victims of wrongful conviction

Contents

Acknowledgements

This book is an outgrowth of the Inaugural Innocence Network UK (INUK) Symposium to mark the 10th anniversary of the Criminal Cases Review Commission (CCRC), held at the University of Bristol on 31 March 2007, at which papers that form the chapters were presented and discussed. Thank you to those who have contributed to the book and the collaborative spirit that has been shown in working together on this project. Thank you to Paddy Joe Hill, Mike O' Brien, Paul Blackburn, Gary Mills and Tony Poole for their participation in the Symposium: in many ways this book is motivated in recognition of your experiences and ongoing struggles. Thank you to Gabe Tan for the many vital tasks that she performed as the editorial assistant and for the comments that she made following a meticulous review of the entire manuscript. Thank you, too, to Michael Zander and Gregor McLennan for their encouraging and constructive feedback on the manuscript. Finally, thank you to Amanda, David and Olivia for understanding my absences whilst I was assembling the pieces of this book.

MICHAEL NAUGHTON

Notes on the Contributors

Steven Bird established Bird & Co. solicitors in October 2000. He specializes in serious criminal cases and deals with potential miscarriages of justice and other matters in the Court of Appeal (Criminal Division) (CACD) or by way of application to the Criminal Cases Review Commission (CCRC). He also represents victims of miscarriages of justice in claims for compensation from the Home Office. Steven is a member of several professional bodies, including the Criminal Appeal Lawyers Association (CALA) where he is a committee member and treasurer. He was a police station duty solicitor from 1992 to 2004 and is a member of the Funding Review Committee and Costs Appeal Committee for the Legal Services Commission.

Kathryn Campbell is Associate Professor in the Department of Criminology at the University of Ottawa, Ontario, Canada. Professor Campbell's research focus has been mainly on issues of social justice, including explorations of miscarriages of justice, youth justice and Aboriginal conceptions of justice. She has written extensively on the Canadian experience of wrongful convictions and has published several articles and book chapters on this topic. She is the author of *Miscarriages of Justice in Canada: Causes, Responses, Remedies* (2009).

Dennis Eady is the Campaign Officer for South Wales Against Wrongful Convictions, a derivative of South Wales Liberty (SWL). Since its establishment, members of the organization have, in a few cases, assisted the CCRC and applications for criminal appeals by providing case analyses and liaison work. The group has also made numerous responses to government consultations on criminal justice issues and has lobbied the authorities in relation to a number of perceived injustices at national level.

Andrew Green is the co-founder of United Against Injustice (UAI), a federal organization of miscarriage of justice victim-support groups. Andrew also co-founded INNOCENT, a Manchester based victim-support organization made up of families, friends and supporters of prisoners alleging that they have been wrongly convicted. He is the author of *Power, Resistance, Knowledge*.

C. Ronald Huff is Professor of Criminology, Law and Society as well as Sociology and previously served as Dean (1999–2009) of the School of Social Ecology at University of California, Irvine, USA. Prior to joining the UCI faculty in 1999, he taught at The Ohio State University, USA (1979–1999), where he directed the John Glenn School of Public Affairs and the Criminal Justice Research Center; at Purdue University, USA (1976–1999); and at UC Irvine, USA (1974–1976). He was also a Visiting Professor at the University of Hawaii, USA (1995). The most recent of his 12 books include *Wrongful*

Conviction: International Perspectives on Miscarriages of Justice; Youth Violence: Prevention, Intervention, and Social Policy; Gangs in America (3 editions); and *Convicted but Innocent: Wrongful Conviction and Public Policy* (which won an Academic Book of the Year Award).

Hazel Kierle has over 20 years' experience as a legal assistant in criminal and civil cases. She was also the regional manager for Victim Support in the Midlands. For the last ten years she has been the Director of Miscarriages of Justice Organisation (MOJO) (England and Wales). MOJO is a human-rights-based organization that was founded in 1999 by Paddy Joe Hill (of the Birmingham Six case) and Mike O'Brien (of the Cardiff Newsagent Three case) to support miscarriage of justice victims and their families, and to attempt to redress the lack of welfare and aftercare provision for the wrongly imprisoned. MOJO (England and Wales) is affiliated to MOJO (Scotland) set up by Paddy Joe Hill and John McManus, a registered charity that is funded by the Scottish Executive to deliver aftercare services to qualifying clients.

Kevin Kerrigan is a Reader and Associate Dean at the School of Law, Northumbria University. He is also a practising solicitor and Human Rights Act consultant with experience of conducting criminal and human rights cases in courts at all levels. His teaching and research interests are in the fields of criminal litigation, human rights and legal education. In particular, he has an active interest in clinical legal education and runs a criminal appeal clinic at Northumbria University's Student Law Office. He has written numerous articles and text books and delivered papers at academic conferences and training courses for professionals, including the police, lawyers, social workers, mental health professionals and court clerks.

Glyn Maddocks is a Partner and the Head of the Civil Litigation Department of Gabb & Co. He specializes in all aspects of civil litigation, including, and in particular, personal injury, clinical negligence, public law and judicial review. Glyn has developed a special expertise in miscarriage of justice cases after initially having cases referred to him by Liberty's Criminal Justice Network. Over the last 15 years he has represented a number of prisoners and former prisoners who have long protested their innocence. He was recently named Lawyer of the Year in Private Practice at the Welsh Law Awards for his pro bono assistance to Paul Blackburn who spent 25 years in prison maintaining innocence, overturning his conviction in May 2005.

Campbell Malone is a Partner of Stephensons, one of the largest law firms in the UK, based in Wigan. He has extensive experience in challenging miscarriages of justice. He was a Consultant in the Crime Special Cases department which has achieved a significant number of referrals to the CACD from the CCRC. The work is undertaken alongside the Prison Law team which developed as a result of the appeal work and difficulties commonly faced by those maintaining their innocence. Campbell is also the chair of CALA, a body he helped set up.

Michael Mansfield, QC, founder of Tooks Chambers, is one of the leading barristers in the UK. As a criminal barrister, he represented and played an instrumental role in overturning a series of high-profile miscarriages of justice, including the Guildford Four, the Birmingham Six, Judith Ward and Angela Cannings, and many more. Michael is also a notable civil-rights lawyer and has acted for the family of Stephen Lawrence both in the Public Inquiry and private prosecution, the families of victims in the Bloody Sunday Inquiry and the family of Jean Charles de Menezes. Michael chaired an Inquiry into the Northern Ireland's 'Shoot to Kill' policy in the North of Ireland at Cullyhanna. He has presented a number of television documentaries and series, including *Presumed Guilty*, for BBC1. He is a regular contributor to television and radio current affairs programmes and was a panel member of *The Moral Maze* for many years. He has published numerous articles for all the major broadsheets and law journals, a legal handbook, *The Home Lawyer*, and, most recently, the book, *Memoirs of a Radical Lawyer*.

Paul Mason is Director of Postgraduate Research in the School for Journalism, Media and Cultural Studies (JOMEC) at Cardiff University. Broadly, his work is in the fields of crime and the media and media discourses on political violence. He has recently edited *Captured by the Media: Prison Discourse in Popular Culture* and he runs the Prison Media Monitoring Unit in the School. He is the Editor of *Journal for Crime, Conflict and Media Culture*. He is a member of the prison abolition group 'No More Prisons' and a regular contributor to the prison newspaper *Inside Time*. He is a founder member of the Addis Research Group, based at the University of Addis Ababa, Ethiopia.

Michael Naughton is Senior Lecturer in the School of Law and Department of Sociology at the University of Bristol, specializing in the area of miscarriages of justice and the wrongful conviction of the innocent. He is the Founder and Chair of INUK, which exists to support and encourage the creation of member innocence projects in universities in the UK, to undertake and facilitate academic research on the various related problems of wrongful convictions, and to inform public and policy debates. He set up and directs the University of Bristol Innocence Project (UoBIP), the first innocence project in the UK, through which he coordinates student investigations into cases of alleged wrongful imprisonment. He has written widely on issues related to miscarriages of justice and the wrongful conviction of the innocent for academic journals, broadsheet newspapers and specialist magazines, and he is a regular contributor to radio and television. He is the author of *Rethinking Miscarriages of Justice: Beyond the Tip of the Iceberg*.

Mark Newby is a solicitor and the Director of the Historical Abuse Appeal Panel (HAAP). Launched in September 2003, the HAAP is a national group consisting of solicitors and barristers who specialize in appealing against wrongful abuse convictions and defending people falsely accused of abuse.

Richard Nobles is Professor in Law at Queen Mary, University of London. Since 1990, Professor Nobles has been researching jointly with David Schiff on criminal appeals and miscarriages of justice. Together they obtained an Economic and Social Research Council (ESRC) Research Award in 1991/92 to investigate the role of the CACD in remedying miscarriages of justice involving the reassessment of expert evidence. The research led to a submission to the Royal Commission on Criminal Justice (RCCJ). More recently their collaboration has involved numerous publications and seminar papers on diverse topics applying autopoietic systems theory. Professor Nobles is currently researching the application of autopoietic systems theory to jurisprudence, in general, and appeal systems within law, in particular. He is the co-author of *Understanding Miscarriages of Justice*.

Robert Schehr is Professor of Criminal Justice in Northern Arizona University. He is the Founder and Director of the Northern Arizona Justice Project (NAJP) in Flagstaff and the Executive Committee Member of the international Innocence Network, the affiliating organization for innocence projects in the United States, the United Kingdom, Australia and Canada. Robert has published widely on the topic of wrongful convictions and has given numerous lectures on the causes and remedies of wrongful and unlawful convictions to law schools in the US, as well as in Australia, Scotland and England.

David Schiff is Professor in Law at Queen Mary, University of London, specializing in criminal appeals and miscarriages of justice. Together with Richard Nobles, he obtained an ESRC Research Award in 1991/92 to investigate the role of the CACD in remedying miscarriages of justice involving the reassessment of expert evidence which led to a submission to the RCCJ. More recently their collaboration has involved numerous publications and seminar papers on diverse topics applying autopoietic systems theory. He is currently on the editorial Board of the *International Journal of the Sociology of Law*. In the past he has been involved in the media, having appeared many times on radio and television, and having written a number of newspaper articles. He is the co-author of *Understanding Miscarriages of Justice*.

Satish Sekar has worked as a freelance journalist since 1990. Based in London, his work has appeared in *The Guardian* and *The Independent* and has been used by television and radio stations throughout England and Wales. Satish specializes in criminal justice issues, racism and miscarriages of justice. His book *Fitted In: The Cardiff 3 and the Lynette White Inquiry* details his meticulous investigation into the Cardiff 3 case and the flaws of the legal system that led to this wrongful conviction, the first case in British legal history in which the real perpetrator in a miscarriage of justice case was subsequently brought to justice.

Gabe Tan is the Database Manager and Research Officer of INUK. As an undergraduate law student at the University of Bristol, she was one of the founding members of the first innocence project in the UK, the UoBIP, which she currently manages. Gabe recently obtained an MSc in Socio-Legal Studies with Distinction, also at Bristol.

Clive Walker is Professor of Criminal Justice Studies and former Dean of the School of Law at the University of Leeds. He has written extensively on criminal justice issues, with many published papers in the United Kingdom and several other countries. He has served as a visiting professor at George Washington University, the University of Connecticut, Stanford University and Melbourne University. His books have focused on miscarriages of justice, and he is the co-author of *Justice in Error* and *Miscarriages of Justice* as well as many academic papers on the subject. He has also published on terrorism and emergencies, with recent books including *The Anti-Terrorism Legislation* and *The Civil Contingencies Act 2004: Risk, Resilience and the Law in the United Kingdom*. He has frequently been called on to provide advice to UK parliamentary committees on terrorism and to the UK government's independent adviser on terrorism and, in 2003, he was a special adviser to the UK Parliamentary Select Committee.

Michael Zander is Emeritus Professor of Law at the London School of Economics. His main fields are criminal procedure, civil procedure, legal system, legal profession and legal services. He was a member of the RCCJ (1991–93), the Report of which led to the establishment of the CCRC. He also conceived and conducted the RCCJ's largest research project – The Crown Court Study – the biggest study ever carried out in the English courts. He was made Honorary QC in 1997 and was appointed a Senior Fellow of the British Academy in 2005. Between 1963–1988 he was also Legal Correspondent of *The Guardian*, for whom he wrote over 2,000 articles. He is the author of several books, including *The Police and Criminal Evidence Act 1984* (London: Sweet & Maxwell, 5th edn, 2005); *The Law Making Process* (Cambridge: Cambridge University Press, Cambridge, 6th edn, 2004); *Cases and Materials on the English Legal System* (10th edn, 2007); and *A Bill of Rights?* (London: Sweet & Maxwell, 4th edn, 1997). He has also been regularly invited to respond to government consultations and official reports on criminal justice issues, including the Home Office consultation on the future of the Police and Criminal Evidence Act 1984 (PACE) (May 2007); Department of Constitutional Affairs Consultation Paper on Jury Research and Impropriety (April 2005); Home Office Consultation Paper on Defence Disclosure (September 2002); and Lord Justice Auld's Review of the Criminal Courts (November 2001).

List of Abbreviations

AEM	Acute Exhaustive Mania
CACD	Court of Appeal (Criminal Division)
CALA	Criminal Appeal Lawyers Association
CCRC	Criminal Cases Review Commission
CCRG	Criminal Conviction Review Group
CID	Criminal Investigation Department
CPS	Crown Prosecution Service
CRM	Case Review Manager
ECHR	European Convention on Human Rights
ECT	Electroconvulsive Therapy
ESRC	Economic and Social Research Council
FSS	Forensic Science Service
GCC	General Criminal Contract
HAAP	Historical Abuse Appeal Panel
HIV/AIDS	Human Immunodeficiency Virus/Acquired Immune Deficiency Syndrome
HOLMES	Home Office Large Major Enquiry System
INUK	Innocence Network UK
IPCC	Independent Police Complaints Commission
IRA	Irish Republican Army
JOMEC	School for Journalism, Media and Cultural Studies
LSC	Legal Services Commission
MOJO	Miscarriages of Justice Organisation
NAJP	Northern Arizona Justice Project
NCCRC	Norwegian Criminal Cases Review Commission
NCIIC	North Carolina's Innocence Inquiry Commission
NMS	Neuroleptic Malignant Syndrome
NSCB	National Safe Conviction Board
NTSA	National Transportation and Safety Administration
NTSB	National Transportation and Safety Board
OED	Oxford English Dictionary
PACE	Police and Criminal Evidence Act 1984
PCA	Police Complaints Authority
PTSD	Post Traumatic Stress Disorder
RCCJ	Royal Commission on Criminal Justice
RCCP	Royal Commission on Criminal Procedure
SBS	Shaken Baby Syndrome
SCCRC	Scottish Criminal Cases Review Commission
SOCO	Scene of Crime Officer
SRA	Solicitors Regulation Authority
SWL	South Wales Liberty
UAI	United Against Injustice
UoBIP	University of Bristol Innocence Project

Foreword by C. Ronald Huff

University of California, Irvine, USA

The increasing number of exonerations of the wrongfully convicted in many nations has brought with it greater awareness of the fact that criminal justice systems throughout the world are imperfect and that such errors not only inflict great harm on the victims of these miscarriages of justice but also endanger public safety by allowing guilty offenders to remain free to continue victimizing others. What has not been so apparent is how best to identify those who have been wrongfully convicted and assist them in overturning their convictions. And so, with the establishment of the Criminal Cases Review Commission (CCRC) in Great Britain in 1995 following the highly publicized wrongful convictions of the Guildford Four and the Birmingham Six, it seemed to many that this model would provide a feasible method of identifying and correcting such errors. It was even hoped, by many, that the CCRC might become a model to be emulated by other nations searching for a proper public policy response to these injustices.

According to this book, that hope has not been realized. Moreover, it is argued, the very foundation of the CCRC – the governing statute by which it was created – imposed on the CCRC critical constraints such as the 'real possibility test' (is there a real possibility that fresh evidence, if it had been available, might have made the original conviction unsafe?) and a subsequent clarification of 'fresh evidence' known as the 'jury impact test', which requires the Court of Appeal (and, by extension, the CCRC, since it must 'second guess' what the Court of Appeal would do) to give great deference to the trial jury's decision. These constraints and others, it is asserted, precluded the CCRC's becoming 'the answer to the problem' of wrongful conviction. Those constraints forced the CCRC to adopt a highly legalistic and conservative approach to such cases, requiring it to determine whether convictions were 'safe' as opposed to identifying, based on original investigations, for example, whether a wrongful conviction had occurred. To make matters worse, the establishment of the CCRC and the attendant expectations that accompanied it may have resulted in a diminution of public concern, since many believed that the problem would now be 'taken care of' by the CCRC.

All of this is conveyed to the reader via 16 chapters written by a collection of contributors, including academics, practitioners, investigative journalists, and victim support workers whose papers were initially presented at the Inaugural Innocence Network UK Symposium, held on the 10th anniversary of the CCRC. This rich representation of the innocence/wrongful conviction perspective provides detailed analyses and case discussions that form a powerful critique of the CCRC. The book's editor, Dr. Michael Naughton, is the founder and director of the Innocence Network UK, and a widely regarded expert on the causes and consequences of wrongful convictions in the UK. The primary aim of this book, he states, '... is to alert the reader to the fact that the CCRC is not doing what it is widely believed to have been set up to do – help alleged innocent victims of wrongful conviction, who may be innocent, overturn their convictions in the interests of justice.'

That criticism stems from expectations that followed the recommendations of the Runciman Royal Commission that called for a new body, independent of the government and of the Court of Appeal '...to consider alleged miscarriages of justice, to supervise their investigation if further inquiries are needed, and to refer appropriate cases to the Court of Appeal.' Such a body, it was thought, would also be able to avoid the inherent 'separation of powers' conflict that faced the Home Office, which had previously had responsibility for reviewing allegations of miscarriages of justice, since such inquiries by the executive branch necessitated some encroachment on the responsibilities of the judiciary, especially the Court of Appeal. But the new body, the CCRC, operates in a manner that appears to be far more conservative than what was envisioned by the Runciman Commission. In fact, it is alleged that the criteria utilized by the CCRC today may actually mean that it would not decide to refer some of the most infamous miscarriages of justice, such as the Birmingham Six, based on the 'real possibility test'. If so, and if the public's thirst for justice has been quenched by the establishment of the CCRC, the search for a proper public policy response to wrongful conviction must continue via reforms to the CCRC or the emergence of a new approach.

Finally, readers should understand that this is not a book that is intended to produce a balanced presentation of the work of the CCRC and its accomplishments. Rather, it is a book that is intended to provide a strong critique of the CCRC and to suggest the need for ongoing reforms. Readers will want to inform themselves of the CCRC's own assessments of its work, consider the critiques in this book, and reach their own conclusions concerning how societies might develop appropriate public policy responses to the problem of wrongful conviction. Free democratic societies should be aggressive in preventing, detecting and punishing crime but they must also be equally aggressive in correcting their errors when actual innocence results in conviction, imprisonment, and perhaps even execution in some nations.

C. RONALD HUFF

Foreword by Michael Zander

The challenging thesis of this book is that the Criminal Cases Review Commission (CCRC) is not doing the job it was intended to do and that something should be done about it.

The CCRC was established to deal with miscarriages of justice following the 1993 report of the Runciman Royal Commission on Criminal Justice (RCCJ). It was the unanimous recommendation of the Royal Commission based on the virtually unanimous view of those who gave evidence to the Commission. The recommendation was greeted with universal approval and was implemented in the Criminal Appeal Act 1995.

Prior to that time the problem of miscarriages of justice was the concern of C3, a small and poorly resourced Division of the Home Office. Under the Criminal Appeal Act 1968, s.17, the Home Secretary had the power to refer cases back to the Court of Appeal 'if he thinks fit', but few such referrals were made. Persuading the Home Secretary to use the power was extremely difficult. The Home Office itself would not undertake proactive investigations of alleged miscarriages of justice. Very occasionally it asked the police to reinves-tigate the case. Usually what was required to get the Home Secretary to move was the intervention of distinguished public figures based on a campaign led by JUSTICE, an investigative journalist, a television programme or public-spirited individuals, such as Ludovic Kennedy. What fuelled most such campaigns was a belief that the person convicted had been wrongly convicted in the sense that he or she was wholly innocent.

The Runciman Royal Commission, of which I was a member, had no difficulty in reaching the conclusion that a better system had to be found. That was urged even by the Home Office and by several former Home Secretaries who gave evidence to the Royal Commission. The main reason given by the Commission was the unwillingness of the Home Office, because of the constitutional separation of powers, to investigate such cases. ('The scrupulous observance of constitutional principles has meant a reluctance on the part of the Home Office to enquire deeply enough into the cases put to it.'[1]) The RCCJ recommended that a new body, adequately resourced and independent of government and of the Court of Appeal, should be set up 'to consider alleged miscarriages of justice, to supervise their investigation if further inquiries are needed, and to refer appropriate cases to the Court of Appeal'.[2] It called the proposed new body the Criminal Cases Review Authority.

Under the old system, the Home Secretary only referred a case back if there was 'new evidence or some other consideration of substance which was not before the trial court'.[3] The Royal Commission's report did not attempt a definition of the cases that should be referred back:

> We are reluctant to set specific criteria by which the Authority should select cases for further investigation. In practice, it will need no further justification for investigating a case than a conclusion on the part of its members that there is, or may be on investigation, something to justify referring it to the Court of Appeal. The Authority will need to devise its own rules and procedures for selecting cases.[4]

The complaint of this book is that whereas the campaign to replace C3 Division by a new body was based on a concern for the innocent victim of a miscarriage of justice, the CCRC was not properly set up to promote the cause of the innocent.

The book is the outcome of a symposium to mark the 10th anniversary of the CCRC organized by the Innocence Network UK (INUK).[5] The contributors write from a variety of perspectives – practitioners who have worked in this field, academics and the voluntary sector. The prime mover behind the symposium and the editor of the book, Dr Michael Naughton, was the founder of INUK. He explains that the purpose of the book is to alert people to the fact that 'the CCRC is not doing what it is widely believed to have been set up to do – help alleged innocent victims of wrongful convictions in the interests of justice'. The book understandably reflects the nature and purpose of the symposium, which was to explore where the CCRC was failing in its mission. It does not claim to be a rounded appraisal of the work done by the CCRC.[6]

As to the topics dealt with, Michael Naughton says in his Introduction that the book deals with the limitations placed on the CCRC:

> by its governing statute in terms of the kind of cases that it may refer; its ability to investigate cases thoroughly; its arrangements for the support of those claiming innocence that would allow them to present their cases; its apparent unwillingness to act proactively; its evident difficulty in responding to claims of defence deficiencies; its overly deferential attitude to the appeal courts.

He says, rightly in my view, that the setting up of the CCRC led to a marked reduction in public concern about wrongful convictions. JUSTICE gave up that part of its work. The media stopped investigating such cases. Miscarriages of justice were now being handled by the CCRC. Michael Naughton's concern is that this is not so. He ends the book by arguing that the CCRC is inappropriate for dealing with claims of innocence and raises the question whether a new body is needed 'that places overturning the wrongful conviction of the innocent at the heart of its operations'.

The issue raised by Dr Naughton was not addressed in those terms by the Runciman Royal Commission. The Royal Commission simply recommended that there should be a new body to investigate cases it thought required investigation and refer back to the Court of Appeal cases that it thought justified referral. It left it to the government to devise the formula that would constitute the basis of a referral. It added that there should be a reserve power, to be used exceptionally, to refer to the Home Secretary for consideration of a Royal Pardon, cases the Court of Appeal was unable to deal with because of the existing rules. This power was included in s.16(2) of the 1995 Act but it has never been used.

The formula devised by the draftsman regarding referrals restricts them to cases where the CCRC considers that there is a 'real possibility' that the conviction would be quashed as 'unsafe'. The 'real possibility' test understandably resulted in the CCRC being guided primarily by its sense of what the Court of Appeal will do in light, first, of existing case-law and beyond that, of the general attitude of the Court to its role in reconsidering jury verdicts. The Court of Appeal has on a number of occasions given the CCRC clear indications of how it should go about considering whether to refer cases. (Some of the criticisms of the CCRC in the book could perhaps with more justice be directed at the Court of Appeal.)

This book should be of interest to anyone concerned about the problem of how to deal with alleged miscarriages of justice. It upsets any comfortable impression that the present operation of the CCRC is beyond improvement. More significantly, it raises for consideration whether the system could be better organized to deal with cases where someone who has been convicted is actually innocent.

MICHAEL ZANDER

Notes

1. Report of the Royal Commission on Criminal Justice, 1993, p. 182, para. 10.
2. Ibid., p. 182, para. 11.
3. Ibid, p. 181, para. 6.
4. Ibid, p. 185, para. 24.
5. INUK has branches in over 20 universities with hundreds of students working under the supervision of practising lawyers on the post-appeal cases of prisoners who claim to be factually innocent. For a wide-ranging review of this movement see C. McCartney, 'Liberating Legal Education? Innocence Projects in the US and Australia' [2006] 3 Web JCLI, at http://webjcli.ncl.ac.uk/2006/issue3/mccartney3.html
6. For the first such, written by a former Commissioner, see Laurie Elks, *Righting Miscarriages of Justice? Ten years of the Criminal Cases Review Commission*, JUSTICE, 2008, pp. 58–71.

Foreword by Michael Mansfield

Over the last 30 years I have handled a large number of cases considered to be miscarriages of justice. Several of those are cited in the pages of this book. Whilst many of the causes underlying these cases have been addressed, there remains a real risk of wrongful conviction if for no other reason than human frailty, fallibility, misjudgement and misdemeanour.

Every participant at every level of the criminal justice system has, therefore, to be alive and alert to human vulnerabilities. Before the establishment of the Criminal Cases Review Commission (CCRC), I was one of a small band of lawyers, solicitors and barristers, who struggled to cope with the steady stream of requests from prisoners who wanted their convictions re-examined. This was, and is, a massive undertaking, and the CCRC has done some remarkable work successfully referring cases back to the Court of Appeal.

There is, nevertheless, in my view, still a significant gap which needs to be filled. The Innocence Network UK (INUK) is admirably placed to do this. Identifying, researching, collating and communicating evidence on the deficiencies of the criminal justice system which can cause miscarriages of justice and obstruct them from being overturned is a vital contribution to improving our criminal justice system and preventing such cases from occurring in the first place. In addition, the growing number of innocence projects over the last five years which investigate and seek to present only meritorious cases for the attention of the CCRC as well as the general public also serves to provide the much needed casework assistance and media attention that are crucial in seeking to overturn alleged miscarriages of justice. Rarely do prisoners have lawyers or legal assistance, because those who were involved originally at trial or appeal have long since departed. It is often difficult to engage a fresh legal team in what may be regarded as an onerous and financially burdensome exercise.

I have found the trickiest judgement call relates to sorting the wheat from the chaff. This cannot be achieved by a cursory or superficial appreciation of the initial approach – usually a prisoner's letter. It requires weeks and months of detailed investigation merely to assess the merits, let alone achieve resolution.

Matters have become more complex in the recent past because of the emergence of Forensic Science and expert evidence as critical factors in the evidential claim. Some of the science is at the cutting edge, not always fully tried and tested, and some of the experts stray beyond their accredited areas of expertise. Added to this is the voluminous increase in criminal law legislation, which requires careful analysis, especially in the context of human rights. Commonly, there is a need to trace witnesses, both old and new, both lay and expert, to conduct interviews and to produce focused, relevant and admissible statements.

To facilitate these initiatives, and to carry out a preliminary review, it is essential to pull together all the paperwork, retrieve documents, statements and exhibits. These may have been destroyed, wrongly filed or dispersed among a number of different bodies. It is a frustrating and time-consuming task but without it there can be no sensible assessment of eligibility, nor any ordered and intelligible submission to the CCRC.

Indeed, there is a clear message from this book and the rationale underpinning the establishment of the INUK: despite the CCRC, there are cases where strong evidence of innocence, or serious doubts of the conviction, exist, which do not meet the stringent criteria of the CCRC and the appeal courts. The INUK and this book, then, present an imperative attempt to resurrect alternatives for such cases where the CCRC can offer no hope to, such as petitioning the Secretary of State for a Free Pardon under the Royal Prerogative of Mercy and re-connecting the media and the public to such cases – non-legal channels that can help resolve possible miscarriages of justice which have been largely forgotten with the creation of the CCRC.

MICHAEL MANSFIELD

List of Cases

List of Statutes

1
Introduction

Michael Naughton

The Criminal Cases Review Commission (CCRC) is a recent development in a long line of attempted remedies against miscarriages of justice. It was established by the Criminal Appeal Act 1995, replacing the Criminal Case Unit of the C3 Division of the Home Office where the Home Secretary (C3) had the power to order reinvestigations of alleged miscarriages of justice and send them back to the Court of Appeal (Criminal Division) (CACD) under s. 17 of the Criminal Appeal Act 1968. The CCRC followed a recommendation by the Royal Commission on Criminal Justice (RCCJ) in 1993 (see RCCJ, 1993) that was prompted by the public crisis of confidence in the entire criminal justice system (Colvin, 1994) that was caused by the cases of the Guildford Four (Conlon, 1990)[1] and the Birmingham Six (Hill and Hunt, 1995),[2] and a string of other notable cases in which Irish people were wrongly convicted upon suspicion of being connected with terrorist crimes that were committed by the Irish Republican Army (IRA).[3]

In particular, it was found that successive Home Secretaries were failing to refer potential miscarriages of justice back to the CACD for political, as opposed to legal, reasons. To remedy this apparent constitutional problem, the CCRC was established formally on 1 January 1997 as an independent public body that would receive applications from alleged victims of miscarriages of justice in England, Wales and Northern Ireland who have previously failed in their appeals against criminal conviction but continue to question the validity of those convictions (see CCRC, 2008b).

The CCRC assumed the responsibilities for reviewing alleged or suspected miscarriages of criminal justice – previously exercised by the Home Office and the Northern Ireland Office – on 1 April 1997, although it received 279 outstanding case files from C3 on the day before in readiness. Since that time, it has received 11,287 applications,[4] approximately a thousand each year. It has referred an average of around 4 per cent of its applications, or 409 cases, to the relevant appeal courts, out of which around 382 appeals against conviction have been heard and 271 have been quashed.[5] This equates to a 'success' rate of around 70 per cent, or an annual average of approximately

20 convictions a year that have been overturned following a referral by the CCRC, which certainly appears as an increase on the previous system under C3 which contributed to an annual average of five cases being quashed upon referral between 1980 and 1992, for instance (Pattenden, 1996: 363).[6]

Such a crude statistical comparison of the CCRC's supposed success rate over its failed predecessor, however, needs to treated with caution as it includes convictions that are quashed by the CACD but sent for retrial and which are, subsequently, reconvicted (see Naughton, 2003). It includes cases that the CCRC refers back to the CACD on technicalities that are not deemed eligible 'claims of innocence' by Innocence Network UK (INUK) to be referred to one of its member innocence projects for further investigation.[7] And it includes cases such as Dino the German shepherd dog which the CCRC helped to reprieve from 'Death Row' in September 2004 after he was put under a destruction order, imposed under the Dangerous Dogs Act 1991, three years earlier by Northampton Magistrates' Court in July 2001.[8]

Moreover, notwithstanding the recent news that staff are already 'dispirited' and the proposed budget reductions will mean that staff numbers will have to continue to fall, the CCRC still has over four times the staff (including Commissioners) working on alleged miscarriages of justice than was the case at C3,[9] and the budget of the CCRC is almost ninefold that of C3 Division (CCRC, 2008a), so more referrals than C3 might well be expected (see Chapter 11).

Perhaps most crucially, though, and as will be demonstrated in great detail in the pages that follow, unlike C3 – which was petitioned by human rights organizations such as JUSTICE, following its own investigations that led it to believe that the people it represented were *factually innocent* victims of wrongful conviction and imprisonment and who should have their cases sent back to the CACD by the Home Secretary – the CCRC does not seek to refer cases of applicants that it finds or believes to be factually innocent. On the contrary, it reviews alleged miscarriages of justice in a legal sense, which is not to be confused with the wrongful conviction of the innocent as miscarriages of justice are popularly understood (as discussed in Chapter 2; see, also, Naughton, 2007b: 14–26), to determine if there is a 'real possibility that the conviction, verdict, finding or sentence would not be upheld were the reference to be made' (s. 13(1)(a) Criminal Appeal Act 1995): the CCRC is about the correctness or otherwise of convictions according to the legal process.

As such, the CCRC is, in practice, subordinate to the criteria of the appeal courts in a way that was not envisaged by the RCCJ, in its recommendations for a new post-appeal body to investigate claims of miscarriages of justice, nor by the subsequent Report by JUSTICE (1994), the all-party human rights organization, which is widely held to have provided the blueprint for the CCRC (discussed in detail in Chapter 2). The CCRC strives to second-guess how referrals may be viewed, referring only those cases that are deemed to meet the strict terms of s. 23 of the Criminal Appeals Act 1968, for example, which governs the requirements for appeals at the CACD. In this sense, the CCRC can be said to act as a filter for the CACD and sanction the successful appeals of guilty offenders if their convictions satisfy the requirements of the appeal courts, whilst, at the same time, if it turns up evidence that indicates an applicant's factual innocence that was available at the original trial it may not constitute grounds for a referral (Nobles and Schiff, 2001: 280–99). This derives from the CCRC working under narrower referral powers than those held by the Home Secretary under the C3 system, which, despite its apparent shortcomings, operated in the interests of justice that was more in line with public notions of miscarriages of justice, that is, it was concerned with alleged wrongful convictions of the innocent, as opposed to the CCRC which works entirely in the realm of legal technicalities (explicated further in Chapter 2).

The CCRC, then, contrary to popular belief, was not designed to rectify the errors of the criminal justice system and cannot ensure that innocent victims of wrongful conviction will obtain a referral back to the appeal courts, let alone overturn their wrongful convictions. It operates entirely within the parameters of the criminal appeals process in the role of a 'legal watchdog' to ensure that its decisions meet with its rules and procedures in the global interests of upholding its integrity – it seeks to determine whether convictions are lawful. Crucially, it does not question the possibility that the rules and procedures of the criminal justice system can cause miscarriages of justice and/or the wrongful conviction of the innocent and/or act against them being corrected (Naughton, 2005b, 2006).

This is not to advocate the return of C3, which presented a constitutional problem that had to be resolved with the separation of post-appeal investigations of alleged wrongful conviction from politics. Rather, it is to make clear that comparing the work of the CCRC and that of C3 is comparing apples and oranges: they each have (had) different premises on what actually constitutes a miscarriage of justice, which determined that they deal (dealt) with alleged miscarriages of justice in different ways – they work (worked) with different levels of resources and with different referral powers at their disposal. To be sure, the aim here in the introduction of this book is to outline some of the key characteristics of the CCRC and introduce the idea that the replacement of C3 with the CCRC is not the final solution to the problem of the wrongful conviction of the innocent: it appears that we have shifted from a problem with the political sphere – failing to refer the cases of potentially innocent people if those cases were thought to conflict with political interests – to a problem with the legal sphere failing to refer cases of the potentially innocent if they are believed to conflict with the interests of the legal system.

Despite this, as the first statutory independent post-appeal body of its kind, the CCRC has been hailed as 'that rare thing – a public body of which the UK can be proud, indeed which is envied in many countries around the world' (McCartney *et al.*, 2008) and has been the subject of much interest from other jurisdictions that see it as a possible solution to their own miscarriages of justice problem. For instance, the Scottish Criminal Cases Review Commission (SCCRC) started its work in April 1999 under the terms of s. 194A of the Criminal Procedure (Scotland) Act 1995 (see SCCRC, 2008b)[10] and the Norwegian Criminal Cases Review Commission (NCCRC) came into force on 1 January 2004 (see NCCRC, 2008). Moreover, there is an on-going debate for a CCRC-type body in the US (see Chapter 15; also see Scheck and Neufeld, 2002; Schehr and Weathered, 2004), in Australia (for example, see Weathered, 2007), in Canada (see Chapter 14; also see Campbell, 2008: 130–3;) and in New Zealand (for example, see Ellis, 2007) in the hope that it might resolve the perennial problem of the wrongful conviction of the innocent in those jurisdictions.

However, the implementation of CCRC-style bodies in other jurisdictions, and the debate for more of the same in the US, Australia and Canada, apparently fails to take account of the critical literature on the deficiencies of the CCRC from the standpoint of the wrongful conviction of the innocent. It seems blind to the establishment of almost 25 innocence projects in universities in the UK over the last five years, where students work on cases of alleged wrongful convictions in response to the failings of the CCRC to guarantee that it will refer the cases of applicants found to be innocent back to the CACD (discussed in detail in Chapter 2). Indeed, it seems that the desperation for a solution to the problem of the wrongful conviction and imprisonment and, in the US, the execution of the innocent, has created something of a rosy view of the CCRC, tending to see it as a *prima facie* progressive development in the law on criminal appeals, that their own criminal justice systems and, therefore, from which their own innocent victims of wrongful convictions would benefit.

Yet, as already indicated, the CCRC has structural failings that significantly impact on the scope of its investigations, meaning that it can even be conceptualized as a step backwards from its forerunner, C3, in its inability to refer potentially meritorious cases back to the appeal courts. This derives from its statutory straightjacket that is placed on it by the 'Real Possibility Test': the CCRC undertakes *reviews* of applications in its pursuit of legal grounds of appeal, as opposed to forms of *investigation* that operate in the interests of justice, as commonly held, and which seek to get to the bottom of claims of innocence, to determine their credibility, and to right apparent wrongs. Perhaps most disconcertingly, then, despite the fact that the CCRC was set up in the wake of a public crisis of confidence, induced by notorious cases such as the Birmingham Six amid a widespread concern for victims believed to be innocent, it is unlikely that such cases would be referred back to the appeal courts by the CCRC today. This is because the evidence of police misconduct and incorrect forensic expert testimony that led to the quashing of their convictions in the third appeal was available at the time of the original trial and appeal, so does not constitute the kind of 'fresh evidence' normally required by the CCRC to encourage a referral (see Naughton, 2008b).[11]

This highlights the incompatibility between the operational remit of the CCRC and the public belief that it exists to help potentially innocent victims to overturn their wrongful convictions, which, as will be shown, also relates to prominent criminal appeal practitioners who are frustrated by the CCRC's unwillingness to refer the cases of their clients back to the CACD who they believe to be innocent (see Chapters 7 and 8). It is significant that representatives from the CCRC have openly conceded that it is often unable to assist innocent victims of wrongful conviction if they do not fulfil the Real Possibility Test in the eyes of the Case Review Managers (CRMs) and/or the Commissioners reviewing the application.[12] And, yet, senior figures at the CCRC continue publicly to defend it on the grounds that to refer such cases would be a waste of time as, whether the applicant is innocent or not, the case is unlikely to be overturned (see Chapter 12).[13] Against this, I argue that this overlooks the conditions for the establishment of the CCRC and undermines other possible impacts that sending such cases back to the appeal courts might have, even if they were not to be overturned under the existing arrangements. Such cases could, for instance, raise public awareness of the inability or unwillingness of the CACD to overturn cases of appellants thought (even by the CCRC after its impartial investigations) to be innocent. Historically, such public awareness of the failings of the criminal justice system in the face of cases that give evidence to those deficiencies have led to changes to protect us against wrongful convictions or the introduction of new remedies, such as the CCRC, to assist in overturning them when they occur (Naughton, 2001, 2007b: 79–94; Chapter 2).

Aim

Against this background, the primary aim of this book is to alert the reader to the fact that the CCRC is not doing what it is widely believed to have been set up to do – help alleged innocent victims of wrongful conviction, who may be innocent, overturn their convictions in the interests of justice. It is the product of the papers given at the Inaugural Innocence Network UK Symposium on the tenth anniversary of the CCRC, 31 March 2007 (for details, see INUK, 2008a).[14] The Symposium brought together a range of different critical voices: victims of miscarriages of justice, campaigners and victim support organizations, practising lawyers and academics.

The challenges set out in the symposium are brought together in this book. Rather than an analysis of how the CCRC should interpret its role in the appeals process,[15] the analyses offered here focus on different aspects of the CCRC's tasks: the limitations placed on it by its governing statute in terms of the kind of cases that it may refer; its ability to investigate cases thoroughly; its arrangements for the support of those claiming innocence that would allow them to present their cases; its apparent unwillingness to act proactively; its evident difficulty in responding to claims of defence deficiencies;

its overly deferential attitude to the appeal courts; and so on. In reference to the ongoing discussion about its suitability for other jurisdictions, there are also wider chapters that compare the CCRC with the existing systems in Canada and the US for dealing with alleged wrongful convictions, giving the analyses that make up the book an important significance for these jurisdictions, too.

Overall, it becomes increasingly evident that the critical challenges to the CCRC are now reaching a climax as, after more than ten years, its ability 'to restore public confidence in the criminal justice system', on the basis that it is the necessary safeguard to assist in overturning the wrongful convictions given to innocent people, is no longer sustainable.

Structure

The book is presented in five parts. Part I (Setting the Scene) gets the book underway properly with Chapter 2 where I, first, outline the fundamental importance of the discourse of innocence for the criminal justice system, charting milestone changes that have occurred in response to widespread public crises of confidence in its workings that were prompted by the belief that innocent people have been wrongfully convicted and imprisoned. Then, in a critical assessment of how the CCRC compares with the body that was recommended by the RCCJ and JUSTICE, the CCRC is shown to be at variance in terms of how it *defines* a miscarriage of justice, its lack of *independence* and its inability to *investigate* cases in the way that the RCCJ and JUSTICE envisaged. It is argued that despite its serious deficiencies, however, a consequence of the CCRC has been that, as alleged miscarriages of justice are now dealt with behind closed doors and away from the public eye, there has been a diminishment of public interest in the problem of wrongful convictions. In particular, the vital channels which played the imperative role of informing the public debate about the failings of the criminal justice process have suffered detrimentally: the press have scaled down their reportage and assistance, that was offered by human rights and law reform organizations, has been terminated due to a mistaken widespread belief that the machinery of the CCRC is capable of resolving the wrongful conviction of the innocent. In noting the need to revive the concept of innocence and reconnect the conduit between public discourse and progressive changes to the criminal justice system, the chapter charts the recent formation of INUK and a growing network of innocence projects in universities around the UK in direct response to the apparent limitations of the appeals system and the CCRC to guarantee that alleged innocent victims of wrongful conviction will have their cases referred back to the appeal courts. The chapter concludes with a critical summary of the inappropriateness of the CCRC for dealing with claims of innocence, raising the question of the urgent need for a new body that places overturning the wrongful conviction of the innocent at the heart of its operations.

Part II (Voluntary Sector Perspectives) contains four contributions by individuals who are at the forefront of the voluntary sector's contribution against the wrongful convictions and imprisonment of alleged victims believed to be innocent. They have each personally helped to overturn wrongful convictions through their investigative and campaigning efforts and continue to strive for justice for alleged victims of wrongful conviction who they believe to be innocent. The shared theme of Part II is the failure of the CCRC to investigate adequately the cases of applicants who may be innocent, due to its limiting its reviews to finding possible legal grounds for appeal and compliance with the Real Possibility Test, as opposed to getting to the truth of whether applicants are, in fact, innocent as they claim. This resurrects a form of analysis regularly employed by JUSTICE, for instance, that was given up when the CCRC was set up on the basis that it was believed to be the long-awaited solution to the problem that it had fought so long and so hard for (discussed further in Chapter 1): to present publicly the findings of investigations to show the shortcomings of C3's ability to investigate claims of wrongful conviction, which played a major part in its replacement by the CCRC. The importance of the contributions that together form Part II, then, is that they lay bare some of the key failings of the CCRC's reviews from the perspectives of investigations that seek the truth of claims of innocence, as opposed to the CCRC's refusal to refer the cases of potential innocent victims who may not fulfil the required legalities.

Chapter 3 is culled from an interview with Hazel Keirle, Director of Miscarriages of Justice Organisation (MOJO) (England and Wales). Its significance is that it presents a critical evaluation of the CCRC from the perspective of the organization that was set up by Paddy Joe Hill, one of the Birmingham Six, one of the key miscarriages of justice that prompted the RCCJ and the subsequent setting up of the CCRC. In particular, Keirle notes how the CCRC is not concerned with whether applicants are innocent but, rather, with whether the conviction or sentence is sustainable in law. She concludes that the CCRC's poor performance can be improved in lots of different ways to ameliorate the overall quality of its work.

In Chapter 4, Andrew Green begins by offering some hope for overcoming the practice of the CCRC of interpreting deficiencies by defence lawyers, in particular their failure to adduce matters of significance at court, as indicative of a case being inappropriate for investigation and referral. In a detailed analysis of the case of Andrew Adams – a leading successful appeal case that was recently overturned, in part because of poor defence – and by Green's own theoretical approach to the production of forms of knowledge that lead to criminal convictions, he shows how the CCRC, perhaps inadvertently, used the method of knowledge production in its review, which, ultimately, broke the prosecution narrative and, thus, was able to present the case to the CACD in a way that rendered the conviction unsafe. On the downside, however, Green sees such cases as the exception rather than the rule, with the

CCRC generally reluctant to investigate unused evidence that might correct wrongful convictions that stem from poor defence representation due to its narrow interpretation of its role. In this light, he sees little hope of the case of Andrew Pountley being referred by the CCRC and, therefore, overturned by the CACD, despite evidence unearthed by Green to cast serious doubts on the conviction.

In Chapter 5, Dennis Eady asks to what extent the CCRC can live up to its stated values, such as independence, impartiality, thoroughness, transparency and accountability, in its reviews of alleged wrongful convictions. This is illustrated by the case of Michael Attwooll and John Roden – the longest case to date at the CCRC, which took ten years from application to a referral to the CACD – through Eady's own lens as a key campaigner for the case. In particular, Eady highlights areas of continuing concern in the case that he claims were not adequately investigated by the CCRC for what was, ultimately, an unsuccessful referral. He reaches the unequivocal conclusion that the CCRC will never be able to live up to its ideals, no matter how genuinely intended they may be, so long as it is statutorily tied to the apron strings of the criteria of the appeal courts.

Continuing the critique of the CCRC's failures in its case reviews, in Chapter 6 Satish Sekar presents a critical analysis of the CCRC's review of the possible miscarriages of justice that may have been caused by the discredited forensic pathologist Michael Heath. As a background, Sekar lists a trail of poor practice by Heath and a plethora of overturned convictions almost from the day that he became accredited by the Home Office in 1991. Through an examination of the case of Neil Sayers and other cases where Heath was involved and which were not referred by the CCRC, Sekar argues that the CCRC's review of Heath's cases was insufficient to capture all of the potential wrongful convictions that he may have been responsible for. He concludes that justice requires that such reviews must be carried out by the appropriate experts, rather than unqualified CCRC Commissioners who lack understanding of the consequences of Heath's conduct and knowledge of forensic pathology-related issues.

In Part III (Practitioner Perspectives), the dominant theme that emerges is an apparent shared frustration by leading criminal appeal lawyers about the statutory limitations placed on the CCRC which thwart the referral of cases of potentially innocent clients back to the CACD. This situation is exacerbated by the routine practice of the CACD to overturn cases at first appeal which would be unlikely to be referred by the CCRC. It is further hampered by the insufficiency of funding applications to the CCRC at the post-appeal stage, which is needed to represent clients in an appropriate manner.

More specifically, in Chapter 7, Mark Newby looks at the particular difficulties caused by the Real Possibility Test for his bulging caseload of clients who have been convicted of historical abuse. Using the successful appeal of Anver Sheikh as a gauge to assess the likelihood, or otherwise, of a CCRC referral for alleged innocent victims that are convicted of historical abuse offences, he argues that there is a significant divergence between how the CACD received and, ultimately, overturned the case as compared with the chances of such cases being referred by the CCRC. He shows how this stems from the way that the CCRC operationalize the Real Possibility Test as opposed to a more common-sense approach taken by the CACD that works in the interests of justice as popularly understood. To be sure, Newby illustrates that the CACD applies a much wider 'miscarriage of justice' test that can deal with cases that the CCRC will often decide against referring. As a way forward, Newby proposes a realignment between the tests employed by the CACD and the CCRC; only then, he contends, will possible innocent victims of historical abuse convictions, who are unable to generate forms of fresh physical evidence, have a realistic chance of having their convictions overturned.

Campbell Malone continues in a similar vein to Newby in Chapter 8 in a discussion of the CCRC's problematic interpretation of its statutory role by evaluating its inconsistency with the CACD as to what, precisely, constitutes 'fresh' evidence, particularly in the area of competing opinions by forensic-science expert witnesses. Citing failed appeals that routinely appear in the CCRC's Statements of Reasons for why it has decided not to refer a case back to appeal, he cites other successful appeals that the CCRC could just as easily rely on, which could lead to more potentially meritorious cases being referred and, possibly, overturned. Overall, for Malone, the CCRC frequently takes an overly cautious approach as it tends to overlook the discretion exercised by the CACD in the overriding interests of justice to receive evidence, even though all the criteria set out in s. 23 of the Criminal Appeal Act 1968 may not have been met, i.e. it may not actually be 'fresh' evidence that was not available at the time of trial. He illustrates his position through an analysis of the cases of Graham Huckerby, Jong Rhee and Alan Cherry, the latter two of whom continue to maintain innocence in prison due to an apparent reluctance by the CCRC to refer the cases, despite strong expert witness evidence that indicates serious flaws in the convictions.

In Chapter 9, Glyn Maddocks and Gabe Tan take a wider perspective on the role of the solicitor in the CCRC processes in an evaluation of the findings from an innovative focus group meeting with various personnel at the CCRC that explored its often thorny relationship with solicitors acting for applicants in the case review process. Maddocks and Tan's research validates many of the hunches that practising solicitors report from their experiences with the CCRC, revealing, for instance, a lack of specific and systematic training for Commissioners and CRMs who carry out the reviews on alleged miscarriage of justice, who are, instead, left to devise their own caseworking methods. This renders the case review process something of a lottery, with the best hopes for alleged victims of wrongful conviction resting on the allocation of a proactive and committed CRM. It also highlights a gulf between CCRC staff and applicant solicitors and a general failure on both sides to understand

and/or appreciate the role of the other, which can contribute to 'communication breakdowns' with CRMs who are, apparently, reluctant to inform solicitors of the progress of case reviews to their satisfaction, who they often view as a hindrance rather than a potential help. Overall, it is argued that, as the final gateway to the CACD for applicants who may be innocent, the CCRC is in need of urgent reform to ensure that its case reviews are of the highest quality and are consistent, which cannot and must not be a matter of chance or luck.

Concluding Part III, Chapter 10 by Steven Bird, a specialist in making applications to the CCRC, considers in detail the limitations of the 'legal aid' funding available for solicitors to provide advice and assistance to their clients who maintain that they are innocent victims of wrongful conviction. He highlights the monetary disincentives for undertaking criminal appeal work, noting the closure of firms that cannot make ends meet and the knock-on impacts for those seeking a quality criminal appeal service. He makes a clear case for the need for a raft of changes, not only in terms of more appropriate and adequate overall rates of pay, but, equally, in the way in which the Legal Services Commission (LSC) determines what is claimable and who should claim it. Bird's conclusion is stark: wrongful convictions are likely to go uncorrected due to the severe lack of funds available for criminal appeal lawyers to investigate properly claims of innocence in pursuit of grounds of appeal that fit with the remit of the CCRC.

Part IV (Academic Perspectives) presents five chapters from academic colleagues which are vital for explaining the reasons for the apparent frustrations that were presented in the foregoing chapters, by practitioners and those working in the voluntary sector, to assist alleged innocent victims of wrongful conviction and the intransigence of the CCRC to responding to such forms of critique.

In Chapter 11, Richard Nobles and David Schiff offer three perspectives by which the CCRC might be measured after its first decade in operation. First, they argue that without a definitive idea of the total number of miscarriages of justice that occur it is difficult to say if the CCRC has been successful in correcting all of the possible miscarriages of justice that occur. However, with an annual contribution of just 0.058 per cent of all of the successful appeals at the CACD, it seems that the CCRC makes such a minute difference to the total problem of miscarriages of justice that any claims to success are difficult to sustain. Moreover, if the CCRC is judged against the Scottish Criminal Case Review Commission (SCCRC), albeit that they each have differently worded tests for referring cases, it is shown to refer about half as many cases back to the relevant appeal court with a similar rate of overturned convictions, again rendering the CCRC as, apparently, less adequate than its Scottish counterpart at overturning miscarriages of justice. Second, Nobles and Schiff consider the CCRC's relationship to the CACD, seeing the CCRC as 'successful' in these terms, as it is constrained, by statute and its working practice, to a cautious approach to only refer cases with a strong possibility of being overturned, hence its high level of quashed convictions following a referral. Third, Nobles and Schiff discuss the likelihood of innocent victims of wrongful conviction who cannot point to any significant error in the trial proceedings or find fresh evidence or new arguments for having their cases referred. By this criteria, the CCRC can be conceptualized as failing: whilst the CACD will overturn first appeals on a 'lurking doubt', there is little, or no, real possibility that such cases will be returned back to the CACD by the CCRC, simply because it may have doubts as to the accuracy of the jury's verdict. Instead, it requires an identifiable legal argument or piece of fresh evidence that was not put to the jury, which, effectively, closes the only door of hope to innocent victims that their cases will be overturned.

In Chapter 12, Kevin Kerrigan also analyses the Real Possibility Test, focusing on the way that it is defended by the CCRC on the grounds of its compatibility with the test of the CACD. In accepting the current failings of the appeals regime as they relate to the problems that potentially innocent victims face, he argues that the CCRC currently performs a predictive, not a normative, role, meaning that it has very limited capacity to challenge those failings. To support his contention, he examines three alternative tests for referral, maintaining that lowering the threshold of the Real Possibility Test might increase the number of referrals but will not increase the number of quashed convictions, as the CACD will assess the safety of convictions from a legal perspective. He concludes that much of the criticism of the CCRC's Real Possibility Test is misplaced and may serve to mask the real obstacles of overturning miscarriages of justice that are posed by the CACD.

In Chapter 13, Paul Mason looks at the newspaper reportage of the CCRC between January 1996 and December 2006, applying a 'crime and the media' perspective. In support of the argument in Chapter 1 about the loss of the media voice with the establishment of the CCRC, his discussion shows how coverage that is critical of the CCRC has waned since its creation and is, instead, mainly restricted to reports of cases that it refers to the CACD. Applying Steve Chibnall's (1977: 23) analysis, Mason suggests that 'celebrity', 'novelty', 'simplification', 'sex' and 'death' all sell newspapers, and so are key considerations in how a crime story is written, who is quoted and what perspective the story is told from, which accounts for the amount of reporting when cases have a 'celebrity' (Barry George, for example) or are 'notorious' (cases such as Ruth Ellis, James Hanratty and Derek Bentley, for instance). These are the underpinning values or 'professional imperatives which act as implicit guides to the construction of news stories', to explain how and why certain stories about the CCRC reach the press and others do not, and, therefore, why forms of critique about the failures of the CCRC to investigate claims of innocence adequately, or the ways in which its procedures may act as a barrier to referring cases of alleged victims of wrongful conviction who may be innocent, are unlikely to be published. The overall implication of this chapter is that miscarriages of justice are no longer the cause of great public concern that they once were: if the CCRC refers cases that are overturned at appeal they are presented as indicative of the success of the CCRC; if CCRC referrals fail at appeal they are depicted by the press as guilty offenders on whom the CCRC should not have wasted taxpayers money.

In Chapter 14, Clive Walker and Kathryn Campbell turn attention from the CCRC in a domestic context to a comparative analysis with the system of alleged wrongful conviction review in Canada under the Criminal Conviction Review Group (CCRG). Seeing the CCRC as a step forward from the CCRG, they point to the existing executive-based review system in Canada under which applications are made to the Minister of Justice who is also the Attorney General of Canada and the Chief Prosecutor arguing that the CCRG suffers from the apparent constitutional problems that were the reason for why the CCRC replaced C3 Division. Noting the need to account for the limits of the CCRC under clauses such as the 'real possibility test' and the need to comply with the criteria of the appeal courts, it calls for a new body for Canada that mirrors the independence from government that is enjoyed by the CCRC but which can improve on its shortcomings, too. This, it is contended, would entail more resources, reform of the CACD, and a more holistic approach that seeks to learn lessons from the whole gamut of miscarriages of justice that are routinely overturned through the normal appeal process, as well as exceptional cases that are overturned through post-appeal routes, which the CCRC has yet to engage in. However, in recognising the public confidence and policy gains obtained by the Canadian custom of commissions of inquiry into the circumstances that cause wrongful convictions, Walker and Campbell caution that the move to a CCRC-type body may well deflect against such inquiries and render systemic failings with the criminal justice system less visible.

In the final chapter of Part IV, Robert Schehr discusses the approach to wrongful convictions in the United States, which makes clear the focus on the concept of factual innocence. Although he claims that the US has a tendency of looking inwards and is generally unaware of developments in criminal law outside of its own boundaries, Schehr notes the roots of the conversation on the suitability of a CCRC-type body for the US at the turn of the century by the creators of the first innocence project, Barry Scheck and Peter Neufeld. However, the notion of a CCRC for the US was decided against by these two, who favoured, instead, 'innocence commissions' – with full subpoena authority, access to investigative resources and political independence – for conducting inquiries into the apparent wrongful convictions that are overturned by innocence projects, in the way that there are investigations of aeroplane and other major transportation accidents in the US, and for making policy recommendations to eliminate the identified cause of the wrongful conviction. Utilizing the concept of 'parrhesia', as outlined by Michel Foucault, he argues the importance of innocence commissions as examples of truth-seeking that privileges the voices of exonerees and a commitment to institutional change to improve the criminal justice systems in the US. Schehr concludes by building on an analysis of the existing innocence commissions in the US to put forward his idea of a schematic for a tripartite system of innocence projects and innocence commissions that overlap on a state and federal level.

The Conclusion, Part V, draws from the foregoing chapters to provide a summary of the key findings and conclusions of the book. It shows that the CCRC is not at all what the RCCJ and JUSTICE called for: there is nothing wrong *per se* with the CCRC as a 'legal watchdog' to ensure that the criminal justice system is operating in line with its own rules and procedures and, therefore, that criminal convictions are correct in law; however, the CCRC is not to be confused with the urgent need – almost two decades since the public crisis of confidence in the apparent inability of the criminal justice system to protect the innocent and guarantee that, when discovered, they would have their cases referred back to the appeal courts – for a specific body to deal with claims of innocence.

Finally, with the reader in mind, it must be acknowledged that the chapters that together make up this book derive from a diverse group of the wrongful-conviction and miscarriage-of-justice community. As such, the chapters display differences of style, ranging from recognizable academic chapters that are rich with references that point to sources of information and/or other points of reference, to chapters from practitioners that cite key cases in detailed discussions of points of law for giving insights into the workings of the CCRC and the CACD, to chapters from investigative journalists and victim support workers that are largely devoid of references, instead standing as their own authority on the matters upon which they speak by the very nature of the engagement of the author(s) with the criminal appeals process in attempts to overturn alleged wrongful convictions. Despite this difference in the presentational style, however, taken together the chapters do share a coherent perspective that identifies the key deficiencies of the CCRC from the perspective of the delivery of justice for innocent victims of wrongful convictions and imprisonment. It is hoped that these forms of critique can form a forceful body of counter-discourse on the existing arrangements that can feed into the debate about the continuing need to introduce further changes to the criminal justice system, so that it contains the necessary mechanisms to overturn the convictions of the innocent, as and when they occur, thus truly acting as it should and as we want it to.

Notes

1. In essence, the RCCJ was an extension of the inquiry by Sir John May into the events surrounding the conviction of the 11 people, mostly family members, who

were convicted in the cases of the Guildford Four and the Maguire Seven (see May, 1990, 1992, 1994).

2. The RCCJ was announced on the day that the Birmingham Six overturned their convictions in the CACD: 14 March 1991.

3. See, for example, Woffinden, 1987; Mullin, 1986; Kee, 1986; JUSTICE, 1989; Ward, 1993; Maguire, 1994; Callaghan and Mulready, 1995; Rose *et al.*, 1997; Walker and Starmer, 1999b; Kennedy, 2002.

4. Including the cases transferred from the Home Office when the CCRC was set up.

5. This figure includes referrals for appeals against sentence as well as against conviction for appeal. It is also interesting to note that the number of referrals is on the decline with only 27 referrals in 2007–08, as compared with 38 in 2006–07, representing only 2.5 per cent of completed cases (see CCRC, 2008a: 6).

6. Although the CCRC's jurisdiction is not confined to the CACD, as it also encompasses alleged miscarriages of justice from magistrates' courts that can be returned to the Crown Court sitting as an appeal court, this book is directed to its operations in the Higher Court of Appeal (see Kerrigan, 2006).

7. INUK is the umbrella organization for member innocence projects in universities in the United Kingdom. Innocence projects see students work on cases of alleged innocent victims of wrongful conviction with pro bono lawyers (see INUK, 2008b; discussed further in Chapter 2). For information on INUK 'typology of claims of innocence' and its eligibility criteria, see Naughton (2007a, 2008a). For reasons of data protection and confidentiality I am not permitted to name the actual cases that the CCRC has referred but which were rejected by INUK.

8. Dino had bitten Elizabeth Coull who tried to intervene in a fight between him and her pet terrier, Ralph. The legal battle over Dino's case passed from Northampton Magistrates' Court to Northampton Crown Court to the High Court to the House of Lords to the European Court of Human Rights and, finally, to the CCRC which looked into the case and referred it back to Northampton Crown Court, whereupon the destruction order was rescinded (see Rozenberg, 2004).

9. In 1994, C3 had 12 case workers and two and a half senior staff working full-time on miscarriages of justice and related issues (Pattenden, 1996: 349) compared with a current cohort of 43 CRMs and 11 Commissioners (including those working part-time) at the CCRC (CCRC, 2008a).

10. As amended by s. 25 of the Crime and Punishment (Scotland) Act 1997.

11. This was acknowledged by John Weedon, Commissioner, CCRC, speaking in a personal capacity at the 2006 Annual Socio-Legal Studies Association Conference, held at the University of Stirling during 28–30 March.

12. Inaugural Innocence Projects Colloquium, held at the University of Bristol on 3 September 2004, which was attended by the Principal Legal Advisor, the Public Relations Officer and four CRMs from the CCRC.

13. As presented by John Wagstaff, Principal Legal Advisor, CCRC, speaking in a personal capacity at the UAI 3rd Annual Miscarriage of Justice Day Conference, held at Conway Hall, Holborn, London, on 9 October 2004.

14. All royalties from the sale of this book will go to INUK.

15. For such an analysis, see Elks, 2008.

Part I
Setting the Scene

2

The Importance of Innocence for the Criminal Justice System

Michael Naughton

Introduction

If you were to ask the 'person in the street' what he or she wants from the criminal justice system, the reply is more than likely going to be that it should convict the guilty and acquit the innocent; and, if it should happen that an innocent person is convicted in 'error', then most people would probably think that the appeals system should operate to overturn the conviction in a speedy fashion to reduce the harm that was caused to the victim and his or her family and friends and restore the legitimacy of the criminal justice system. The idea that the criminal justice system should be about convicting the guilty and acquitting the innocent is reflected in political statements about how the system should function and it is transmitted in portrayals of wrongful convictions and wrongful acquittals in the media. Perhaps most significantly, the history of the criminal justice system is peppered with high profile media campaigns for alleged victims of wrongful convictions who were believed to be innocent, which have helped to shape some of the most significant changes to the structures that govern how the system operates.

This chapter sets the context for the book by considering the importance of the discourse of innocence for the criminal justice system. It charts landmark changes to the system in response to widespread public crises of confidence in its workings in response to the belief that victims of wrongful conviction and imprisonment are innocent. It compares the Criminal Cases Review Commission (CCRC) to the kind of body that was recommended by the Royal Commission on Criminal Justice (RCCJ) (1993) and the subsequent report by JUSTICE (1994), 'Remedying Miscarriages of Justice', to demonstrate that it is not at all what was envisaged. Moreover, it argues that the establishment of the CCRC signalled the silencing of innocence as an organizing counter-discourse against miscarriages of justice amid a mistaken widespread belief that it was, indeed, the body recommended by the RCCJ and JUSTICE to remedy the wrongful conviction of innocent people. With the setting up of the CCRC the term 'miscarriage of justice' went through what can be called a *legalification* process, shifting it from a concern with the possible wrongful conviction of the innocent to an entirely legal notion that sees miscarriages of justice in terms of the need for convictions to be safe in law. On a more promising note, the chapter charts the recent formation of Innocence Network UK (INUK) and a vibrant network of innocence projects in universities around the UK in direct response to the deficiencies of the CCRC to confirm that alleged innocent victims of wrongful conviction who may be innocent will have their cases referred back to the appeal courts, which has resuscitated innocence as a lens through which to judge the legitimacy of the criminal justice process.

Innocence and changes to the Criminal Justice System

The importance of the discourse of innocence in criminal justice policy is evident in the extent to which it has shaped the key remedies against wrongful convictions, and/or the safeguards that exist to prevent innocent people from being wrongly convicted, or to help them to overturn wrongful convictions (see Naughton, 2001). For instance, the Court of Criminal Appeal was established in 1907 in response to the combined counter-discursive public pressures exerted by the cases of *Maybrick* (Ryan and Havers, 1977), *Edalji* (Lahiri, 2000) and *Beck* (Cathcart, 2004). These cases exemplified the urgent need for a court of criminal appeal, as they provided the necessary evidence to the public that people such as *Edalji* and *Beck* had been wrongly convicted and imprisoned – for mutilating a pony and obtaining by deception, respectively – and that others, as exemplified by the *Maybrick* case, were given the death penalty for crimes that they may not have committed.[1] Taken together the *Maybrick*, *Edalji* and *Beck* cases served to diminish public confidence in the criminal justice system to the extent that a Committee of Inquiry was established to investigate the Beck Affair. Subsequently, a court of criminal appeal had to be established to dispose of the crisis and restore public confidence that the criminal justice system was operating as it should. Indeed, in announcing the establishment of the Criminal Court of Appeal under the Criminal Appeal Act (1907) the then Home Secretary, Herbert Gladstone, made clear the dynamic link between the public desire for a criminal justice system that could correct the apparent wrongful convictions of those believed to be innocent in the following terms to the House of Commons in 1907:

> the only way to reverse the public belief that miscarriages of justice were an every-day occurrence ... was the establishment of a court capable of hearing appeals of fact, law and sentence. (Herbert Gladstone, Parl. Deb (HC) 31 May 1907, cc. 193—5; quoted in Pattenden, 1996: 31)

Similarly, the Police and Criminal Evidence Act (PACE) (1984), the code to guide police investigations and suspect interviews, was an outgrowth of a recommendation by the Royal Commission on Criminal Procedure (RCCP)

(1981) that was set up in response to the public crisis of confidence in the criminal justice system induced by the successful appeals of three youths, Colin Lattimore, Ronnie Leighton and Ahmet Salih, in a case known as the Confait Affair. In particular, the Fisher (1977) inquiry into the case had been especially critical of the police practices that led to the wrongful convictions of the three youths for the murder of Maxwell Confait. The whole prosecution, argued Fisher, was geared simply to providing the case against the boys, i.e. 'fitting them up' (Fisher, 1977; Price, 1985; Price and Caplan, 1976). In recommending what would become the PACE Act, the RCCP argued that the case exemplified the need for police accountability, both in the interests of greater reliability of evidence and the enhancement of suspect's rights (Report, RCCP, 1981: para. 10.1).

More recently, as outlined in Chapter 1 above, in the late 1980s and early 1990s a spate of high profile cases including the Guildford Four (Conlon, 1990), the Birmingham Six (Hill and Hunt, 1995), the Maguire Seven (Maguire, 1994), and so on, generated a crisis of confidence in the ability of the criminal justice system to overturn the convictions of those believed to be innocent. In response, and on the day that the Birmingham Six had their convictions overturned by the Court of Appeal (Criminal Division) (CACD), the Government established the RCCJ to 'examine the effectiveness of the criminal justice system in England and Wales in securing the convictions of those guilty of criminal offences and the acquittal of those who are innocent' (RCCJ, 1993: i). These cases had raised a number of serious issues with the criminal justice system and the RCCJ observed the vital link between public expectations and the legitimate operations of the system: 'Public confidence was undermined when the arrangements for criminal justice failed to secure the speedy conviction of the guilty and the acquittal of the innocent' (RCCJ, 1993: 1).

The main recommendation of the RCCJ (1993) was the replacement of C3 Division, which investigated alleged miscarriages of justice at the time, and the Home Secretary's role in referring post-appeal cases back to the CACD. In specific terms, the CCRC was established under the Criminal Appeal Act 1995 as:

> an independent public body set up to review possible miscarriages of justice and decide if they should be referred to an appeal court. It was set up as a non-departmental body on 1 January 1997 and took over responsibility from the Home Office and Northern Ireland Office for reviewing suspected miscarriages of justice on 31 March 1997. The Commission has jurisdiction over criminal cases at any Magistrates' or Crown Court in England, Wales and Northern Ireland. Our main job is to review the cases of those that feel they have been wrongly convicted of criminal offences, or unfairly sentenced. (CCRC, 2008e)

Following the RCCJ, JUSTICE (1994), as the principal source of support for alleged victims of miscarriages of justice in terms of assisting them to make applications to C3 Division and its record on overturning them (discussed further below), filled in some of the details as to how the body recommended by the RCCJ should operate in its report *Remedying Miscarriages of Justice*, which is widely held, even by JUSTICE itself, to be the blueprint for the CCRC. But, is the CCRC really the kind of post-appeal body that was recommended by the RCCJ and JUSTICE?

Is the CCRC what the RCCJ and JUSTICE envisaged?

To be sure, although the CCRC is claimed, and widely accepted, to be the new post-appeal body to deal with alleged wrongful convictions of the innocent that the RCCJ and JUSTICE had called for, a closer analysis reveals just how far it diverges from the actual recommendations that these bodies had proposed.

Definition

The way in which the RCCJ and JUSTICE had defined a miscarriage of justice was very clear and in line with lay understandings: it was either the wrongful conviction of the factually innocent and/or the wrongful acquittal of the factually guilty (see Naughton, 2007b: 14–26). Moreover, although the remit of the RCCJ was far reaching, 'to examine the criminal justice system from the stage at which the police are investigating an alleged or reported criminal offence right through to the stage at which a defendant who has been found guilty of such an offence has exhausted his or her rights of appeal', its considerations referred to the issues raised *'only to the extent that they b[ore] on the risks of an innocent defendant being convicted or a guilty defendant being acquitted'* (RCCJ, 1993: 1; my emphasis). Likewise, JUSTICE only assisted alleged victims of miscarriages of justice if 'the allegation [was] of actual, rather than technical, innocence' (JUSTICE, 1989: 1–2).

This requires a clear distinction to be made between miscarriages of justice as understood by the RCCJ and JUSTICE in the everyday sense and how they are understood by the legal system (see Naughton, 2005b). Indeed, the CACD's grounds for receiving evidence in its decisions about allowing and dismissing appeals, for instance, is set out in s. 23 of the Criminal Appeal Act 1968[2] as follows:

> (1)   For the purposes of an appeal under this Part of this Act the Court of Appeal may, if they think it necessary or expedient in the interests of justice:
>
> >   (a)   order the production of any document, exhibit or other thing connected with the proceedings, the production of which appears to them necessary for the determination of the case;
> >
> >   (b)   order any witness who would have been a compellable witness in the proceedings from which the appeal lies to attend for

      examination and be examined before the Court, whether or not
      he was called in those proceedings; and
(c) receive any evidence which was not adduced in the proceedings
      from which the appeal lies.
(2) The Court of Appeal shall, in considering whether to receive any
      evidence, have regard in particular to:
      (a) whether the evidence appears to the Court to be capable of belief;
      (b) whether it appears to the Court that the evidence may afford any
            ground for allowing the appeal;
      (c) whether the evidence would have been admissible in the proceed-
            ings from which the appeal lies on an issue which is the subject
            of the appeal; and
      (d) whether there is a reasonable explanation for the failure to adduce
            the evidence in those proceedings.

These criteria not only render legal notions of miscarriages of justice in continual flux, as the rules and procedures of the appeals system change over
time with amendments to the statutes that govern them, but also illustrate
how far removed this is from a public understanding of what would constitute a miscarriage of justice – that is, the wrongful conviction of the innocent
or the wrongful acquittal of the guilty – and that it differs from how the legal
system decides miscarriages of justice based entirely on the prevailing rules of
evidence: s. 23(1)(c) highlights how appeals in the CACD are not full rehear-
ings of criminal trials but, rather, require that the evidence adduced must *not*
have been heard in the original trial, that is, 'fresh evidence', in the criminal
appeal process. In addition, further caveats apply to the admissibility of such
fresh evidence in criminal appeals in s. 23(2) to the effect that the CACD must
believe in the validity of the evidence, see it as having a bearing on the appeal,
decide whether it would have been admissible in the original trial and accept
that there is a 'reasonable' reason why the evidence was not offered in the
original trial. These requirements emphasize the technical nature of the criminal appeals process, which often presents insurmountable barriers to overturning wrongful convictions. Overall, in considering the validity of criminal
appeals, the CACD is not concerned with correcting the wrongful conviction
of the innocent but, rather, with deciding if the fresh evidence, if it fulfils the
admissibility clauses, renders criminal convictions 'safe' or 'unsafe' in law:

(1) Subject to the provisions of this Act, the Court of Appeal:
      (a) shall allow an appeal against conviction if they think that the
            conviction is unsafe; and,
      (b) shall dismiss such an appeal in any other case. (Criminal Appeal
            Act 1968, s. 2)

Contrary to the RCCJ's and JUSTICE's vision for the new post-appeal body,
as will be developed further below, the CCRC's definition of a miscarriage of

justice works entirely within the parameters of the legal system and is not concerned at all with whether applicants are innocent or guilty: 'We do not consider innocence or guilt, but whether there is new evidence or argument that may cast doubt on the safety of an original decision' (CCRC, 2008e).

Apparently, this is not something that troubles the CCRC's Principal Legal Advisor, as is evident in the following answer to the question as to how the CCRC defines a 'miscarriage of justice': 'I don't even know what a miscarriage of justice is. We simply consider whether convictions are reliable and refer cases back to the appeal courts if we believe that there is a real possibility that the conviction will be overturned' (John Wagstaff, Principal Legal Advisor, CCRC).[3]

This almost flippant approach to the core question about the CCRC's role and purpose suggests that the CCRC has lost sight of its historical context: the CCRC was set up in the wake of a public crisis of confidence in the criminal justice system's (lack of) ability to overturn the wrongful conviction of people believed to be innocent. Moreover, given that the RCCJ, which gave life to the CCRC, was set up on the day that the Birmingham Six overturned their convictions in the CACD, it seems geographically symbolic that the CCRC is based in Birmingham: it is a permanent reminder that it was set up – in part, in governmental response to one of the most notorious miscarriages of justice in British legal history – to restore public confidence that the criminal justice system could rectify such miscarriages of justice, understood as the wrongful conviction of the innocent, when they occur.

Independence

A particular problem identified by the RCCJ related to the lack of independence in the existing post-appeal referral system at the time and the very limited way in which successive Home Secretaries practised their discretion to return cases back to the appeal courts where it was suggested that there had been a miscarriage of justice:

> There is in theory no restriction on the numbers of categories of cases which the Home Secretary may refer to the Court of Appeal under section 17 [of the Criminal Appeal Act 1968] since the section gives him discretion to refer cases 'if he thinks fit'. In practice, however, ... the Home Secretary and the civil servants advising him operate within strict self-imposed limits. These rest upon constitutional considerations and upon the approach of the Court of Appeal itself to its own powers. The Home Secretary does not refer cases to the Court of Appeal merely to enable that court to reconsider matters that it has already considered. He will normally only refer a conviction if there is new evidence or some other consideration of substance which was not before the trial court. Successive Home Secretaries have adopted this approach, and not only because they have thought that it would be wrong for Ministers to suggest to the Court of Appeal that a

different decision should have been reached by the courts on the same facts. They have also taken the view that there is no purpose in their referring a case where there is no real possibility of the Court of Appeal taking a different view than it did on the original appeal because of the lack of fresh evidence or some other new consideration of substance. (RCCJ, 1993: 181–2)

As such, the RCCJ was acutely alive to the possibility that there might be cases where applicants to the new proposed Authority would not be able to muster grounds for appeal under the limited scope of the Court of Appeal, that is, fresh evidence and/or fresh argument normally not available at the time of the original trial (Criminal Appeal Act 1968, s. 23). As such, it was especially critical of the custom of successive Home Secretaries to show undue deference to the appeal courts and the self-imposed practice of not referring cases back to the CACD where it was thought that there was no 'real possibility' that it would take a different view than it did at the original appeal.

For these reasons, the RCCJ called for the 'creation of a new body *independent of both the Government and the courts* to be responsible for dealing with allegations that a miscarriage of justice [i.e. wrongful conviction of the innocent] has occurred' (RCCJ, 1993: 182; my emphasis). Given the reason why the RCCJ was established, that is, successive Home Secretaries failing to refer potentially meritorious cases back to the CACD, it is, perhaps, unsurprising that the new system for correcting the wrongful conviction of the innocent was to be independent of the government. Equally, whilst the RCCJ felt that the CACD ought to be able to quash the convictions of the innocent, it recognized that it operates within a realm of legal rules and procedures that mean it is not 'the most suitable or the best qualified body to supervise investigations of this kind' (RCCJ, 1993: 183).

In line with the RCCJ, JUSTICE (1994: 3) spelt out the need for the new body to be independent in the following terms:

The Home Secretary's power to reconsider and refer cases to the Court of Appeal has always been used sparingly. This is in part at least because of the Home Secretary's reluctance to interfere with the judicial process. The increased robustness of the Court of Appeal in its readiness to quash convictions has thrown into relief the continuing caution of the Home Office in referring cases to the Court ... the setting up of a new body, independent of the courts and the Executive, provides an opportunity to deal with these problems. It is important for the operation of that body, and for public confidence in its decisions, that its independence from the police, the Home Office and the courts is jealously guarded. This will affect both its structures and its procedures.

Taken on face value, the CCRC appears to fit with what was envisaged by the RCCJ and JUSTICE, as is evident in the following quotation from its website:

> We are completely independent ... entirely independent of government ... [and] entirely independent ... of the adversarial justice system and represent neither the prosecution nor the defence. (CCRC, 2008e, 2008h)

Contrary to this, however, the CCRC's operations are chiefly governed by s. 13(1)(a) of the Criminal Appeal Act 1995 which requires that it cannot refer applications to the appeal courts unless 'there is a real possibility that the conviction, verdict, finding or sentence would not be upheld were the reference to be made'.[4] This means that the CCRC must try to second guess how the appeal courts would consider any referrals that it may make, significantly impeding any supposed independence that it may have (Naughton, 2006).

Most critically, then, the principal problem that the RCCJ and JUSTICE found with the existing practice of successive Home Secretaries working within the parameters of the Court of Appeal criteria, and seeing no point in referring a case where there was no real possibility of the CACD taking a different view than it did on the original appeal, has not been rectified in accordance with its recommendations. On the contrary, what was *self-imposed* by successive Home Secretaries has become *statutorily formalized* by the 1995 Criminal Appeal Act. As a result, the present arrangements for post-appeal referrals back to the appeal courts under the CCRC can be conceived to be more restrictive than the system it replaced. The CCRC is subordinate to the rules of evidence of the appeal courts and does not have 'unrestricted discretion conferred' on the Home Secretary under s. 17 of the Criminal Appeal Act 1968 to refer cases 'if he thinks fit', as this power has been removed from the statute books (RCCJ, 1993: 181). Rather, the CCRC's 'discretion' is confined to the narrow terms of working within the parameters of the terms of the Criminal Appeal Act 1995, and its subsequent amendments, as it deals with applications.

However, although the general idea was, rightly, that the Home Secretary would cease to have any function in attempting to overturn the possible wrongful conviction of the innocent, the RCCJ saw that he or she would retain ministerial responsibility for the Royal Prerogative of Mercy, where the CACD is unlikely to be able to overturn an alleged wrongful conviction under the existing appeals criteria. In particular, the RCCJ found that this might happen:

> if the Court of Appeal were to regard as inadmissible evidence which seemed to the Authority to show that a [wrongful conviction of an innocent] might have occurred ... We therefore recommend that the possible

use of the Royal Prerogative be kept open for the exceptional case. (RCCJ, 1993: 184)

Accordingly, a possible door remains open for the CCRC under s. 16(2) of the Criminal Appeal Act 1995 to refer applications to the Secretary of State if it is of the opinion that the applicant is innocent but lacking the necessary legal grounds for the appeals system. There should, instead, be a recommendation to exercise the Royal Prerogative of Mercy and give the applicant a full and free pardon. In practice, however, this route has yet to be taken by the CCRC, which may not see its relevance to its work as it reviews applications for possible grounds for appeal as it acts as a filter for the appeal courts. To be sure, as it does not actively seek out evidence of factual innocence, but rather fresh evidence that questions the safety of the conviction, it is, perhaps, not surprising that it will automatically favour the appeal avenue over that of an application for a free pardon on behalf of an applicant (discussed further below).

Investigations

For the RCCJ, the new Authority that it called for would be one that would, where it thought it appropriate, supervise thorough re-examinations of alleged miscarriages of justice, i.e. alleged claims of the wrongful conviction of the innocent, that failed to be overturned at their appeals:

> The applicant's approach to the Authority would normally be made either after his or her conviction had been upheld by the Court of Appeal or after he or she had failed to obtain leave to appeal. In cases which seemed to the Authority to call for further investigation, it would ensure that that investigation was launched ... Where the Authority instructed the police to conduct investigations, it would be responsible for supervising the investigation and would have the power to require the police to follow up those lines of inquiry that seem to it necessary for the thorough *reexamination* of the case. (RCCJ, 1993: 182–3; my emphasis)

This was echoed by JUSTICE (1994: 21–2) which outlined the 'Mission Statement' of the proposed new body in terms of its ability to 'undertake comprehensive investigations in criminal cases where miscarriages of justice may have occurred' and to examine 'the totality of the case to seek to assess whether there is prima facie evidence of a miscarriage of justice' (with all references to miscarriages of justice to be read as meaning the possible wrongful conviction of an innocent).

Contrary to this, as discussed above, the statute that dictates the operations of the CCRC is not about full re-examination of the entire case that might ascertain whether applicants are innocent or guilty. Instead, it will 'investigate' or *review* only partially, within the terms of the Real Possibility Test and the general criteria of the criminal appeals system to seek out possible forms of fresh evidence that may suggest that convictions may be unsafe in law. In its reviews, the CCRC seeks to find fresh evidence that undermines the reliability of the evidence that led to the conviction, as opposed to evidence of innocence or, even, guilt. In the case of Barry George, for instance, the CCRC referred the case back to the CACD on the basis that the Firearms Discharge Residue evidence, that played a large part in his conviction for the murder of Jill Dando, was unreliable, which the CACD then decided made his conviction unsafe – not that it showed that he was factually innocent of the murder (see *R* v. *George*). This is, generally, true of all successful appeals. However, in cases where the evidence that led to the convictions cannot be undermined by such forms of fresh evidence – for example, juries believing the word of the accuser against the defendant in the absence of any physical evidence in historic sexual abuse cases (see Chapter 7), or convictions based on purely circumstantial evidence put before a jury – the applications are unlikely to be referred and/or the injustice corrected, as there is a lack of the kind of fresh evidence required by the CCRC for it to determine that the case has a real possibility of being overturned. Indeed, whilst the RCCJ acknowledged that juries can play a part in 'mistaken verdicts' (RCCJ, 1993: 3), the CCRC, in line with the practice of the CACD, will generally not seek to undermine jury verdicts *per se* – tending, instead, to reflect the CACD's underpinning position of jury deference and to see such claims as generally lacking the potential to constitute legal grounds – as juries would have heard the evidence in the context of the trial, regardless of how unsubstantiated it may have been, and decided to convict anyway. Specifically, the CCRC must assess how the CACD will see a case in the light of the House of Lords ruling in the case of *R* v. *Pendleton*, which introduced the 'jury impact test' to fresh evidence in the following terms:

> the Court of Appeal ... is not and should never become the primary decision-maker ... the Court of Appeal ... has an imperfect and incomplete understanding of the full processes which led the jury to convict. The Court of Appeal can make its assessment of the fresh evidence it has heard, but save in a clear case it is at a disadvantage in seeking to relate that evidence to the rest of the evidence which the jury heard. For these reasons it will usually be wise for the Court of Appeal, in a case of any difficulty, to test their own provisional view by asking whether the evidence, if given at the trial, might reasonably have affected the decision of the trial jury to convict. If it might, the conviction must be thought to be unsafe. (*R* v. *Pendleton* [2001] UKHL 66, para. 19)

Moreover, the RCCJ saw the new Authority as referring cases back to the Court of Appeal under the existing terms of s. 17 of the Criminal Appeal Act (1968) where the appeal would be considered as referred by the Home Secretary and treated for all purposes as an appeal to the Court by that person, i.e. a first appeal:

> Where the result of the investigation indicated that there were reasons for supposing that a miscarriage of justice might have occurred, the Authority would refer the case to the Court of Appeal, *which would consider it as though it were an appeal* referred to it by the Home Secretary under section 17 [of the Criminal Appeal Act 1968]. (RCCJ, 1993: 183; my emphases)

However, CCRC referrals are not regarded as first appeals and must take account of the appeal judgements in any cases that it considers. In the context of the Real Possibility Test, this means that the CCRC is not merely looking forward in a predictive attempt to second guess how the appeal courts might view potential referrals, it is also looking backwards at how the appeal courts have previously considered the applicant's appeal, whereby, inevitably, possible lines of inquiry are likely to be excluded by the CCRC if they relate to evidence already considered but rejected by the appeal courts. A recent observation by a CCRC Commissioner[5] about the unlikelihood that the Birmingham Six case would be referred today, emphasizes the gap between the CCRC and the body that the RCCJ hoped for. Although the case of the Birmingham Six was twice referred back to the CACD by the Home Secretary under the old s. 17 powers of the Criminal Appeal Act 1968 after it had failed in its first and second appeals, each appeal was considered as a first appeal and, hence, it was immaterial that the grounds of appeal for all three of the Birmingham Six appeal hearings were fundamentally the same and not fresh in the eyes of how the CCRC would presently see it (see *R v. McIlkenny and others*).

If this logic is applied to the general need for successful appellants in the CACD to produce fresh evidence that was not adduced at the original trial, it places an onus on the CCRC to find even fresher evidence, since the fresh evidence that formed the basis for the first appeal will not be fresh enough for the CCRC to be able to make a referral, which will need, instead, to be fresh, fresh evidence (see Chapter 8). This is contrary to JUSTICE's (1994: 12) assertion of a 'consensus' at the time of the RCCJ, 'that what is considered as fresh evidence should no longer be subjected to the restrictive approach adopted by the Court of Appeal in the past', which 'must be prepared to take account of new considerations or lines of argument which were not put, or not adequately put, at trial'. From this perspective, the CCRC can be conceived as a regressive step in the apparatus for overturning alleged miscarriages of justice with more restrictive powers and methods of referring cases back to the CACD than the system that it replaced.

Stemming the flow of counter-discourse against the wrongful conviction of the innocent

As indicated above, public awareness that victims believed to be innocent of being convicted of, and imprisoned for, criminal offences that they did not commit or, even, when there had been no criminal offence at all (Naughton, 2005a), has resulted in some of the most significant changes to the criminal justice system aimed at new mechanisms for preventing alleged wrongful convictions or at overturning them. However, with the establishment of the CCRC, the vital channels that inform the public debate about the failings of the criminal justice process were severed due to a widespread belief that the machinery was now in place to overturn the wrongful conviction and imprisonment of the innocent as and when they occur. In consequence, there was something of a stemming of the free flow of information to the public that might contribute to the production and deployment of counter-discourse against the deficiencies of the criminal justice system that might lead to changes to address the causes of the wrongful conviction of the innocent or act to obstruct them from being overturned.

To be sure, the discourse on wrongful convictions took a perverse turn. They no longer were seen as newsworthy as they once had been because we now had an official body to deal with them. Where newspapers previously invested in investigative journalists to examine alleged miscarriages of justice and follow their progress, or lack thereof, through the appeals system, it was felt that this was now an unnecessary expenditure in time and money as the CCRC was the appropriate body, funded by government, to undertake such investigations. Moreover, when newspapers did cover stories about miscarriages of justice, it was in the context of the reporting of successful appeals against criminal convictions that had been referred back to the appeal courts by the CCRC (see Chapter 13), which can be conceptualized as serving as a kind of 'celebration' of the criminal justice system and the CCRC in righting apparent wrongs, strengthening the idea that the CCRC *is* the solution to the problem of miscarriages of justice. This was at the expense of reportage on miscarriages of justice and wrongful convictions as damming indictments of the failures of the criminal justice system that caused the wrongful conviction and the accompanying suffering to the victims and their loved ones in the first place.

Where there was once a sustained television presence in terms of reconstructions of crimes to raise awareness of the possible wrongful convictions of the innocent and the escape from justice of the real perpetrators of those crimes, such programmes disappeared from our screens almost overnight, again under the belief that such programmes were no longer required as we now had the CCRC. At the forefront of the media campaign against wrongful convictions was David Jessel, who had spent 15 years exposing miscarriages of justice through his television programmes – BBC's *Rough Justice* and Channel 4's *Trial and Error* – which were instrumental in helping to overturn numerous wrongful convictions, including Johnny Kamara (see Carter and Bowers, 2000); Thomas Campbell and Joseph Steele (The Glasgow Two) (see Kelbie, 2001); Danny McNamee (Woffinden, 1999b); Mary Druhan (see Jessel, 1994: ch. 2); Mark Cleary (see Jessel, 1994: Chapter 1); Peter Fell (see Jessel, 1994:

Chapter 4); Sheila Bowler (see Devlin and Devlin, 1998); Raymond Gilmour (see Carroll, 2007); Vincent Hickey, Michael Hickey and James Robinson (Bridgewater Four case) (see Foot, 1986); Paul Esslemont, Gary Mills and Tony Poole (see Jessel, 1994: ch. 7); Paul Blackburn (see Naylor, 2004); and George McPhee (see Howie, 2006). However, in 2000, Jessel hung up his campaigning hat and joined the CCRC as a Commissioner, accepting the proviso that he no longer had any involvement with any cases that he had previously worked on – and the television coverage of alleged wrongful convictions suffered another fatal blow (Bennetto and Nunes, 2005).

Politicians had previously been mobilized in support of their constituents who were claiming to be innocent victims of wrongful convictions and regularly joined campaigns to put pressure on the Home Secretary to revisit cases with a view to a referral back to the appeal courts or to the Secretary of State for a free pardon under the exercise of the Royal Prerogative of Mercy. However, with the separation of the CCRC from the political sphere, political interest was disconnected and, even, seen as inappropriate, in favour of allowing it to do its job unhindered – 'independently'.

On a practical level, as already mentioned, prior to the establishment of the CCRC, JUSTICE had led the way in assisting alleged innocent victims of wrongful conviction and imprisonment in England and Wales (JUSTICE, 1989: 2). Since its inception in 1957, JUSTICE had received requests for help by, and on behalf of, hundreds of prisoners alleging that they were innocent. Initially, because of the voluntary nature of the organization, and the lack of staff and resources, it was decided that it would not investigate individual cases. However, the sheer volume of requests eventually convinced Tom Sargant, the organization's secretary for its first 25 years, that there was a real need to investigate where he could and assist with appeals and petitions to the Secretary of State (JUSTICE, 1989: 1). Crucially, and in line with the working premise of the RCCJ, JUSTICE only assisted alleged victims of miscarriages of justice if 'the allegation [was] of actual, rather than technical, innocence' (JUSTICE, 1989: 1–2). In terms of 'results', JUSTICE had a hand in helping to overturn such landmark cases as those of Michael and Patrick McDonagh (see Hill *et al.*, 1985), Paul and Wayne Darvell (see BBC News, 2002a), John McGranaghan (see Woffinden, 1997: Appendix 1), Jackie Fletcher (see Naylor, 2001), Andrew Evans (Duce, 1997) and Ashley King (Dyer, 1999).

Just as significantly, perhaps, before the CCRC, JUSTICE was also central in terms of its critique of C3 and the call for a new statutory post-appeal body to investigate alleged wrongful convictions that might provide a better resourced and more effective remedy than JUSTICE's own voluntary efforts: it first called for an independent statutory body to investigate miscarriages of justice in 1964; it repeated the call in 1989 with its report, 'Miscarriages of Justice'; it offered evidence to the RCCJ in 1993 which again repeated the call; in 1995 it submitted 'Remedying Miscarriages of Justice', which set out a blueprint for what is claimed to be the CCRC's and JUSTICE staff were consulted for advice in the early stages of setting up the CCRC (see JUSTICE, 2008a). Against this history, it is, perhaps, not surprising that when the CCRC was established JUSTICE ceased to assist alleged innocent victims of wrongful conviction as it believed that it had finally achieved the criminal justice reform that it had fought so long and hard for.[6]

Yet, as already shown above, the CCRC does not resolve the problem of the wrongful conviction of the innocent, which was the focus of JUSTICE's casework in the area of miscarriages of justice. On the contrary, the Real Possibility Test subordinates it to the criteria of the appeal courts to receive fresh evidence and the legal definition of a miscarriage of justice, instead of a lay perspective that truly seeks to help potentially factually innocent victims of wrongful conviction to overturn their convictions and obtain redress. As such, the perennial problem of the wrongful conviction of the innocent remains, despite the CCRC's and JUSTICE's abandonment of its casework for alleged innocent victims of wrongful conviction and imprisonment was not only premature, it closed a vital door of hope to the hundreds of alleged victims who continue to this day[7] to contact it for assistance, but who are directed, instead, to seek justice through the CCRC.

INUK and the release of the discourse of innocence

INUK, the umbrella organization for member innocence projects based in UK universities, was launched in September 2004.[8] It was set up in direct response to a growing awareness of the inherent deficiencies of the CCRC to help alleged innocent victims of wrongful conviction who may be innocent overturn their wrongful convictions and the extent to which it acts to silence the discourse on factual innocence. It operates in a synergy of casework, research and communications to release the discourse of innocence from its shackles. It seeks to re-establish the bridge between the public and the legitimate operations of the criminal justice system in its attempts to unearth evidence of the wrongful conviction of the innocent through research and casework by its member innocence projects that may be deployed as counter-discourse for contributing to further improvements in their remedy, prevention and/or redress (INUK, 2008c).

Originating in the US in the early 1990s (see, for example, Scheck and Neufeld, 2002; Scheck et al., 2000), an innocence project is a group of students, predominantly law, but also including other disciplines such as criminology, journalism, sociology, forensic psychology, and so on, investigating, normally under academic supervision and guidance by a practising lawyer working on a pro bono basis, cases of convicted persons, usually prisoners serving life sentences or indeterminate sentences who maintain their innocence and who have exhausted the appeals process.[9]

Against this background, the remainder of this section will reflect on the foregoing discussion of the divergence between what the RCCJ called for and the working realities of the CCRC, using the same subheadings to show the extent to which the underlying principles and mode of operation of the INUK and its member innocence projects fits more closely with the vision of the RCCJ than the CCRC.

Definition

As discussed above, the RCCJ was only concerned with correcting the criminal justice system insofar as it bore on the possibility of the factually innocent being convicted for crimes that they did not commit and/or the factually guilty evading conviction. In total correspondence with this stance, INUK member innocence projects are only and entirely concerned with claims of factual/actual innocence, as opposed to allegations of technical miscarriages of justice. For instance, and in line with JUSTICE's rationale, member innocence projects do not consider claims that murder convictions should have been convictions for manslaughter, for instance (see Naughton, 2006).

A pertinent question that is always asked of innocence project casework is: how do you know that the case you are working on is the case of a factually innocent person? It is important to emphasize that INUK and its member innocence projects are *not* safe houses for the guilty and *do not* work on the basis that their 'clients' *are* factually innocent. On the contrary, they seek to explore *claims of innocence*, that may, *potentially*, be genuine – bearing in mind the flaws with the criminal justice system at the pre-trial and trial stages, police and/or prosecution errors and/or misconduct, malicious allegations, mistaken forensic-science evidence by expert witnesses, poor defence, and so on (Naughton, 2007b: ch. 3) – and that fall within the horizon of the limits of the criminal appeals system and the CCRC for guaranteeing that innocent victims of wrongful conviction will have their convictions overturned.

Moreover, in an attempt to isolate claims of factual innocence from other claims of innocence by applicants who are not factually innocent, the INUK undertakes centrally for its members a process for deciding eligibility through the application of an innovative 'typology of claims of innocence' based on the responses to its questionnaires from applicants. In this process, the following categories of applicant are excluded from further investigation: ignorance of criminal law (applicants who claim innocence because they do not *know* that they have committed a criminal offence); disagreement with criminal law (applicants who claim innocence because they do not *believe* that their behaviour is, or should be, regarded as criminal); claims of technical miscarriages of justice (applicants who claim innocence because they think they have a chance of *appeal*) (Naughton, 2007a, 2008a). It goes without saying that if evidence turns up in the course of an innocence project investigation that a 'client' is not innocent, the case is terminated with an explanation of the reasons for withdrawal from the case that makes clear her/his legal culpability/guilt.

Investigations

Resembling the RCCJ's and JUSTICE's recommendation for a body to thoroughly re-examine claims of factual innocence, the INUK member innocence projects attempt to conduct full investigations of the claims of innocence in the cases that they take on. Unlike the CCRC, the aim is not merely to find legal grounds.[10] On the contrary, innocence projects are not hindered by the requirements of the legal system and, rather, seek to get to the truth of innocence claims, exploring the possibility for wrongful conviction at each stage of the criminal justice process from the initial police investigation of the crime or alleged crime through to the trial proceedings. Key questions that govern innocence project investigations include: How was the police investigation conducted and the case constructed against the alleged innocent victim of wrongful conviction/imprisonment? Were there any other suspects for the crime/alleged crime and were they appropriately eliminated in line with police protocols or was the entire investigation orientated towards getting a conviction of the alleged innocent? How credible is the evidence that led to the charge and the conviction (for example, circumstantial evidence or unsupported or uncorroborated allegation versus physical evidence such as DNA or fibres or fingerprints,[11] and if it is the latter form of evidence have there been any advances in forensic science technology, for example, that might exonerate (or confirm the guilt) of the alleged innocent)? Are there any other possible lines of inquiry that can be gleaned from the unused evidence that could lead to evidence of innocence that need to be investigated or reinvestigated (such as alibi evidence)? Are there any factors at the trial that could lead to the conviction of an innocent person (such as the misrepresentation of evidence not adequately challenged by the defence, conduct of the trial judge, etc.)?

The true extent of the practical difference between innocence project investigations and CCRC reviews emerged in a recent submission to the CCRC by the University of Bristol Innocence Project (UoBIP).[12] A student caseworker found that the failure of the original DNA tests conducted by the Forensic Science Service (FSS) to produce any positive results may be due to the unsuitability and inadequacy of the technique that was used. The student then proposed that the biological samples obtained from the deceased victim and the crime scene be retested, utilizing a relatively recent DNA testing technique which has been extremely successful in securing the exoneration of appellants in similar cases in the United States. It was proposed that if the samples were subjected to this new testing technique, it may be able to show that the alleged innocent victim of wrongful conviction may, in fact, be innocent or, alternatively, may have an association with the murder that he was convicted of and which he has always denied any involvement with at all. The response from the Case Review Manager (CRM) dealing with the case was one of surprise by the submission on the grounds that as the DNA evidence that was found at the murder scene was not part of the evidence that led to the conviction and, therefore, he was unclear of its relevance to his review of the case. More specifically, the CRM stated:

> Perhaps ... [the name of the UoBIP student caseworker] ... could assist in explaining how this [submission] is ... relevant to [the applicant's] case and how it could undermine the safety of the conviction? I am mindful that no DNA was found that related to [the applicant] and absence of DNA linking [the applicant] to the offence was a point put by the Defence to the jury.[13]

This exposes how CRMs at the CCRC confine their reviews to attempts to find legal grounds as required by the Real Possibility Test, as opposed to full reinvestigations that seek the truth, or otherwise, of claims of innocence by innocence projects. In restricting his review to largely circumstantial and highly questionable evidence that led to the conviction, the CRM was not only unlikely to find the kind of fresh evidence to enable him to recommend referring the case back to the CACD, he failed to recognize forensic reports which suggest that DNA possibly belonging to the assailant may have been present but could not be profiled due to the limitations of the (outdated) technique used by the FSS; he was failing to see the potential of the unused evidence at his disposal and the possible utility of new DNA tests that could answer, once and for all, who committed the murder, which could, possibly, help not only to exonerate the applicant but, even, lead to the capture of the real murderer.

Of course, there are significant limitations to the extent of the investigations that innocence project students can undertake. Aside from their general lack of investigative training and/or experience, innocence project student caseworkers do not have the formal powers to instruct inquiries or obtain documents from persons serving in public bodies such as police forces, government departments, local authorities, and so on, that may assist them in their investigations, which are afforded to the CCRC under ss. 17–21 of the Criminal Appeal Act 1995. This is a particular impediment when investigating cases that involve claims that police misconduct contributed to the alleged wrongful conviction, as it would require access to all of the police records of the investigations, such as police notebooks or diaries, disciplinary records and/or the Home Office Large Major Enquiry System (HOLMES) database of all data and information on a case, including information from members of the public (Johnson and Cross, 2005).

And yet, despite these obvious limitations, as the brief discussion above has shown, innocence project student caseworkers can bring fresh eyes and minds to investigations that are unconstrained by the requirements of the criminal justice system, truly attempting to operate in the interests of justice in the RCCJ and JUSTICE (1994) sense.

Independence

As a university-based initiative, INUK and its member innocence projects exist as a resource for student education about the ills of the criminal justice system through the investigation of real cases. Moreover, INUK's member innocence projects serve to meet the unmet caseworking needs of possible innocent victims of wrongful conviction and imprisonment and those whose cases fall outside the scope of legal aid. However, INUK and its innocence projects do not have the same kind of responsibilities that lawyers have for ensuring the 'best outcome' for their clients, understood in terms of pragmatic legal outcomes, and they are not paid for their efforts. Rather, the primary interest is an objective investigation that, simultaneously, seeks to educate the students and wider society about the failings of the criminal justice system to determine the truth of the case in the interests of justice as popularly understood.

In this sense, the INUK and its member innocence projects are truly independent in the way that was set out by the RCCJ and JUSTICE (1994) as they are not subordinate to a financial relationship with their clients, to governmental interference or to the courts and the structural limitations of the criminal appeals process and/or the CCRC. Instead, whilst acknowledging the pragmatic need to find grounds of appeal and, where appropriate, make applications to the CCRC on behalf of 'clients', innocence projects can also make applications to the Secretary of State for a Free Pardon through the exercise of the Royal Prerogative of Mercy, reconnecting the public domain with the possible wrongful conviction and imprisonment of the innocent that was prematurely given up when the CCRC was set up.

As such, member innocence projects can be conceptualized as more akin to public inquiries into alleged wrongful convictions of the innocent as they try to uncover what may have gone wrong to cause the conviction and/or imprisonment of an innocent, which can never be said to be in the public interest. Aside from supporting its member innocence projects, the INUK combines the case working aspect undertaken by its innocence projects with academic research on the issue of the wrongful conviction of the innocent and other associated problems, communicating its research findings widely in the hope that this synergy of casework, research and communications can collectively contribute to effecting changes to the criminal justice system that will reduce the possibility of wrongful convictions/imprisonment in the future and improve the ways in which they are addressed and corrected when they occur (INUK, 2008c).

Overall, the INUK and its member innocence projects work together in synergy to produce counter-discourses against the wrongful conviction of the innocent that releases the discourse of innocence that had been stemmed by the establishment of the CCRC to create an environment that might be receptive to change when cases are unearthed that show the failings of the system. This corresponds with the general position of the RCCJ that was expressed as follows: 'If innocent people are convicted the real criminals, who may be very dangerous people, remain undetected' (RCCJ, 1993: 2–3).

Conclusion

The logic of this chapter points to the need to be semantic about the CCRC, which is not at all the kind of post-appeal authority for the full re-examination of alleged wrongful conviction of the innocent cases that the RCCJ and JUSTICE (1994) proposed. Firstly, the CCRC works on the cases of applicants who are pitched as *criminals*, hence 'Criminal Cases'. As such, the cases of criminals who are claiming a miscarriage of justice, as opposed to an alleged innocent victim of a wrongful conviction, is the given object at the core of the CCRC's work. In working on criminal cases it does so in line with the working premises of the criminal appeals system, seeing them in terms of a general presumption of legal guilt, as all of the people in the cases that it reviews are legally guilty of the crimes of which they allege that they are innocent of committing (cf. Naughton, 2008a). Further, the CCRC must find technical forms of fresh evidence to construct legal grounds for appeal and not evidence of innocence.

Secondly, the CCRC does not *investigate* cases in the way that the RCCJ and JUSTICE (1994) envisaged the necessary body would, in terms of trying to get to the bottom of whether alleged innocent victims of wrongful conviction are innocent. Instead, it is a *review*-orientated exercise of criminal cases, hence 'Criminal Cases Review' body that operates on the terms of the criteria of the appeal system. To be sure, the Oxford English Dictionary (OED) gives the literal meaning of 'review' as to 'inspect again' or to carry out 'a retrospective survey or report'. The CCRC conducts such reviews under the specific terms of s. 13 of the Criminal Appeal Act and the criteria of appeals system, and according to whether or not there is a belief that 'a real possibility' exists that the conviction would not be upheld if it were to be referred – and not investigations that seek to ascertain if the wrongful conviction of an innocent person has, in fact, occurred.

The final part of the semantic analysis of the CCRC relates to the fact that it does not have the kind of *authority* that was called for by the RCCJ, but rather is entirely subordinate to the authority of the appeal courts in its attempts to second guess what it might do in the cases that it reviews. Hence, it is the 'Criminal Cases Review Commission', with 'Commission' understood in its literal OED sense as a body which functions on 'an instruction, command, or duty', whose authority extends only to the 'perform[ance of] a task', in this case not straying outside of the task determined by the precise statutory powers that it has been given (no matter how unsuitable they may be) to decide if alleged miscarriages of justice (understood in a legal sense) that have already failed in appeal have a 'real possibility' of not being upheld if they are referred back to the appeal courts, and, thus, having no independent power of its own.

Of course, the CCRC still retains the option, in theory, of sending cases in which it is believed that the innocent have been wrongly convicted to the Secretary of State for a Free Pardon and the exercise of the Royal Prerogative of Mercy if it is felt that the evidence of innocence does not provide admissible grounds for a referral back to the appeal courts under the strict terms of the Real Possibility Test. However, due to the way that the CCRC review applications in the pursuit of legal grounds for appeal, CRMs are not likely to uncover evidence of innocence that would provide the confidence necessary to seek to ask for a Free Pardon on behalf of an applicant. As such, it is not surprising that after almost 12 years of casework, the CCRC has yet to use the Royal Prerogative of Mercy route,[14] further restricting public knowledge of alleged wrongful convictions.

Along with the establishment of the CCRC, the concept of innocence all but disappeared from public discourse as an organizing counter-discourse against wrongful convictions. For a considerable time, this was not adequately understood by those individuals, groups and organizations that stand opposed to the wrongful conviction and imprisonment of innocent people as the concept of factual innocence went through a kind of legalification process and the critical distinction between a miscarriage of justice as understood as a wrongful conviction of an innocent (lay discourse and the definition of the RCCJ) became blurred with the notion of a miscarriage of justice as understood in its technical legal sense (legal discourse and the definition of the CCRC) (Naughton, 2006).

This is to some extent understandable. We tend to see the world the way that we want to see it and through the spectacles that we are wearing (cf. Naughton, 2008a). As this relates to the establishment of the CCRC, at first there was a widespread belief that it was, indeed, the body that was recommended by the RCCJ and JUSTICE, and was better placed and resourced to carry out the vital investigations into claims of wrongful conviction to determine their validity and appropriateness for returning back to the appeal courts. This was enhanced by the setting up of the RCCJ on the day that the Birmingham Six walked free from the CACD, which was viewed as an indicator of real change, and it was fully embraced by organizations such as JUSTICE as the long awaited solution to the problem that it had struggled against for almost 40 years. As time has passed, however, its deficiencies have become increasingly apparent and the challenges against it have, likewise, been amplified.

What has become clear is the urgent need for a concerted effort by the media, politicians, voluntary sector groups, practitioners, academics, and so on, to further revive the lens of innocence to reconnect the arteries that are the channels of the life blood of public information on the legitimate workings of the criminal justice system; to rebuild the damaged bridges between the public and the legal system. This will be aided by forcing cases that indicate that innocent people may have been wrongly convicted and/or imprisoned, but who do not have legally admissible grounds of appeal, back into the public domain by side-stepping the CCRC, which is not appropriate for dealing with such cases, and, instead, sending them to the Secretary of State for consideration for the Royal Prerogative of Mercy and a Free Pardon.

Most significantly, we still need statutory change to our system of criminal justice and a specific body that can address the continuing problem of the wrongful conviction of the innocent and deliver what the RCCJ and JUSTICE (1994) recommended all those years ago: the machinery that can guarantee to investigate fully alleged wrongful convictions and get to the bottom of whether such claims are genuine (and an innocent person has been convicted) or fallacious (and the alleged innocent is, in fact, guilty).

Notes

1. Due to continued public pressure, Maybrick, who was convicted of murder and sentenced to death in 1889, subsequently had her sentence commuted to life imprisonment and was released after 14 years in prison in 1904.
2. As amended by the Criminal Appeal Act 1995.
3. In a meeting at the CCRC on 16 September 2003.
4. However, the CCRC *can* refer cases back to the appeal courts under s. 13(2) of the Criminal Appeal Act 1995 'if it appears to the Commission that there are exceptional circumstances which justify making it'. To date, however, the only conviction referred to the CACD under s. 13(2) was the case of Anthony Stock, which was also the first case in which the CCRC referred a case to the CACD for a second time. Mr Stock's conviction was upheld, making it his fourth unsuccessful appeal (CCRC, 2008f).
5. John Weedon speaking in a personal capacity at the Socio-Legal Studies Association Annual Conference held at the University of Stirling, 28–30 March 2006.
6. It is, perhaps, surprising that JUSTICE have not noticed that the CCRC does not fit with what the RCCJ recommended or that it outlined in 'Remedying Miscarriages of Justice'.
7. JUSTICE's telephone voice message suggests that callers seeking help with miscarriages of justice, who have failed in their appeals, to try contacting the CCRC (JUSTICE, 2008b).
8. For details and a list of member innocence projects, see INUK (2008b).
9. At the time of writing, INUK has over 20 member universities, each of which either has an active innocence project or is in the process of establishing one. This equates to several hundred students at universities around the country working on almost 50 cases between them.
10. There is evidence of a tension between criminal lawyers working with innocence projects who sometimes do not understand the ethos of innocence projects and see them as 'criminal appeals projects' and who can prematurely dismiss cases as they fail to see any grounds for appeal.

11. Having said this, it needs to be acknowledged that physical evidence such as DNA, fingerprints, fibres, and so on, are, effectively, circumstantial in nature, amounting to evidence of association and not concrete evidence of guilt.
12. As this is an on-going matter at the CCRC and I have not obtained express permission from the UoBIP 'client' or the CRM working on the case to give their names, the following account will be anonymized.
13. Culled from an email from the CRM at the CCRC to me as Director of UoBIP.
14. Confirmed by John Wagstaff, Principal Legal Advisor, CCRC, in a phone call on 19 December 2008.

Part II
Voluntary Sector Perspectives

3

Thoughts from a Victim Support Worker

Hazel Keirle

The following is culled from an interview with Hazel Keirle, Director of Miscarriages of Justice Organisation (MOJO) (England and Wales). It was conducted by Gabe Tan at the MOJO conference, 'Limits to Reparation', held at City Chambers, Glasgow, on 21–22 April 2008. Its significance is that it presents a critical evaluation of the Criminal Cases Review Commission (CCRC) from the perspective of the organization that was set up by Paddy Joe Hill, one of the Birmingham Six, the case which was one of the key miscarriages of justice that prompted the Royal Commission on Criminal Justice (RCCJ) and the subsequent setting up of the CCRC.

Q: What do you think the CCRC was set up to do?

The CCRC was set up to take over the functions of the former C3 ... C3 was a section of the Home Office where you applied if you needed an out of time appeal and you required the Secretary of State to refer your case back to the Court of Appeal via C3. So C3 was a necessary function, but because it was political, because the references all came via the political agenda, it was seen as not independent ... the Criminal Cases Review Commission was set up to be an independent, non-governmental body to take over from C3 and be independent ... its function is to refer cases to the Court of Appeal where ... former applications in the Court of Appeal have failed.

Q: So they will be looking at cases with genuine claims of innocence?

No ... the CCRC is for you to go to the Court of Appeal where your previous appeals have failed ... the CCRC also refer sentences as well as convictions and it isn't to do with innocence and is not to do with guilt. It is simply to do with whether the conviction [or sentence] and the previous process is sustainable in law.

Q: What do you think is wrong with the CCRC?

I think the problem for the CCRC is that because it is independent the amount of applications it gets is ten times more than C3 ever got. To get through C3 you really needed a very high profile lawyer or political pressure ... because of the independence of the CCRC, all those who years ago wouldn't go to C3 do go to the CCRC [which] is under-resourced entirely to do what they are doing.

The other problem for the CCRC ... is that it has a funding master, and the funding master is the government, and that will always affect its independence. For instance, during this current year, it's had, in real terms, a funding cut, and that funding cut has affected its resources and so it's also affected its criteria and how and when it will get cases back to the Court of Appeal ... Whilst it's supposed to be independent, the political agenda that is controlling the finances is actually controlling the CCRC and how it operates ... it needs to be entirely independent of Government, its funding needs to come from a different route so that its independence is better established.

Q: In terms of their referral criteria?

The [CCRC] doesn't have a criteria. Its criteria as you may call them, is framed within the 1995 [Criminal] Appeal Act. It is framed by statute and they can't go outside it. The CCRC does have some flexibility, and I think one of the problems with the CCRC is that in trying to increase its flexibility ... they send some cases back that they shouldn't send back because the evidence base isn't strong enough ... and then other cases where the evidence base is strong, they don't send back.

I think another problem for the [CCRC] is they do not fully grasp what a really skilled QC can do with grounds of appeal ... and something that the CCRC may feel as fairly weak and not affording a ground of appeal, a top skilled lawyer/QC can take that through the Court of Appeal ... they don't recognize that, in spite of the fact they think they do, they don't.

Q: They think that they are better than lawyers?

The [people] at the CCRC believe that they understand the Court of Appeal. I think they do understand the Court of Appeal, and that actually is their problem because like many other people they study the judgments that come out of the Court of Appeal and then they use their personal analyses of those judgments to frame what they will do in the future. But, the reality for anybody who works in appeals is, you know, that reading the Court of Appeal judgment is pointless. You need to have been in the court and to have heard the whole appeal and understand all the arguments that led to that judgment before you can really, fully understand what you are on about, and I think they lack that. I think they don't spend enough time in the Court of

Appeal on ordinary appeals ... I think there is maybe an education lack there amongst the case workers and commissioners.

Q: *What changes do you think the CCRC should make so that it can do what it has set out to do?*

I don't think they should be dealing with sentence appeals. Whilst I accept that unlawful sentences and things like that do need to be dealt with, because there is no issue about innocence or guilt at all in relation to a sentence appeal, I think an entirely different body should deal with those. I think the Criminal Cases Review Commission should only be there to service those who may be wrongly convicted.

I think they have got to work far more with lawyers, QCs and academics, and they've got to send more cases back and try and stretch and push the Court of Appeal to overturning more convictions so that the criterion is lower. I don't think, like many others, the Court of Appeal doesn't overturn sufficient convictions to convince the public that the safety net is actually working. I think they lose track of what the electorate and the general public feel. They wrongly assume that if there are only a few cases overturned each year then that enhances public confidence in the system because they will believe the system is almost perfect, and the few little bits that go wrong are sorted out in the Court of Appeal. That is very naïve. Generally, people are far better educated than that these days, and what it actually sends out is the opposite message: what happens to the people who must be wrongly convicted each year because we are not a perfect system? There is not enough being overturned, therefore the system actually isn't working, therefore, I have less confidence in the system ... it's function, which is to uphold public confidence in the system, I think is actually having a complete opposite effect and they don't realize or understand that at all.

Q: *Anything more about the CCRC?*

I do think they need some internal changes. I think one of their huge problems, and they do need to face it, is that when an applicant makes an application to the CCRC, as an independent body, the CCRC has no liability to that applicant – it's not the applicant's lawyer. Because of that, they must encourage applicants to be legally represented and they *must not* send out the message that says 'you don't need to be legally represented to come here' ... Applicants must be legally represented to ensure that they are being properly protected within the law ... that's the first thing that I think they've got to change. They must recognize that and know that.

The law was recently changed so that only the CCRC's grounds of appeal could formulate the formal grounds of appeal and you now need leave to put anything else in. Since that rule change, which may or may not be proper,

I think another process they can change within the CCRC itself is when they make a referral to the Court of Appeal, 'I think that what they should make [is] a provisional referral, not a straightforward referral [directly to the Court of Appeal].' It should be a provisional referral and I think the applicant's lawyers and the people who are then going to take it through the Court of Appeal should have the opportunity to look at that document, to interact with the CCRC, to put additional grounds in if they feel they're necessary ... by the time the CCRC do their final referral, what the Court of Appeal gets is precisely what the statute says ... the thing that is going to then go through the court. That will allow the court to expedite those cases and hear them within six months. At the moment they can't do that. They've got a chicken and egg situation, somebody hasn't thought it through. It's a bad piece of policy, a bad piece of practice, and a bad piece of procedure, and that can be changed.

Q: How is the SCCRC different from the CCRC?

In real terms it isn't that different, apart from the fact that it's a much smaller operation: there are less miscarriages of justice, there are fewer commission members, fewer case workers and a lot more part-time. The main difference, really, with the Scottish CCRC is that the Commission members are all QCs, so they all come from a legal background and they are also QCs that are still currently sort of in practice ... I think they've got a slightly different perspective on it. They also have the time and the resources to go out and visit all the applicants which is quite good. But, there are very few lawyers in Scotland able to represent applicants and the legal aid in Scotland is so diabolically poor that nobody in Scotland wants to take up that work in any description ... the Scottish applicants in prison are totally reliant on the Scottish CCRC to act as their advocates when, in fact, they can't. So, the Scottish CCRC has more problems.

The Scottish court of appeal [the High Court] is a very strange place that hears cases when it wants to, can make you wait 12 months or 12 years if it wants to: the criteria is different, the rules that govern appeals in Scotland are also that once a referral is made to [the High Court] the appellant then has total charge of his case ... you don't have the situation you've got in England where you've got to mess around trying to get extra grounds in leave. In Scotland, it is down to the appellant's lawyer, and he can change or alter it. He can even take the CCRC's grounds out if he wants to put his own in. So, the process in the Appeal Court from the Scottish CCRC reference appears to be fairer within [the High Court]. But getting a case through the Scottish CCRC is just as difficult. They still have a lot to learn. There are still not enough people within the Scottish prison system making applications to the Scottish CCRC. I think if MOJO were to raise its profile in Scotland as it has done in England [the] Scottish CCRC would have some problems. They would have hundreds and hundreds of cases.

Again [the SCCRC] are independent, but they are funded by the Justice Ministry within the Scottish government so they are not entirely independent. That is something that is going to affect them. They will end up with the same problems as the English CCRC if they don't learn some lessons quite quickly. But, they are thorough in what they do when they do it, but they can also be very easily misled from an investigation point of view ... the investigative system in Scotland is different than in England ... one of the things that the Scottish Commission can do is to order the local sheriff or the procurator fiscal to go out and make inquiries on its behalf. In England that, of course, is a big problem. If the CCRC in England wants to physically have an element of the crime investigated, they can't do it. They have to commission an outside police force to make inquiries and the criteria for them doing that is very high. So, if you've got one or two issues that need to be inquired on, I think in the English system those inquiries often fail and don't even get off the ground because the English CCRC can't do it, whereas the Scottish CCRC can ... there are some interesting comparatives between the two.

The referral rate in Scotland is slightly higher, but the result in [the High Court] ratio is too difficult to tell because the Scots take so long to come to a decision. There are so many cases pending that haven't been heard yet, we can't really do an analysis yet on what the outcome in the court is. So, the Scottish system has some pros that will be useful for England and vice versa. A good mix of the two would work well, but because the jurisdictions are completely different, the processes are different, the investigation processes are different, I don't think it will ever happen. I think there will be two bodies that will go off on slightly different routes altogether.

Q: Any final thoughts?

My overall view ... is that the English judicial system is supposed to be one of the best in the world ... The CCRC is a small fragment, but it can be improved on in lots of different ways. We need to improve on its quality so that it [is] not letting the system down by poor performance.

4
Challenging the Refusal to Investigate Evidence Neglected by Trial Lawyers[1]

Andrew Green

Introduction

People claiming to have been convicted of crimes they did not commit give one explanation more than any other for their wrongful conviction: their lawyers did not prepare or conduct their defence adequately. Those who apply to the Criminal Cases Review Commission (CCRC) to have their cases referred for an appeal against conviction cite poor defence work as a reason for their claimed wrongful convictions more frequently than any other reason (CCRC, 2008h). Almost all of those who seek help from the non-governmental organizations which help those believed to be innocent victims of miscarriages of justice say that the defence provided by their lawyers was inadequate. These allegations against lawyers should perhaps be treated with caution: those who believe themselves to have been wrongly convicted are looking for someone to blame for their perceived predicament; and when people are found to have actually been wrongly convicted then those directly responsible are likely to be the police, prosecutors, incompetent experts, mistaken or malicious witnesses or the operation of a system which is defective or not designed to secure the acquittal of the innocent. Poor defence work in such cases merely failed to prevent the wrongful conviction. But, its consequence is that the wrongful conviction is much harder, if not impossible, to rectify through the appeals process.

This chapter considers the limits of defence lawyers in the preparation of their cases which can lead to wrongful convictions. It examines how unused evidence if investigated appropriately by the CCRC can fulfil the tests required by the appeal courts. It argues, however, that the production of such knowledge is uncommon for the CCRC, with the norm being to see the failures of defence lawyers as part and parcel of the adversarial contest in criminal trials. As a result, potential wrongful convictions may never be corrected.

The faults of defence lawyers

The main faults said to have been committed by defence lawyers, who have not prepared cases adequately or presented cases fully in court, are failures to use relevant, admissible and significant evidence which would have supported defence cases, or to obtain such evidence in the first place. Since such evidence was always available to the defence, it is generally not regarded as 'fresh evidence' for the purposes of appeals. The Court of Appeal (Criminal Division) CACD will only admit fresh evidence if it satisfies the criteria set down in s. 23(2) of the Criminal Appeal Act 1968. This section requires the Court 'in considering whether to receive any evidence, to have regard in particular to ... whether the evidence would have been admissible in the proceedings from which the appeal lies ... and whether there is a reasonable explanation for the failure to adduce the evidence in those proceedings.'

The main explanations for not adducing evidence that defence lawyers could have obtained and/or used in earlier court proceedings is that they were negligent, incompetent, indifferent or made poor judgments about how to conduct their clients' cases. Such allegations are frequently made by those who believe themselves to have been wrongly convicted, but they are very hard to substantiate. There appears to be an assumption that defence lawyers are competent and do in practice carry out their work diligently, and that decisions not to obtain or use evidence which might support defence cases are made for carefully considered tactical reasons. If the alleged negligence of trial lawyers becomes an issue in appeals, the lawyers concerned may be called to give evidence, and will use this opportunity to defend themselves.

The Criminal Appeal Act 1995, s. 13 rules that the CCRC should not refer a conviction for review by the CACD unless 'there is a real possibility that the conviction ... would not be upheld were the reference to be made' (known as the 'Real Possibility Test'). The CCRC appears to take the view that an appeal based on the admission of evidence, which can only be regarded as fresh because of trial lawyers' failure to make use of it, would be unlikely to succeed, and so routinely refuses applications which depend on such evidence. Further, it is unwilling to investigate leads which were ignored by defence lawyers, however likely such investigations might be to produce significant evidence not previously known to the lawyers concerned. In the 'Statements of Reasons' it issues in support of its decisions on applications, it may quote the CACD in *R* v. *Thakrar*:

> The mere fact that an appellant's solicitors may have failed to carry out their duties to the appellant in a proper manner does not itself mean that a conviction is automatically unsafe ... The test is whether, in all the circumstances, the conviction is safe.

The problem that faces applicants who wish to rely on available but unused evidence is: how can they persuade the CCRC to acknowledge that such evidence can be significant and to refer their applications to the appeal court? This is a problem which can perhaps be solved by persuading the CCRC of two things: first, that it should obtain such evidence; second, that the court will be prepared to admit such evidence – if it results from appropriate investigations and is properly presented.

It will be necessary to review why the problem arises in the first place: why is relevant evidence not used or not even obtained by defence lawyers? Despite the CACD's assumptions about the competence and diligence of defence lawyers, research indicates that lawyers may not always provide the service expected of them. McConville *et al.* (1994) found, following detailed research into the working practices of nearly 50 criminal law firms, that legal advisers had a deficient overall grasp of clients' cases, that they tend to assume their clients are guilty, that police and prosecution versions of events were true, that clients' allegations of police malpractice which could be used as the basis for challenging the admissibility of evidence were 'almost invariably ignored or met with a bland response' (ibid.: 95–6, 137, 143; see also McConville and Hodgson, 1993: 80). McConville *et al.* (1994) argued that these assumptions and practices derive from the closeness of defence and prosecution lawyers' and the police's working circumstances, attitudes, culture and ideologies, compared with the lack of empathy between defence lawyers and their clients, and so poor defence work is predictable. Defence lawyers are often said to be inadequately funded to prepare cases for legally aided clients (see Chapter 10). Tracy Cook reported in *The Guardian* that:

> Most criminal lawyers have not had a fee increase since 2001. Many practices already subsidise legal aid work and rely on continual overdrafts ... In the past five years, over a quarter of criminal law firms and 670 civil firms have closed. (Cook, 2007)

The apparently inadequate funding of defence lawyers is perhaps unsurprising, deriving as it does from the attitude expressed by Lord Devlin: 'if [criminal defences] were prepared as thoroughly as a civil defence the bill would be very large: since the police are there to investigate, why double the cost?' (Devlin, 1981: 75).

McConville *et al.* (1994: 68) found that defence cases are normally constructed from prosecution material and that defence solicitors carried out little independent investigation. In addition, there are few checks (if any) on the quality of defence lawyers' work, and clients have limited avenues of redress following poor work by their lawyers if they are wrongly convicted. Under these conditions, it seems possible, if not probable, that the poor defence work of which CCRC applicants so frequently complain has actually occurred. While the CACD may have, as Lord Bingham CJ put it in *R* v. *Campbell*, 'repeatedly underlined the need for defendants in criminal trials to advance their full defence before the jury and call any necessary evidence at that stage', actual defendants are frequently incompetent to know what case preparation should be done, unable to persuade their solicitors to carry out adequate preparation, and powerless to persuade counsel that their cases should be conducted as they, rather than counsel, wish. Some examples will illustrate what can happen and why it poses a serious problem for CCRC applicants.

Case illustrations

Andrew Pountley was convicted of the abduction, rape and murder of a five-year-old child, Rosemary. A key part of the prosecution case was that Pountley had taken Rosemary from her bed in a house which he had visited many times previously. The evidence which supported this contention was that fibres from Pountley's scarf were found on the duvet used on Rosemary's bed. The prosecution expert said that these 'findings would support a view that there had been recent contact between [Pountley's] scarf and...the duvet cover from the bedroom of Rosemary'. A forensic scientist instructed by the defence said, however, that it was 'very debatable as to what "recent" means': '[it was likely that the fibres] had accumulated over a period of time and as a result of Mr Pountley's visits to the house' (*R v. Pountley*). Counsel for Pountley explained to him that he could use the expert's findings in his cross-examination of the prosecution expert, and so would not need to call their own witness. Pountley appears to have accepted this advice. The result appears in the judge's Summing Up: the fibre evidence showed 'that the defendant had recently been in the bedroom of [Rosemary] from the large quantities of blue fibres on the sheet' (there is no mention of any challenge to this evidence) (*R v. Pountley*, 18H–19A).

A single fibre from the scarf was found on the bag in which Rosemary's body was found. The prosecution expert speculated that 'this could have been the last of a large number since washed away'. The defence expert thought that the fibre's presence on the holdall 'could have arisen as a result of secondary transfer'. But the jury did not hear his opinion. The judge told them the fibre 'could represent the remains of initially a much larger number' (*R v. Pountley*, 16F).

The prosecution expert said, of six hairs found on a sheet from Pountley's house which probably originated from the victim, 'all have been broken [and this] suggests that these hairs have ... been subject to a forceful pulling action causing them to break'. The prosecution case was that Pountley raped and murdered Rosemary in his own house. The broken hairs provided the only evidence that this violence occurred in this place. But the defence expert concluded: 'the broken ends of these hairs could be produced in a variety of ways. The possibility cannot be excluded that these hairs could have persisted from the time that Rosemary and her mother were occupants of [Pountley's house]'. The judge said that the prosecution's 'conclusions are the most likely in his expert opinion. You are not obliged to accept that, members of the jury, but it is there for you to consider' (*R v. Pountley*, 18E). The jury, not having heard from the defence expert, accepted the inferences drawn by the prosecution expert.

Pountley applied to the CCRC. Its Statement of Reasons on the case, which explains its decision not to refer it to the appeal court, concluded that defence counsel 'must have ... made a tactical decision not to call' the defence expert, and that there would be no real possibility that the CACD would receive his evidence.

An important exhibit in the same case was a pyjama top found in Pountley's house, and said by the prosecution to have been worn by Rosemary when she was abducted. It was produced in a police interview of Pountley, when his solicitor was present. A photograph of the item which was to be exhibited at the trial was disclosed to defence before the trial. Both Pountley and his solicitor thought that the pyjama top in the photograph was distinctly different from the one they had been shown at the interview. The solicitor made a statement to this effect, and since it was planned that he should testify he was excluded from trial and unable to advise his client or instruct counsel during the trial. Pountley himself gave evidence that the item exhibited was not the one produced in the interview, expecting to be supported by his solicitor. Counsel, however, decided not to call the solicitor to give evidence. Junior counsel later told the CCRC: 'we were advised by the Prosecution that they had material which would significantly undermine our case and which would be put to [the solicitor] in cross examination' (CCRC Statement of Reasons, para. 62(f)(vii)). Pountley said that he understood that the reason for not calling his solicitor was because there were differences between their accounts. After the trial he conferred with the solicitor and found there were no differences. The CCRC chose to accept junior counsel's recollection, did not interview the trial solicitor and concluded that the CACD would not hear the solicitor's evidence.

In another alleged wrongful conviction case that is currently supported by INNOCENT,[2] the applicant was a woman convicted of murder. She had been present when a man had killed her father. The two were tried jointly. During the trial, the man changed his plea to guilty. Subsequently, he testified that the woman had persuaded him to commit the crime. She argued that she had not known in advance of his intention to kill her father. A witness statement by the man's own father was disclosed, which gave an account of the man's long history of psychiatric problems and propensity to violence. Junior counsel, preparing the case for trial, advised the woman's solicitor to obtain, if possible, her co-accused's medical records, arguing that these might support the client's account of the man's unpredictable violence. But the solicitor did not apply for the records. In her application to the CCRC, the woman asked for these records to be obtained. The CCRC has the power, under s. 17 of the Criminal Appeal Act 1995, to obtain copies of documents held by any public body. They may choose not to disclose such documents, but the applicant expected that the CCRC would in her case obtain her co-defendant's medical records and assess whether they did, in fact, contain material which would have supported her defence. The CCRC, however, formed the opinion that the applicant's defence lawyers had clearly made a forensic decision *not* to apply for disclosure of the medical records (although it could not consult the solicitor concerned, since he had died) and that the CACD would not admit the records as fresh evidence. It did not attempt to obtain the records.

Interpreting 'fresh evidence'

The meetings of organizations which offer to help those who believe themselves to have been wrongly convicted[3] are frequently attended by people who say that evidence they expected to be used by the defence in the cases in which they were involved was not used. They are advised that such evidence is not to be considered by the CCRC, and that they must find fresh evidence, as the legal system defines it. These organizations, often echoing advice from solicitors, relay the clear message from the CCRC that evidence available at trial but unused cannot constitute fresh evidence for the purposes of appeals. The position appears to be entrenched and intractable: but is this really the case?

The CACD can hear any evidence it wishes to hear, as long as the evidence accords with the rules of evidence which apply to any criminal case hearing. The restrictions given in s. 28 of the Criminal Appeal Act 1968 are not absolute and are not invariably observed. Lord Bingham CJ observed when conducting a judicial review of a CCRC decision:

> The exercise of [the CCRC's] discretion cannot be circumscribed in a manner which fails to give effect to the statute or undermines the statutory objective, which is to promote the interests of justice; the Court will bear in mind that the power in section 23 [of the 1968 Act] exists to safeguard defendants against the risk and consequences of wrongful conviction. (*R* v. *Criminal Cases Review Commission, ex parte Pearson*)

If an appellant made a clear choice not to give evidence in his or her own defence at trial, and then sought to testify at his or her appeal, anything he or she might say would clearly be evidence available at the trial with no explanation for why it was not adduced there. Yet, for example, in the case of *R* v. *Murphy and Brannan*, overturned on appeal following a CCRC referral, the CACD permitted John Brannan to testify at his first appeal, although he had not done so at his trial and had not answered questions in his police interviews. It might be argued, in cases such as that of Angela Cannings (*R* v. *Cannings*), in which an expert provides fresh evidence at appeal, that diligent defence lawyers when preparing for the trial could have found the same expert and, therefore, that the evidence is not strictly fresh; but fortunately no one was so foolish as to consider this argument.

Reflecting the power of the CACD to hear any evidence it wishes, so long as it is in the interests of justice, the Criminal Appeal Act 1995, s. 13(2) gives the CCRC a general power to refer cases: nothing in the previous, restrictive s. 13(1) 'shall prevent the making of a reference if it appears to the Commission that there are exceptional circumstances which justify making it'. The Real Possibility Test still applies, but, in the face of differing attitudes towards the admission of unused defence evidence adopted by variously constituted appeal courts, how can the CCRC assess what, from the mass of such evidence available, will be admitted by the Court?

Clearly, the CACD does not wish to spend its time considering cases in which the incompetence of lawyers has led only to the failure to adduce evidence which would not have made any difference to the jury's decision if they had in fact heard it. As the CACD explicates it:

> In order to establish lack of safety in an incompetence case the appellant has to go beyond the incompetence and show that the incompetence led to identifiable errors or irregularities in the trial, which themselves rendered the process unfair or unsafe. (*R* v. *Day*)

Nonetheless, if such failures have prevented an appellant from having a fair trial, within the meaning of Article 6 of the European Convention on Human Rights, that will normally mean that the conviction is unsafe and should be quashed (see *R* v. *Togher*). Therefore, the first question is whether the appellant received a fair trial or whether such a trial was prevented by the failings in preparation on the part of her or his solicitors. Such an issue is to be determined by considering the proceeding as a whole, as one cannot confine one's attention merely to the solicitor's preparations in isolation (*R* v. *Thakrar*).

In 2005, the CCRC referred the case of Andrew Adams to the CACD on three grounds, the first of which was:

> Inadequate legal representation by solicitors and counsel, particularly in relation to ... the failure to view relevant unused material and pursue lines of enquiry arising from it and the failure properly to proof and call potentially significant defence witnesses. (CCRC, Statement of Reasons, para. 399)

According to Ben Rose, Adams's appeal solicitor, the evidence of inadequate preparation by the trial solicitors was 'overwhelming'. His opinion was that this case had not extended the law, and so the CCRC would not change the way they assessed other applications alleging poor defence preparation.[4] Only when the evidence of blatant incompetence was presented to the CCRC would it be able to treat the evidence, not heard by the jury as a result of that incompetence, as fresh evidence. Allowing the appeal, Lord Justice Gage said:

> None of the evidence which was not deployed ... can be described as fresh evidence. It was all available to the defence before trial. But the failure to use this evidence, in our judgment, demonstrates that, for whatever reason, the legal advisers at trial had failed in those respects in their pre-trial preparations. (*R* v. *Adams*, para. 155)

No doubt Rose is right to advise caution. It is probable that in any case in which CCRC applicants blame lawyers for their perceived wrongful convictions, the CCRC's staff, and, if the case is referred, appeal judges, are more likely to believe lawyers' versions of events than applicants'. In *R* v. *Adams*, the court had before it very clear evidence of poor trial preparation. But, in the end, what demonstrated clearly to the judges that there was poor defence preparation was the *failure to deploy* significant evidence. This is in accordance with the injunction in *R* v. *Thrakar* to 'consider the proceedings a whole'. The CACD appears to be indicating that, in addition to some evidence that lawyers did not carry out work competently (in the case of *R* v. *Adams* solicitors did not read prosecution unused material or interview witnesses, while counsel failed to instruct them to carry out important preparation work), the failure to adduce significant evidence is, *in itself*, evidence that defence preparation has been inadequate.

What the judgment in *R* v. *Adams* does is direct attention to the nature of that evidence put before it which, if defence counsel had been familiar with it, would probably have been put before the jury at the trial: evidence sufficient to possibly render the conviction unsafe in the judgment of the appeal court. What is perhaps most unusual about the CCRC's review of this case is the thoroughness of the investigation. The Statement of Reasons supporting the decision to refer is long and detailed. According to Rose, the Case Review Manager (CRM) who investigated the case spent 'a huge amount of time' examining the Home Office Large Major Enquiry System (HOLMES) – an extensive database which records all information relating to the police investigation in major incidents. The CRM also interviewed witnesses that had been neglected by defence solicitors. This work provided the fresh evidence which enabled the judges to reach the conclusion that Adams's conviction was unsafe and, at the same time, the demonstration of why that evidence could be considered fresh, namely the defence lawyers' failures. What created the difference between the evidence in this case and that in the other cases in which similar allegations have been made against trial lawyers?

The production of revelatory knowledge

I have argued elsewhere that knowledge which can become prosecution evidence in criminal cases is privileged by its method of production, the structure it has been given and the authentication that accompanies and supports it (Green, 1997, 2008). Briefly, when the police produce knowledge of a suspect, or of anything else that might become evidence in a case, they always do so by using a method, which might be called *testing*, in which they reduce any indicator of possible evidence to a trace, test that trace until it resists, overcome its resistance, and then reveal the truth behind the surface on which the trace lies, and where resistance is found. I have termed this the 'revelatory method', and its product, 'revelatory knowledge'. The police distrust surface appearances and reveal what lies behind them. It is a common idea, but it requires the exercise of power by the police or some other agent or expert working with them to encounter, provoke (if necessary) and overcome the resistance of any object of knowledge. The defence do not have the power to produce evidence which has the same quality and authentication as that produced for the prosecution.

The evidence which is assembled as a prosecution case is grounded in its *authentication*; authentication, the record of investigations, is joined together in a coherent narrative, namely, the narrative of the prosecution, which then gives coherence to the evidence itself. The defence in a criminal case cannot hope to compete by producing a coherent counter-narrative, and rarely attempts to do so. McConville *et al.* (1994: 136) found that solicitors 'discouraged clients from telling their own stories'. Defence work consists entirely of attempts to fracture the prosecution narrative (which is implied by the apparent inadequacies of defence work mentioned above and illustrated by the *Adams* case). The defence is perhaps seen as a supplement to the prosecution, tasked with finding and eliminating errors (Ericson, 1994: 119; Green, 2008: 110–1; McConville *et al.*, 1991: 167). The judgment in *R* v. *Adams* gives an example of what a good defence should be doing:

> Nevertheless, we cannot escape the fact that the prosecution case on this important piece of evidence was not tested to any real extent by the defence lawyers. They ought to have seen A491 [an item in the unused material disclosed to them]. Mr Nolan [prosecution counsel] concedes that it was unacceptable not to have examined the Holmes database. If this document had been unearthed it would have given the defence lawyers a useful tool with which to challenge both the evidence of the two police officers and Kevin Thompson. (*R* v. *Adams*, para. 92)

What the CCRC's investigation in *Adams* did was not defence work. It applied police methods, of revelation and case construction, to the production of defence evidence and construction of a narrative. The disparate items of previously non-investigated, non-deployed potential defence evidence are linked in a coherent narrative by the CCRC's investigation records, and this narrative, instead of being one which demonstrates the guilt of a defendant, as would a police-constructed narrative, now demonstrates the consistent inadequacies of the defence preparation. Each piece of newly revealed evidence becomes 'something which must be put in the balance with other factors when we consider whether this verdict is unsafe' (*R v. Adams*, para. 92).

It is not strictly necessary to adopt the theory outlined in the preceding paragraphs in order to understand what the CCRC achieved in this case (and hence what it could achieve in other cases), but perhaps the theory will assist an understanding of the detail of the case. The appeal judgment admits that a lot of relatively small items of evidence should have been discovered and, if it had been discovered, would have been used by counsel in support of the appellant's version of events (*R v. Adams*, paras. 83–92, 110–17). The CCRC obtained and authenticated these items by following lines of inquiry from their initial traces, through detailed examination of the HOLMES database, to interviews of witnesses concerned, including police officers and the examination of material never previously disclosed by the police and prosecution, to reveal the hidden truth of the unused (because never found) items of evidence. It is not my impression, nor that of police officers with whom I have discussed defence preparation, that many defence lawyers carry out such detailed work: as noted above, they are not funded to do so. They do not have the power to require disclosure of all records held by public bodies, as the CCRC does. They do not interview serving police officers to obtain information relating to active cases. Instead, they frequently pass the responsibility for preparatory work over to their clients (McConville *et al.*, 1994: 145). In contrast, the CCRC can, like the police, produce the kind of privileged knowledge that I term revelatory. This is the kind of knowledge which can be admitted and carry weight in the CACD; the kind of knowledge which in itself can demonstrate to the CACD the inadequacy of defence preparation.

A budgetary problem?

It is possible (although almost certainly unusual) for the CCRC to work in the way it did in *Adams* because of the powers it has been given, and because it is able to act neither as prosecutor nor defender, but as inquisitor. Unusually for the British legal system, the CCRC is an inquisitorial body. It prides itself on being 'utterly independent of every other body' (CCRC, 2007a: 4). The Criminal Appeal Act 1995, s. 8(2) states that 'the Commission shall not be regarded as the servant or agent of the Crown'. It has unique powers to be used in the investigation of applicants' cases. Although it says its job is simply to 'review' cases (CCRC, 2007a: 2), s. 14(2) of the 1995 Act says the CCRC shall 'have regard to (a) any application or representations made to the Commission by or on behalf of the person to whom it relates, (b) any other representations made to the Commission in relation to it, and (c) any other matters which appear to the Commission to be relevant': it does not take instructions and it can act on its own initiative.

Besides, under the same Act, it has s. 17 powers to view records; it has power under s. 19 to require the appointment of investigating officers; and under s. 21 to take 'steps which the [Commissioners] consider appropriate for assisting them in the exercise of any of their functions including, in particular – (a) undertaking, or arranging for others to undertake, inquiries, and (b) obtaining, or arranging for others to obtain, statements, opinions and reports': all of which powers it does in practice use. But it has not explicitly acknowledged that it has an inquisitorial role, and in most cases appears not to consider using its powers – they were not used in the cases cited above. Why does it not always use these powers in the way that the police might do when investigating a crime that comes to their attention?

The answer could be that it has insufficient resources to do so. It is able to spend over £7 million a year (CCRC, 2007a: 62), which, if its only activity were investigating cases, would amount to approximately £7,000 per case. It has other responsibilities, including responding to judicial reviews of its decisions, which must be costly, so the figure per case must be less in practice. It is difficult to find a way of comparing any estimate of the CCRC's expenditure per case with that of the police. In 2006–07 the police spent between £900 and £5,000 per 'incident' (excluding minor crimes such as criminal damage) (House of Commons (Hansard), 2008), but the incidents presumably include cases that were not cleared up or were perhaps only minimally investigated due to lack of leads, and since most cases that result in the charging of suspects are determined by cautions or guilty pleas, they might not require the level of resources that are required by the cases of CCRC applicants, most of whom pleaded not guilty.

The police are prepared on occasion to spend large sums on investigating cases: £800,000 on investigating allegations that donations were made to the Labour Party in exchange for honours (Dodd and Wintour, 2007); £3.6 million on investigating a fire in which four people died (Goulden, 2008) (neither of these cases has resulted in anyone being charged); and £15 million on an investigation into child pornography which resulted in 1,451 convictions (about £10,000 per conviction) (McCue, 2005).

If the CCRC were to reinvestigate fully all the cases in which applicants ask it to follow lines of inquiry – that point to possible significant evidence which was neglected by their defence lawyers – and do so with the thoroughness of the original police investigations, then it might be able to process far fewer cases overall. The cost of the investigation into the death of television presenter Jill Dando was over £2 million, even before anyone was arrested, and it reportedly eventually exceeded £10 million (BBC News, 1999): the CCRC must also have spent a large sum in the course of its investigation of the case of *R* v. *George*, convicted of this murder; and the CCRC investigation that led to a referral of the case for a second appeal, at which the conviction was quashed. Presumably the CCRC balances the large sums it spends on cases like *George* and *Adams* by spending less on others, but overall it considers its funding to be insufficient (CCRC, 2007a: 5). So it may be deterred from full investigations in order to process more cases and to appear efficient and capable of meeting targets.

However, the CCRC does not explicitly acknowledge the existence of budgetary constraints on its investigations, and when I have asked CRMs or Commissioners whether such constraints exist they have told me that they do not. In the examples I have used, the cost of the requested investigations would not be great. In the second case, the cost of obtaining and assessing the co-defendant's medical records would not have been high. In the case of *Pountley* and the specific example of the pyjama-top exhibit, interviewing the defence solicitor and his clerk (who passed messages between counsel, client and solicitor) would not have been difficult or costly, but the CCRC chose not to follow this line of inquiry (although a successful challenge to the authenticity of the exhibit concerned could have led to the failure of a significant part of the prosecution's case, including the fibre evidence, as well as damaging the veracity of key prosecution witnesses). Instead, it accepted counsel's recollection of events and assessment of the significance of the issue and declared that the appeal court would not admit the solicitor's evidence (CCRC Statement of Reasons, para. 62(f)). By interviewing the solicitor and his clerk, the CCRC would have converted the trace of possible defence evidence into authenticated revelatory evidence, which the CACD might well have been prepared to admit.

Conclusion

In general, the CCRC does not recognize the difference between knowledge produced in the course of preparation of defence cases and the knowledge that it has the power to produce and which is the product of its own investigations. It does not see its job as being the conversion of the traces of possible system knowledge into knowledge privileged within the system and therefore admissible in the appeal court, which is also knowledge that can be used to construct case narratives. When it fails to respond to the content of applications by investigating whether the traces they offer can be converted into privileged revelatory knowledge, it becomes instead a player in the adversarial game, taking one side or the other, and the side it appears to take most often is that of the prosecution:

> Applicants experience the response of the CCRC to their applications as dismissive and hostile, often viewing Statements of Reasons ... as reinforcements of the prosecution case ... The adversarial context in which it operates influences the CCRC to assess each item of potential evidence submitted by applicants according to how it would be criticised by the prosecution. (Green, 2006)

If this situation is to change, it will first be necessary for constructive critics of the CCRC to recognize that the problems experienced by applicants, particularly those seeking to introduce evidence neglected by their own trial lawyers, occur neither at the interface between the CCRC and the CACD – governed by the Real Possibility Test and the CCRC's interpretation of what might constitute 'fresh evidence' and possible grounds for referral – nor in the interpretation the CCRC makes of its own role and, hence, how it carries out its own work. Demands for change are better directed at how the CCRC *does* its work, which can be changed, rather than at the Real Possibility Test, which can only be changed by legislation but which is unlikely to occur.

Notes

1. The references to the CCRC's Statements of Reasons, judges' Summing Ups and expert reports, and so on, that are cited in this chapter, which will not appear in the list of references at the end of the book, were available to the author by virtue of his role in working on the case with the organization INNOCENT.
2. Name withheld in line with the wishes of the applicant.
3. For example, see United Against Injustice (2008) for details of the member organizations.
4. From a conversation with the author, 20 April 2007.

5

The Failure to Live Up to its Stated Values? The Case of Michael Attwooll and John Roden[1]

Dennis Eady

Introduction

The Criminal Cases Review Commission (CCRC) claims to adopt certain core values to govern its operations and, most importantly, its case reviews of alleged miscarriages of justice. These values appear variously in its Annual Reports and on its website and are expressed by the words 'independent', 'thorough', 'investigative', 'impartial', 'accountable' and 'transparent'. One might argue that stating noble values could leave any organization or individual open to contradiction when particular instances are examined. However, it is not the intention of this discussion to use these statements in a cynical or ironic way. On the contrary, the use of the CCRC's own key terms to structure the following discussion is intended to illustrate how a particular case, that of Michael Attwooll and John Roden, who waited ten years from the first application to the CCRC in 1997 until referral to the Court of Appeal (Criminal Division) (CACD) in May 2007, can bring into focus some of the fundamental difficulties and systematic limitations that the CCRC faces in enacting and living up to its stated values. This is not to deny that such values may be genuinely desired or pursued but, rather, to acknowledge the internal and external barriers to their achievement and the consequential impact that this has on the ability of the CCRC to overturn the alleged wrongful convictions of potentially innocent people.

Outline of the Attwooll and Roden case

At around 1.30 a.m. on Friday 6 May 1994 the bodies of Gerald Stevens and Christine Rees were found in the office section of a taxi firm called Western Valley Taxis on the Birds Industrial Estate in Risca, South Wales. They had been shot and cut with a sharp weapon and were discovered by a taxi driver returning to the office in the early hours of the morning. Gerald Stevens was the joint owner of the firm with Mike Attwooll, and Christine Rees was a driver with the firm. The two victims had been having an extra-marital relationship.

Attwooll, Gerald Stevens's business partner, was arrested on Monday 9 May 1994. His daughter's boyfriend, John Roden, was arrested on 8 August 1994 (one week after Mr Attwooll's committal proceedings). Both were convicted in June 1995 of the murder of Gerald Stevens and Christine Rees.

Essentially, the prosecution case was that Attwooll was motivated to commit the murders by anger about the relationship between the victims and/or by a feeling that his business partner was cheating him financially (no motive could be attributed to Roden). Apart from some disputed statements, which amounted to little more than local and contextual gossip, such claims, as often is the case with motive, could be implied but not substantiated.

Like many potential miscarriages of justice in serious cases, this case became immensely complicated and littered with confusions and contradictions. Following his conviction in June 1995 Attwooll wrote a document running to 90 pages describing his version of the evidence in the case. This formed the basis of his request for leave to appeal and his initial application to the CCRC; and despite its rigorous and, arguably, compelling content it was largely dismissed as a series of 'jury points', that is, the jury had already heard the evidence and decided to convict regardless.

Due to limitations of space many of the details of, and disputes about, certain pieces of evidence cannot be included here, but some of these may be referred to in the analysis of the CCRC involvement below. The key strands of evidence will be briefly summed up under four headings: timings and sightings; blood traces in Attwooll's car; the gun and the evidence of Vincent Price (against Attwooll) and Carl Perkins (against Roden); and the evidence of David Eaves.

Timings and sightings

It was undisputed that Attwooll left the taxi office around 12.30 a.m. on the night of the murders. This was verified by another driver who left at the same time. Mr Stevens was still at the office and was joined by Mrs Rees who had completed her driving jobs. Attwooll then drove the short distance (less than half a mile) to call at his daughter's flat to confirm taxi arrangements for the next day. At this point the two versions of events diverge. According to Attwooll he then drove the short distance home, arriving at around 12.40 a.m. and retiring to bed at around 12.50 a.m. – a version of events confirmed by his wife in statement and at trial. According to the prosecution Attwooll picked up Roden at his daughter's flat, Roden then lay down in the back of the car so as not to be seen and they drove back to the office and committed the murders.

This version of events was backed by statements from the owner of a garage next to the taxi office who claimed that he heard an argument between the business partners followed by a loud bang at around 12.30 a.m. It was also backed by the evidence of two teenage girls who claimed, after seeing newspaper reports and photographs following Attwooll's arrest, to have seen him driving towards the office in his white Sierra car at the material time. These claims were countered by Attwooll, denying that there had been an argument and suggesting that the loud bang was probably his closing of the roller shutter doors around that time. In addition, a group of young men who were present outside the estate that night claimed to hear gun shots at around 1.15 a.m. These young men were not called to give evidence and only part of their statements were read out in court. On 1 November 2001 one of these men appeared in an HTV 'Wales this Week' documentary confirming his version of events and expressing surprise that he had not been called to give evidence. The evidence of the two girls was inconsistent in both statement and at trial, but may have been seen as an important piece in the prosecution jigsaw. However, since conviction, Attwooll has provided the CCRC with an analysis of timings based on the girls' own statements, their till receipts from the garage outside the estate and the time they themselves said it took them to walk up the road. The analysis seems to provide a compelling argument that they would have been well past the place that they claimed to see his car by the time they claimed to see him. It has also emerged since conviction that evidence of another white Sierra in the vicinity at the time was not utilized by the defence. The timescale available for the prosecution scenario to take place is by any measure very tight – 'an enduring feature of miscarriages' it has been argued (Woffinden, 1998: 28).

Blood traces in Mike Attwooll's car

Following information given to the police by Vincent Price on the Sunday after the murders (see below), Attwooll was arrested the next day and questioned as a suspect and his car was searched and tested. Four tiny areas of faint blood staining were found on the inside of his white Ford Sierra and tests indicated that some of these could be combinations of the blood of both victims. Four pages of the judge's 216-page Summing-Up document discuss the testing that took place and the conclusion is far from clear. The Summing Up only very briefly alluded to the fact that the victims often used the white Sierra and were known to fight and make love in that car. This somewhat crucial point was dealt with by the statement 'remember the evidence we heard from more than one witness that Stevens and Christine Rees used to quarrel with one another'. The likelihood that they could have left small traces of their blood in the car is not insignificant (the blood traces could not be aged).

The other issue relating to this piece of evidence concerns Attwooll's visit to the crime scene, at the request of the police on the morning after the murder, to locate files and describe the normal layout of the furniture in the office. In a statement made before the discovery of the blood traces, and consistently maintained ever since, Attwooll has claimed that he travelled from his home to the office in his own car following a police phone call to agree to this arrangement. Although this call and his departure in the Sierra was witnessed by Mrs Attwooll and another witness, no log of the call has ever been traced and the police maintain that he was taken from his home to the crime scene in the police car. Despite the other possible ways that the blood traces could have got into the car, this began to establish a case against Attwooll, especially in the light of the evidence of Vincent Price.

The gun and the evidence of Vincent Price and Carl Perkins

One of the most curious features of this case is that the key prosecution witness against Attwooll, his brother-in-law, Vincent Price, claimed to have provided the alleged murder weapon and that the key prosecution witness against Roden, Carl Perkins, claimed to have disposed of it. There is no other connection whatsoever between the two defendants and the weapon, other than the word of the two prosecution witnesses who both admit committing the illegal acts of providing an illegal converted weapon (Mr Price) and disposing of a weapon believed to be a murder weapon (Mr Perkins).

Vincent Price had an interest in guns and had a firearms licence. However, he claimed that he had provided bullets to a man called O'Neill to use in a converted air rifle. Mr O'Neill then claimed that he had engaged a friend, Mr Duffy, to convert this gun to fire .22 bullets and to fix a silencer. Having had this done, he gave this now illegal weapon to Vincent Price. These events might be seen as suspicious in terms of motive and were certainly illegal. Mr Price claimed that he had sold this gun to Attwooll some months before the murders and furthermore that Attwooll had visited him on the morning after the murders and, effectively, confessed to the crime by saying he had got rid of the gun and asking Mr Price for advice on how to remove nitro stains from his hands (Statement of Reasons, 2001: paras. 1.24 and 1.25). Mr Attwooll has always denied buying or being in possession of the gun and making such incriminating remarks. Vincent Price, however, gave evidence to this effect, even though he suffered mental health problems at the time of the trial, including having made a suicide attempt (Statement of Reasons, 2001: para. 10.9).

Carl Perkins was a friend of Roden and Attwooll's daughter, Vicky. He had a history of criminal convictions relating to drugs and theft and had suffered mental health problems which had been treated at one point before the trial with ECT (electroconvulsive therapy). Mr Perkins was imprisoned shortly after the murders for non-payment of fines and while there he requested to be placed on the wing for vulnerable prisoners (at that time known as 'Rule 43') apparently because he was fearful of his reputation as a 'grass' (Trial Summing Up, paras. 36G and 37A). When placed in this section, he shared a cell with a man convicted of sex offences, named Woodland. 'Mr Woodland was, or shortly thereafter became, a registered police informant' (CCRC Provisional Statement of Reasons for John Roden, 2004: para. 1.33) and he gave information to the police that Mr Perkins had told him that he (Perkins) had knowledge about the Risca Murders. Following this information, the police visited Mr Perkins at his home on Monday 8 August 1994 and spent almost three hours with him, recording only a few minutes worth of notes (ibid.: para. 9.4). During this time, however, Mr Perkins was able to direct the police to find the two parts of the gun which had been thrown into the river Ebbw, which ran at the back of his house. In fact, the gun was located roughly halfway between the home of Perkins and the home of Price, who lived in the same street, although the two men claimed they did not know each other. Following this, Perkins gave further evidence claiming that Roden had confessed to the murders and had asked him to dispose of the murder weapon which he did by partially burning it in a bonfire and then throwing it into the river. Mr Perkins was never charged with the offence of assisting an offender but gave crucial evidence at trial along with Mr Woodland.

The evidence of David Eaves

After being charged, Attwooll was remanded to Cardiff Prison where he came across a man called David Eaves. Eaves had convictions for violence and sexual offences against young people including incest with his daughter and at the time was on remand on charges of assaults and threats to kill his wife. On 27 May 1994, he gave evidence to the police that Attwooll had confessed to the murders and given him certain details. On 2 June, Eaves was granted bail, the prosecution opposed bail but the judge was told that he had given evidence in the Risca murder case. Following this, his wife dropped the case against her husband and the police did not pursue the matter (Summing Up, 114, para. B). The judge's Summing Up spends 28 pages (111–39) discussing the evidence of Eaves and Attwooll's response to his claims. Inconsistencies and inaccuracies around detail and possible motives are considered along with the possibility that information was gained from newspaper, TV and radio reports. The possibility that detail was obtained from meetings with the police is not considered. Eaves provided considerable detail; much of it contradicted earlier statements and some provided explanations for unexplained factors in the case such as why no blood could be found on any of Attwooll's clothing. He had, according to Eaves, worn 'wet gear ... oils' – but there was nothing to support this accusation. Eaves also made claims that reinforced the motives about resentment and being cheated, which the prosecution were putting forward.

Jury secrecy means that it can never be known whether the jury believed Eaves, but the attention given to his evidence by the judge indicates that it was taken as serious evidence to be considered, even though the use of prison informers has often been used to bolster cases which have later been established as miscarriages of justice (Bridgewater Four, Cardiff Three, Cardiff Newsagent Three, for example). In fairness, the judge warned the jury at one point 'to consider his [Eaves] evidence with the greatest care and caution' (Summing Up, 113, para. D). However, the complexity of the intellectual task faced by the jury and the inevitable role of speculation is well illustrated in the whole of these 28 pages (and throughout the lengthy Summing Up) with all the various possibilities they might consider. To give an example with just one paragraph:

> You will also want to ask: suppose Attwooll were guilty, why should he ever want to confess his guilt to a man who, before they met in prison, was a total stranger? Would a guilty man ever trust a stranger with his guilty secrets? Would he regard a convicted criminal as on the same side, against the law, and someone therefore to be trusted? Would he just want to talk about it?' (Mr Justice Jowitt, Summing Up, 113, para. B)

It might be argued that a jury could never do more than speculate on such questions.

The importance of thorough research and questioning by counsel, including examining previous statements in cross-examination, is also illustrated by Mr Justice Jowitt's directions about the primacy of oral evidence:

> It's only what he [Eaves] said in the witness box which is evidence, and it's important therefore, if you should find something referred to in the statement which he did not speak about in evidence, that you do not treat that as though it were part of the evidence. It isn't. (Mr Justice Jowitt, Summing Up, 117, paras. G and H)

One of the problems with any trial, and particularly with one as complex as this, is how much evidence is included, how much is understood or remembered, how it is treated and, most difficult and obscure of all, what has really gone on behind the scenes of the investigation. In fairness, both the jury and later the CCRC faced a considerable challenge with this case.

Chronology of the CCRC's involvement

Following conviction in 1995, both men applied for, and were refused, leave to appeal. Attwooll's own submission was forwarded from the Home Office C3 Department to the CCRC when it came into operation in 1997, and Roden's solicitors submitted representations on his behalf in June 1998. Further submissions followed from Roden's solicitors and South Wales Liberty (SWL) at various intervals from 1998–2000 and following the CCRC's Provisional Statement of Reasons in May 2001. Despite this, the CCRC confirmed its decision not to refer the case with a Final Statement of Reasons on 14 November 2001.

Faced with potential judicial review proceedings from Roden's lawyers the CCRC decided in April 2002 to place the case before a newly constituted Committee of Commissioners (effectively reopening the case). The reason for this decision was the presence of David Jessel on the original panel of Commissioners, whose former firm, Just Television, had undertaken some investigation work on the case in 1997. The CCRC, therefore wishing to uphold 'the very highest standards of decision making', accepted that there might be a genuine perception of potential bias, although it did not accept that there is 'any evidence of actual bias' resulting from Jessel's 'undisclosed previous involvement' in the case (Letter from CCRC Case Review Manager (CRM) to Mike Attwooll 11 April 2002).

In the second review of the case it appears that the cases were treated separately, although prior to this the CCRC had maintained they would be treated together. More submissions were made by Roden's lawyers at this stage. SWL, after a great deal of searching and persuading, were able to find a solicitor for Attwooll in 2002.

In June 2004, the CCRC issued a Provisional Statement of Reasons declining to refer Roden's case. Responses followed from SWL and Roden's lawyers in October 2004. Both these submissions expressed concern at the CCRC's approach to new evidence about the handling of the witnesses who gave evidence against Roden by the police and the fact that the CCRC's own CRM had recommended that Roden's case be referred to appeal but had been overruled by the committee of three Commissioners.

Since 2004, it appears that the cases have again been reviewed together, and in May 2007 the Commission reversed its previous decisions and referred the case of both men to the CACD.

Analysis of the CCRC's involvement

In assessing the CCRC's handling of the case of Attwooll and Roden, the analysis is structured along the lines of its governing core values in three sections: transparency and accountability; thorough and investigative; and independence and impartiality.

Transparency and accountability

In the early days of the CCRC the applicants tended to feel that there was a willingness to listen to their voice, and both lawyers and voluntary groups were given attention. In this case, the level of communication has fluctuated over the years with long periods of complete silence and apparent complete inactivity. Equally, at times, especially when lawyers or campaign groups have pushed issues, these issues have been taken up to some degree at least and responses given. Communication directly with the applicants has largely been limited to responses to their submissions, rather than any active policy of keeping the applicant informed. The CCRC's policy is only to visit the applicant when there is a perceived reason that might advance the case (see Chapter 9). Roden has never been visited by the CCRC, while Attwooll had one visit in the early stages from the first CRM. (Over the ten years four CRM's have been involved.) While it may be impractical to visit all applicants it might equally be argued that the complexity of this case and the extraordinary length of time it has been with the CCRC would have warranted more visits in the interests of thorough investigation as well as openness and accountability.

In June 2004, the CCRC issued a provisional Statement of Reasons declining to refer the case of Roden to appeal. It came to light as a result of enquiries by SWL that the CRM had recommended referral but had been overruled by the Commissioners. The CRM concerned left the CCRC shortly after this. Efforts by campaigners to acquire a copy of the original Statement recommending referral were met with claims that the document no longer existed. Only a letter from the previous CRM could confirm that this different view of the case existed within the CCRC:

> The complete absence of any indication in the Provisional Statement of Reasons that the Commissioners took a different view to the Caseworker is not in the spirit of openness and fairness that the Commission pronounces publicly. (SWL Response to Statement of Reasons, 2004: 6)

Furthermore, the new Statement of Reasons, it was argued, gave scant explanation as to why the submissions of Roden's lawyers had been rejected, urging that a spirit of transparency required some explanation:

> Openness and fairness surely require full disclosure of the Committee's legal arguments and discussions given that these overcame the case put forward by Mr Birnbaum QC – a case found to be 'compelling' and 'very strong' by the Caseworker. Surely the Commissioners cannot concede on the points made yet simply declare themselves 'unpersuaded' without any rationale. (SWL Response to Statement of Reasons, 2004: 6)

Expediency and an image of credibility were, it seems, in this instance, being given preference over accountability and transparency. The importance of this is, arguably, that those representing Roden should have access to the knowledge that the CRM agreed with Mr Birnbaum QC while the Commissioners apparently did not. So where is the rationale for concluding that there is 'no reasonable possibility' that the CACD might also have agreed with the CRM and the QC? Not to be open with this information, therefore, might deprive Roden of crucial information in support of his case and/or the opportunity for a judicial review application on the reasonableness of the CCRC's decision.

In terms of accountability, while the CCRC report to the Home Secretary, it is hard to identify any real accountability, for example for the delays in this case or for investigations that may not be thoroughly conducted. In practice, it seems that the CCRC feels most accountable to the CACD and responds to the messages it receives from them. The CACD may on occasions be critical of referrals made by the CCRC but, notwithstanding the often expressed views of lawyers and campaigners, there is no 'official body' in any position to be critical of non-referral.

Thorough and investigative

When the CCRC came into being many wrongly convicted people and their supporters expected, or at least hoped, that it would be a proactive investigative body. In fact, in its 2005–06 Annual Report, the CCRC recorded that 38 per cent of applications are considered ineligible, 51 per cent are cleared within five days (often because they can provide no new argument) and thus only 11 per cent could really be said to have a thorough review, unless the case is simple enough to be adequately reviewed in five days (CCRC, 2006a). In practice, the CCRC responds to issues raised by applicants when they see this as appropriate. It does not, generally, review the case as a whole or delve proactively into areas not raised by the applicant, unless its enquiries specifically lead onto other areas.

In this case, the applicants themselves left no stone unturned in their presentations to the CCRC and, faced with the complexity of the case, the CCRC has, effectively, paid little investigative attention to many areas that they saw either as 'jury points', that is, matters that the jury has decided upon and not to be revisited, or as issues of little relevance. This is unfortunate given the view expressed by CCRC Commissioner David Jessel at the conference held in May 2007 to mark the ten-year anniversary of the CCRC. Jessel reflected on how previously, as a journalist, he would have longed for the resources, powers and rights of access to information now available to the CCRC.

Unfortunately, there have been many areas raised by the applicants where the CCRC has not deemed enquiry relevant. These matters include the lack of any thorough examination of the ballistics issue. This is crucial given that whether the alleged murder weapon is in fact actually the murder weapon is, in many ways, the key to the case and the credibility of the two main prosecution witnesses. When enquiries were made following a partial report obtained by the defence it was discovered that the bullets and initially the gun could not be located by the police despite, it is assumed, a CCRC preservation order on the exhibits. In its referral document, the CCRC make no comment on this other than to say 'further examination of the bullets is therefore precluded' (Statement of Reasons for Mike Attwooll, 2007). Apart from Vincent Price, who was interviewed by the CCRC, no other key witnesses have been interviewed; Perkins, Woodland, Eaves or the witnesses who claimed to have seen the white Ford Sierra driving back towards the office, for example, all remain unquestioned by the CCRC review. Numerous issues have not been taken up, such as the informant status or otherwise of Perkins, or his current whereabouts and the 'bullet-like objects' which were referred to at the trial as being found in Attwooll's home, which to this day, and to his great frustration, he has never been given the opportunity to identify.

Despite this, the case was finally referred in May 2007 to the CACD, but on only two grounds that the CCRC saw as relevant, both of which had been raised primarily in Attwooll's submissions. To what extent then does the decision to refer reflect a thorough and investigative approach?

Firstly, they have undertaken a much more thorough and critical view (than the view they had previously taken) of whether Attwooll may have used his own car to travel back to the office with the police in order to enter the crime scene and locate files and describe how furniture had been moved in the incident (this action in itself is not questioned by the CCRC – see below). The CCRC accepted that the jury considered this issue important by asking a question about it and that they were not given full information on this. It was not made clear to the jury, for example:

1. That the main prosecution witness, Price, had stated in his interview and statement that he had met Mr Attwooll coming out of the estate from the office in his own car.
2. That two witnesses who might have supported Attwooll's story were not used by the defence to do this.
3. That Attwooll's movements in undertaking his next taxi run would have meant he would have been travelling in the wrong direction had he met Price at any other time than when he left the office in his own car. As the CCRC put it, the prosecution's version of events on this matter 'was inherently implausible'.
4. That one of the two police officers involved in arranging for Attwooll to travel from his home to the office did not give evidence because he maintained that he could not recall the events of the day at the time of the trial but could recall them later when questioned by the Police Complaints Authority. (CCRC Notification of Referral, 22 May 2007, paras. 170–80)

Thus, a more thorough analysis of this issue now recognizes the significance of these matters in supporting Attwooll's credibility in conflict with that of the police officers. There is, however, nothing here which was not available to the CCRC and argued by and on behalf of Attwooll from the very start of the investigation in 1997. It is more the case that the CCRC have revisited the issue with more rigour, after much pressure, and used its discretion to change its view from the decision not to refer the case in 2001. Sadly it took a further six years to recognize the points made by SWL at the time of that decision. Originally, for the CCRC, 'the relevant facts were before the jury'. SWL, on the other hand, has always disputed that this is the case and that clearly once again important evidence was not provided to the jury that could have made a difference to the jury's decision at the time (SWL Response to CCRC Statement of Reasons, 2001).

The second issue on which the referral is made is that the CCRC came to recognize the importance of a statement from a Mr Rowlands which the defence had inexplicably failed to use at trial. Rowlands spoke to the victim Gerald Stevens earlier on the evening of the murders and gave a statement asserting that Stevens had been very nervous and frightened when a blue Ford Sierra drove past. The statement contained revealing information which might point to other suspects:

> Gerry [Stevens – the victim] had told me previously that he thought that someone was after him ... Gerry appeared very agitated and nervous ... I can remember that Gerry continually looked up the road, in my opinion watching to see if the Ford Sierra was returning toward him ... In my opinion Gerry was waiting for someone to come and confront him. (Extracts from Mr Rowland's statement, 17 May 1994)

Mr Rowlands also stated that Gerry Stevens believed the attack and stabbing of another employee of the taxi firm shortly before the murders had really been meant for him. There is no suggestion that the defendants could have been the occupants of this blue car, Attwooll's white Sierra was elsewhere and Stevens was reportedly completely at ease in the company of Attwooll later that same evening.

As with the issue of transport to the office, the argument about the importance of Rowlands's evidence had been argued by the applicants and their supporters, SWL – since 1997 and, again, in response to the 2001 decision not to refer the case – in the following terms:

> We cannot agree with the conclusion of the single judge and the Commission that the evidence of Mr Rowlands was not of significance. Clearly, if the jury had been presented with the knowledge that Mr Stevens was seriously worried by the presence of other parties on the night of the crime it is likely that this evidence would have raised serious doubt about the involvement of Mr Attwooll and Mr Roden. (SWL Response to CCRC Statement of Reasons, 2001).

Again, the CCRC has looked at the issue more thoroughly and linked Rowlands's statement to the statement of another witness who was refuelling his white Sierra at the garage near the murder scene at around 12.40 a.m. that night. (It has been argued that this white Sierra might have been mistaken for Attwooll's.) This witness also reported a blue Sierra in that garage at that time. Furthermore, the CCRC's examination of police papers found a record of another person, a woman, who saw the blue saloon car with two or three occupants in the garage and who, being made to feel nervous by the car's occupants for some reason, decided not to stop in the petrol station but pulled off and drove home. Thus, there is evidence that the blue car that had so alarmed Stevens earlier may have returned to the area around the time of the murders.

In fairness to the CCRC, both of these issues had been rejected by the single judge in refusing to grant leave to appeal after the original trial, hence the CCRC rationale was to follow that ruling. The CCRC uses cautiously worded legal arguments to justify the referral to the CACD, especially in the always difficult area of defence inadequacies or tactical decisions (see Chapter 4). Herein lies the systemic problem that denies justice because of rulings made in the past which may have been inadequately examined or simply wrong. The CCRC has been reluctant to challenge the way the system interprets fair process and most of all reluctant to challenge the CACD. In this sense, there is a caution about the CCRC referral which manifests itself in the very limited grounds on which this case has been referred. This is particularly serious given the clause (s. 315) in the Criminal Justice Act 2003 which prevents grounds other than those on which the CCRC referral is based from being raised at the appeal, unless the CACD agrees to accept them following a specific application from the defendants. In a case as complicated as this one, where the miscarriage of justice can only really come into focus by taking a holistic view, this could be very serious. The danger is that the CACD may see some merit in the grounds of referral but maintain the conviction on the basis of the other evidence which the CCRC does not appear to question. The catch-22 imbalance here should be obvious: the appeal cannot be argued holistically but it can be rejected on the basis of a holistic argument. In fact, there are numerous other areas that lawyers, supporters and the defendants feel are of equal importance and relevance to those that form the grounds for referral but have not been considered so by the CCRC. In this sense, while years were wasted awaiting the more analytical approach that was finally taken on these two issues, the overcautious approach to other matters, which seems to stem from fear of criticism from the CACD, risks repeating the mistakes of the past. One might argue that if a case is worth referring it is worth referring well, armed with the full range of major areas of doubt.

Indeed, there remain other areas that also call for a further and fuller investigation, including the following.

The gun issue

Following a report from a ballistics expert for the defence, which raised doubts about the likelihood of the gun claimed to be the murder weapon, attempts in seeking further ballistics examination led to the revelation that crucial exhibits (initially the gun and then the bullets) have been lost by the police, despite being, presumably, the subject of a CCRC preservation order. This (1) prevents detailed reinvestigation of the crucial ballistics issue; and, (2) raises the possibility of deliberate concealment to prevent reinvestigation. If there is suggestion of deliberate concealment then this should, surely, warrant investigation and a ground of referral to appeal. The CCRC dismissed this point without comment or analysis in one short paragraph (para. 202) of their referral statement, stating that 'further examination of the bullets is therefore, precluded'. This rather bland acceptance of the situation is further undermined by the acknowledgement in the previous paragraph which suggests that further examination could be of value: 'today's microscopes are more sophisticated than those in use in 1994' (para. 201). The importance of this element of the evidence cannot be overemphasized, because if the gun concerned was not the murder weapon, then both Price and Perkins were lying and the whole case must surely collapse. There would seem to be enough matters that were not fully canvassed before the jury to justify this as a ground of referral given its importance, but the CCRC declined to do this.

Evidence not heard by the jury

The jury did not hear the evidence of eight youths who were outside the estate and did not see Attwooll's car entering it. Nor did they hear evidence that a Mr Francis was driving another white Ford Sierra car in the area at the time or that another similar car (Blue Sierra saloon) was seen at the garage by other witnesses. The CCRC have accepted that the statements of witnesses at the garage give support to Rowlands's evidence in the second ground of their referral. It seems reasonable, therefore, that these issues, that were not before the jury, should also be given the opportunity to support an alternative perspective of the girls' evidence – especially in the light of the timing issue described by Attwooll. Indeed, the whole issue of timings in relation to a number of witnesses is so complex that the jury must have been confused by the mix of information they did receive.

The relationship of a juror to the officer second-in-command of the investigation

It was discovered that a member of the jury was related to the second-in-command of the police investigation and lived close to him. The CCRC have followed the indication of the single judge in refusing leave to appeal, considering the fact that this was discussed with the defendants to be adequate. The alternative position on this issue was summed up in SWL's response to the CCRC's Provisional Statement of Reasons which declined to refer Mike Attwooll's case in 2001:

> The failure to discharge the jury was such a grave failure as to render the trial unfair. It is not sufficient to state that the matter was explored in the presence of the defendants – it is incumbent upon the defence and indeed the Court to ensure that justice is seen to be done. The notion of a 'fair trial' includes concepts such as impartiality and independence (something which is clear from European Court of Human Rights jurisprudence), and the relationship of the juror to such a police officer cannot be seen to be in accordance with these concepts. We, therefore, submit that in the light of human rights standards in force today, the Commission should conclude that there has not been a fair trial, requiring immediate referral to the Court of Appeal. (SWL, 2001, para. 1.12)

Prison witnesses in support of Mr Attwooll re David Eaves

The CCRC argues that evidence from a number of prison witnesses, who might have made statements supporting Mr Attwooll's view of the prison informant David Eaves, would in any event have been inadmissible (CCRC Notification of Referral, 2007: para. 249) with the exception of a Mr Robinson who claimed that Eaves had suggested 'grassing up' someone to him. The CCRC view Robinson's point as 'not a strong point' (para. 250). However, the point may be considerably stronger if the jury were aware that there was something of a culture of claiming cell confessions among certain inmates of Cardiff Prison at that time.

Support for evidence of police impropriety in John Roden's submissions to the CCRC

In October 2004, Michael Birnbaum, QC for Roden, made a response to the Provisional Statement of Reasons declining referral for Roden. This included a schedule of the CCRC's responses to the points made in his submissions. Birnbaum listed 13 points, four of which were accepted as discrepancies in the police handling of Woodland and Perkins, but the other nine are listed as 'not mentioned'. The CCRC had concluded, it seems, that the four points conceded were not significant enough to warrant referral (a view not shared originally by the CRM), while the other nine points were not significant enough to warrant discussion, even though they concerned similar potentially serious questions around police practice. Suggestions such as the possibility that Perkins was offered inducements to give evidence are dismissed as 'speculative'. An investigative approach however cannot, surely, rule out some 'speculation' as a starting point for a detailed analysis? Moreover, Birnbaum's submissions identified a number of aspects that gave considerable contextual support for such 'speculation', not least what seems to be a three-hour 'off-the-record' interview with Carl Perkins at the time the gun was discovered, the record of which is covered by only a few minutes worth of notes. A common complaint from campaigners about the CCRC is the tendency to make value judgements of this kind even when presented with new evidence. In this case, it is conceded by the CCRC in the Provisional Statement of Reasons for John Roden (2004) that:

> There were significant departures, by the police, from the practices set out, then as now, in the PACE (Police and Criminal Evidence Act 1984) codes [para. 9.6] ... It is at least possible that the jury could have been left with the mistaken impression that the CPS (Crown Prosecution Service) was closely involved in deciding how the police should approach Mr Perkins [para. 9.5] ... As with the handling of Mr Perkins, there are several inconsistencies in the information regarding how Mr Woodland was handled. (para. 9.12)

These inconsistencies include two police officers recording entirely different accounts of the same meeting with Mr Woodland.

The treatment of suspects and witnesses is crucial to the validity of their evidence, PACE exists for this very reason. The significant departures and inconsistent accounts conceded here go to the heart of the only evidence against Roden – the testimony of Perkins which was prompted by the registered police informer Woodland. The rejection of this new evidence as not being sufficiently significant to warrant referral to the CACD is the kind of value judgement that many might feel shows a lack of impartiality from the CCRC where the police are concerned or a naivety about the pressure that can be put on witnesses when the rules and records are abused.

Entering the crime scene

In the Final Statement of Reasons of 14 Nov 2001 for Mike Attwooll, the CCRC responded to concerns raised by SWL about the practice of allowing Attwooll onto the crime scene, the morning after the murders, when blood was still present and forensic scientists and scene-of-crime officers were still working at the scene (although the bodies had been removed). As Des Thomas, Forensic Management Consultant and a former Senior Investigating Officer, Head of CID Training and Deputy Head of Hampshire CID, remarked:

> it completely undermines the integrity of any evidence found on him [Attwooll] or found at the scene ... Most forensic experts would agree that you would never, ever take a suspect to a crime scene until it had been completely sterilised, and if you did you couldn't rely on any evidence you got thereafter. It would undermine the credibility of any subsequent prosecution because it must be so evident to everybody that you would have cross–contamination...that's why you guard it, that's why everybody wears suits. (Interview with Des Thomas, 11 July 2007)

It was not, in this case it seems, evident to anyone that cross-contamination would occur; neither did Mr Attwooll wear a protective suit, only paper boots and, to Mr Thomas's further surprise, 'no gloves'! It was pointed out that at that stage Mr Attwooll was not officially a suspect, to which Mr Thomas responded: 'Even then you've got a problem – you wouldn't take anyone onto the scene'.

Independence and impartiality

The CCRC has a limited remit. Under s. 13 of the Criminal appeal Act 1995 it must apply the Real Possibility Test which generally prevents the referral of any case to appeal without new evidence or argument. There is also an 'Exceptional Circumstances' clause, which has only been used once and certainly not in support of a general 'lurking doubt' about the safety of a conviction.

Section 315 of the Criminal Justice Act 2003 (which limits grounds of appeal to those in the CCRC's Statement of Reasons unless the Court grants permission to include other grounds) causes so many problems for a case of this kind, as described above. This section was prompted by pressure from the CACD which felt unhappy about dealing with cases involving too many grounds of appeal. The CCRC seems to have taken this on board by being extremely cautious even in the context of a referral. It might be argued that if a case is going to be referred it is in the interest of all to give it the best chance of a full hearing rather than a restricted one.

Factors such as these support the impression that the CCRC is not and cannot be independent because of its subservience to the CACD. It is the approach and attitude of the CACD that dominates the approach and attitude of the CCRC and, consequently, has limited the ability of the CCRC to truly change the landscape of miscarriage of justice rectification. Three factors are illustrated by the case of Attwooll and Roden and are echoed by many others. These three problems mirror the traditional conservative approach of the CACD:

1. The CCRC is resistant to making a referral based on cumulative factors comprising 'lurking doubt'. The fact that a great many aspects of this case in combination amount to serious doubt about the case is not accepted: there have to be legal points which stand in isolation. Ironically, even such points can be undermined by a superficial view that they are outweighed by other evidence or a value judgement about their significance (see Chapter 11).

2. The CCRC is resistant to making a referral based on serious question marks about police investigation practices even, as in this case, despite admissions of failings in relation to PACE and other inappropriate practices. In this case, there has at last been an admission of some question marks about police integrity but a refusal to view other questionable practices in the light of these. This reflects both the reluctance to challenge police practices and the reluctance to look at a case holistically. It would seem reasonable to conclude that if it is accepted that police and defence failings may well be present in some areas that it might well indicate that other areas of complaint might also have grounds and should be investigated. If some parts of a process are not functioning as they should then other parts of the same process undertaken by the same team should also be looked at critically.

3. The CCRC is resistant to making referrals on the basis of poor defence representation that has resulted in significant evidence not being heard by the jury. Again, in fairness, the referral of Attwooll and Roden did acknowledge some question marks about defence performance but it has taken many years in this case to reach this position and the acknowledgement is still only partial.

A truly independent and impartial CCRC would not be restricted by a fear of criticism from the CACD and would be using its investigatory powers to ensure that police investigations were properly conducted and legal representation did not leave out crucial evidence through negligence or tactical decisions that clearly damaged their client's case. Independence requires the thorough use of investigatory powers, even when this seems to question police and legal establishments. In the case of Attwooll and Roden, the CCRC has accepted bland explanations and tolerated inadequate practices, often it seems because no other body along the way has questioned those practices. This approach does not promote impartiality. In this case, to a large measure, the benefit of the doubt has been awarded to the established authorities and the dice loaded against the applicants. Without the support of lawyers and campaigners it seems doubtful that the case would have been reopened in 2002 and a more thorough investigation leading to referral might never have happened. Independence and impartiality should not depend on the amount of pressure that can be applied.

Conclusion

The Attwooll and Roden case took ten years to achieve a referral. This is not entirely down to the CCRC: there have been long delays, especially for Attwooll, in finding lawyers, obtaining legal aid for experts, commissioning experts and, perhaps most of all, the problem for lawyers in finding the time to do work on such a complex case without the required funding. Furthermore, this case is exceptionally complex, even by the generally highly complex nature of major murder inquiries, with many issues being raised by and on behalf of the applicants.

However, it has to be said that a rigorous investigation, willing to be critical where justified of police and legal practice, should have led to a referral by at least 2001. There is nothing in the current referral rationale that could not have been available from the outset of the CCRC's review in 1997. In any event, the struggle continues and two potentially innocent men remain in prison, in large part because of an overcautious, and in some respects partisan, approach that pervaded the CCRC's review and its limited grounds of appeal in its reference to the CACD.

After nearly 14 years of struggle the CACD finally heard the case on 17 March 2008. Lawyers for Roden had to argue for inclusion of the evidence on his behalf on the day, even though extensive representations had been forwarded to the CACD the previous Autumn – no preliminary hearing had been arranged. The judges declined to include this evidence in their considerations. Thus, only the two grounds relating to Attwooll were allowed, although lawyers were allowed to discuss some of the other issues as background. The appeal, listed for two days, lasted under four hours. The men and their families and friends then faced a tormenting reserved judgment which took over five weeks to be finally delivered on 23 April 2008 (see *R v. Attwooll and Roden*).

Perhaps predictably, the CACD dismissed the appeal on the basis of a holistic argument while refusing to hear a holistic argument from the defence. It maintained that the evidence of Price and Perkins had not been undermined. The judgment appears to accept some validity on the grounds of appeal and some of the other concerns about the gun and the evidence of David Eaves, but it is remarkable in its vagueness, largely failing to comment on the significance of these issues. The overriding claim that the evidence of Price was not undermined conveniently ignores the issues around the missing gun and other matters that were not specifically grounds of appeal. Moreover, the crucial point behind the grounds of appeal, that evidence of a flawed investigation and poor defence should inevitably throw doubt on the potential reliability of all witnesses, is conveniently ignored or sidestepped. Furthermore, denying the jury evidence of alternative suspects, as evidenced in the second ground of appeal, is not seen as significant. As for the claim that nothing undermined the evidence of Perkins – the evidence of police impropriety, which the defence believed fundamentally undermined the evidence of Perkins, is not discussed in the judgment for the simple reason that the judges refused to admit that evidence into the appeal grounds.

There is much that could be said about the judgment, which is beyond the scope of this chapter. Suffice to say, justice has been denied as the CCRC cannot measure up to its stated values so long as it works within the scope of the CACD, which is not interested in properly investigating such cases and is as reluctant as ever to take a serious stand against flawed investigations and poor legal defence.

Note

1. The references to the CCRC's Statements of Reasons, interviews, trial judges' Summing Ups, expert reports, responses from SWL, witness statements, and so on, that are cited in this chapter, which will not appear in the list of references at the end of the book, were available to the author by virtue of his role in working on the cases with the organizations SWL and South Wales Against Wrongful Convictions.

6

The Failure of the Review of the Possible Wrongful Convictions Caused by Michael Heath[1]

Satish Sekar

Introduction

Forensic pathology is, undoubtedly, a very important science, but one that is surrounded by misunderstanding of its limitations and significance. It cannot, for example, tell you precisely when a murder took place. There are far too many variables to enable anything more than a range of times within which death occurred. There are, however, several indicators that should be established and not just the obvious ones such as body weight, body temperature, ambient temperature and the progress of rigor mortis. Analysis of stomach contents and of the rate of dissipation of alcohol content in the body can all assist in establishing a likely range for when death occurred. However, despite ongoing research, no science can give a precise time of death – yet.

In homicide cases, the forensic pathologist will be the first forensic scientist to perform scientific examinations. He or she will also take samples from the body, some of which will be used by other forensic scientists. Consequently, the integrity and competence of forensic pathologists can also affect the ability of other experts to obtain and interpret scientific evidence. Forensic entomology – the study of the life cycles of insects recovered from crime scenes – is a science that can offer useful evidence, enabling investigators to establish the post-mortem-interval. It, too, cannot tell you precisely when a murder occurred, but it can give investigators a range to work with.

However, forensic entomologists are not always available at the drop of a hat. Consequently, they may have to depend on others to establish the environmental information that they require. In such circumstances, they also require others to obtain entomological samples and to treat them in the manner recommended by themselves. Competent forensic pathologists have to be fully conversant with such requirements and, in the absence of a forensic entomologist, be prepared to ensure that the integrity and quality of the entomological evidence is guaranteed so the entomologist gets the best opportunity to establish the optimum evidence that the samples can give. Forensic entomology is capable of establishing a likely range of when a significant post-mortem event, such as burning or partially burning a body or even death, took place, but on occasion that will depend entirely on the efficiency, competence and even integrity of the forensic pathologist who took those samples.

Like any science, forensic pathology depends upon the efficiency and competence of the practitioner. It would be churlish in the extreme not to acknowledge that the vast majority of forensic pathologists perform their duties with due diligence and expertise. Some, inevitably, fall below their usual high standards on rare occasions. There is nothing sinister in that. There are others whose work is simply not up to standard.

Against this background, this chapter considers the limits of the Criminal Cases Review Commission's (CCRC's) review of the possible wrongful convictions that may have been caused by the discredited forensic pathologist Michael Heath. In particular, it highlights cases of continuing concern that may have been insufficiently considered by the CCRC's review of Heath, arguing that potentially innocent prisoners may have been denied justice.

The incompetence of Michael Heath

Michael Heath began working as a forensic pathologist in 1979. He became a Member of the Royal College of Pathologists in 1990. In 1998, he became a Fellow of the Royal College and had been accredited by the Home Office since 1991, when what became the Register was established. Heath was a very experienced, but controversial, pathologist. His evidence caused numerous miscarriages of justice, tipping the scales towards prosecution in cases where the pathological evidence did not warrant it.

As far back as the early 1990s, for instance, a controversial case occurred. Kenneth Carrera stood in the dock charged with murder. He maintained that he had acted in self-defence. Carrera held strong views on mugging. He was accused of stabbing to death a man who tried to mug him. Carrera was represented by an up-and-coming barrister who is now one of the top QCs in the country – Michael Mansfield. Carrera told the jury that he fought with the younger man for his life and in the course of the struggle the mugger fell on his own knife, which went through his chest-bone.

Dr Heath's version was radically different. He told the jury that 'considerable force' had been used. Heath's opinion was that Carrera had deliberately stabbed his attacker using 'considerable force'. But what does this term mean? Considerable force compared to what? Nevertheless, the accounts of the injuries sustained by the mugger given by Heath and Carrera were mutually exclusive. The jury acquitted Carrera. Sadly, the precise reasons for the acquittal cannot be established, but in so far as the case depended on the accounts of Heath and Carrera it is clear that the jury could not have believed Heath and acquitted Carrera, unless this was a perverse verdict.

Nevertheless, years later Heath would claim that 'considerable force' was used in another case. He would also say that the knife Kenneth Noye used to stab Stephen Cameron had gone in to the hilt (see Cheston, 2000). Peter Jerreat, another pathologist who gave opinion on the case, disagreed, arguing that he had not seen any evidence that the knife had gone up to the hilt and that, in his opinion, only mild to moderate force had been used. This should have been easy to resolve. Medical evidence should have proved whether it had indeed penetrated to the hilt as the skin and underlying tissue should have shown requisite damage (see Sengupta, 2000). Consequently, it should not be difficult to establish whether Jerreat's opinion or Heath's should be relied on in this case. It is still unclear if this has been investigated again and resolved.

When Heath gave evidence in Carrera's case he had yet to be appointed a Home Office pathologist. He was making a steady living, but already there were signs that something was not right.

In 1997, Heath gave evidence at the inquest into the controversial death of Gambian refugee[2] Ibrahima Sey in police custody (see INQUEST, 1997). He was cross-examined by Patrick O'Connor QC, exposing Heath's limitations for all to see. Tear gas had been used to restrain Sey after he had been hand-cuffed. Heath suggested Sey had suffered sudden death due to mental illness but was forced to accept that there was no basis for his previous diagnosis of hypertensive heart disease. He also ruled out restraint as a factor in Sey's death, but five other pathologists refused to discount the possibility. The jury concluded that Sey had been unlawfully killed.

It emerged at the inquest that despite practising for several years Heath had not been admitted to Membership of the Royal College of Pathologists because he repeatedly failed his exams. This ought to have raised questions regarding his competence. It should have been used in cross-examination to discredit Heath regularly since. Somewhat surprisingly, however, this did not occur and Heath remained extremely busy and continued to be relied on as an expert witness in many cases after the inquest into the death of Ibrahima Sey. He conducted post-mortem examinations for the police in London, Essex, Kent and East Anglia after his abilities had been called into question. Lawyers failed to cross-examine him effectively. In some cases he was not cross-examined at all, even though his conduct in these cases made him vulnerable to challenge. But there were other cases that would raise serious questions about the competence and efficiency of Michael Heath, both before and since that momentous inquest.

In 1992, Phillip Johnstone sadly lost his life. Dr Heath originally declared the cause of death to be neuroleptic malignant syndrome (NMS). However, during the inquest Heath unexpectedly changed the cause of death to acute exhaustive mania (AEM). Despite all the existing literature establishing that the terms were *not* interchangeable, Heath claimed that they were, and he changed the cause of death to emphasize that use of neuroleptic drugs did not contribute to Johnstone's death. His family had no knowledge that Heath would change his opinion and had cross-examined witnesses on the basis that Johnstone's death was associated with neuroleptic drugs, having had no reason to doubt it until Heath's change of opinion in the witness box. Believing Heath's incorrect claims that NMS and AEM were interchangeable terms, the coroner refused Johnstone's family an adjournment to prepare expert evidence to challenge so remarkable a change of opinion. It would require a judicial review heard by Lord Justice McCowan and a then Mr Justice Buxton to give Johnstone's family the justice that Heath's conduct had so nearly stolen from them. The judges quashed the original verdict and ordered a fresh inquest due to Heath's conduct.

When cross-examined by O'Connor at the Sey inquest about this case, Heath tried to claim that the major issue was that the coroner had wrongly allowed him to hear the evidence which caused him to change his opinion. Perusal of the judgment in the judicial review proceedings swiftly disabuses the reader of that interpretation. It contains strong criticism of Heath's conduct. Yet, there would be many more before Heath would fall from grace.

In 1993, Sheila Bowler (see Devlin and Devlin, 1998) was convicted of the murder of her elderly aunt, Flo Jackson. Time would eventually prove that, more than likely, no crime had actually occurred (see Naughton, 2005a) and Flo Jackson most probably died of accidental causes. Mrs Bowler would lose an appeal and have two documentaries made about her case by Channel Four's *Trial And Error* before her case would be referred back to the appeal court by the CCRC. A retrial would be ordered before she would finally be vindicated by a not guilty verdict. Heath was the pathologist in Bowler's case. The Crown did not rely on him at her retrial – with good reason.

Heath originally claimed that Mrs Jackson had been pushed down a steep bank into the River Brede where she drowned, until a visit to the scene forced a rare change of mind from him as such a scenario required requisite injuries that were not present. He then suggested that Mrs Bowler had helped her aunt down a bank, that clearly would have challenged far more athletic people than Mrs Jackson, before pushing her into the river. Dr Heath's scenario of Mrs Jackson effectively assisting her killer to murder her was dismissed by the judge as 'rather improbable'. His response that his 80-year-old mother could easily have climbed the slope in a couple of steps was treated with derision.

Information such as the weight, height and the temperature of the body, and indeed that of the river, that could have assisted in establishing a range for the time of death, was not recorded. Furthermore, the defence pathologist Dr Vesna Djurovic said that there was no pathological evidence to suggest the use of force, let alone attributing motive to murder as Heath did without any scientific basis. Suffice to say, this was not Heath's finest hour, but worse would follow.

In March 1996, 73-year-old Jocelyn Strutt died in her home in Southborough, Kent. A myocardial infarct had ruptured. She had fractured ribs as well. Petty burglar Craig Kerwin was arrested and charged over her death. The only evidence to justify the charge was the uncorroborated opinion of Heath – an opinion that went far beyond the limits of his expertise. Heath claimed that Strutt's death had been caused by a blow struck with a heavy instrument that had fractured her ribs and caused the myocardial infarct to rupture.

Kerwin had been caught burgling Strutt's home. He claimed that he had not noticed her body in the kitchen, but had noticed a nasty smell. Forensic pathologists Dr Vesna Djurovic and Dr Nat Cary did not share Heath's opinion. During the inquest into the death of Ibrahima Sey, Heath claimed that Djurovic might have agreed with his opinion in the Strutt case. In actual fact, Djurovic had described Heath's opinion as 'unacceptable'. Djurovic wrote: 'There is no pathological evidence whatsoever to suggest that Mrs Strutt suffered a "heavy" blunt impact to the chest'.

Dr Cary agreed with Djurovic, describing Heath's suggestion as 'quite implausible and is readily countered not only by common sense but also by published data in relation to rupture of myocardial infarction'. Cary also wrote, 'I can see no reason whatsoever from any of the evidence presented to suggest that this is anything other than a sudden natural death'. Cary's report also stated: 'There is no evidence of a weapon mark externally visible and, furthermore, there are no general features present to suggest a violent assault such as bruising or laceration to the facial area or defensive type injuries to the hands or forearms'. Cary concluded by saying: 'There is no evidence that any external stimulus either could or in reality did contribute to the development of rupture of the heart in this case'.

In short, there was no pathological evidence at all to support Heath's claim that Mrs Strutt's death had in any way been caused by a violent assault. She had most likely died of natural causes, yet Kerwin spent just over a year on remand awaiting trial. Heath's opinion was the only 'evidence' capable of supporting a charge of murder or manslaughter. The judge decided that Heath's evidence was not fit to be left to the jury. In fact, the jury was ordered to acquit as the judge found no evidence fit to put before them.

In 1996, Malcolm Reid died as a result of injuries sustained during a fight. Victor Boreman, Malcolm Byrne and Michael Byrne were convicted of murder. Their convictions were quashed on appeal, but they were convicted again after retrial. Their next appeal failed. The case was referred back to the appeal court by the CCRC on the basis of Heath's unreliability. Even by Heath's standards this was an extraordinary case. Heath insisted that death had occurred after a fight, but before the fire. However, medical evidence established that there were fire products in the body. On any sensible view this proved that Reid was alive when the fire occurred. The appeal court quashed the convictions in 2008 but substituted convictions for assault (see CCRC, 2005b).

Heath also provided ample evidence of an inability to interpret poor practice by autopsy technicians. Steven Taylor, for instance, spent ten months on remand charged with murdering his wife Beatrice (see BBC News, 2002a). It was a case that would not come to trial. Heath believed that marks on the neck of Beatrice Taylor proved that she had been strangled. He was wrong.

Professor Derrick Pounder of Dundee University was one of two forensic pathologists to disagree strongly with Heath's conclusions in this case. His report of August 1997 says: 'In summary there is a high degree of probability that the haemorrhages observed in the deep neck structures were produced during dissection by autopsy technicians prior to the involvement of the forensic pathologist. There are no other autopsy findings to support an allegation of homicidal strangling. Such an allegation cannot be sustained on the existing pathological evidence'.

At Pounder's suggestion the Crown instructed another forensic pathologist to review the pathology evidence. Dr John Clark supported Pounder's view that the marks on Mrs Taylor's neck were post-mortem artefacts. The charges against Steven Taylor were dropped as a result.

Textbooks show that dissecting the neck at autopsy in the same manner in which other dissections are routinely conducted will produce haemorrhages that can be mistaken for trauma produced in life. It is well known to competent forensic pathologists that special techniques are required for dissecting the neck in such cases. Derrick Pounder was distinctly unimpressed with Heath's performance in this case. 'It is a classical error,' said Pounder. 'I can't imagine any other forensic pathologist in the UK taking the same view as Dr Heath.'

Leon Murphy was beaten to death in his flat in 1999. Darren Cullen was found guilty of Murphy's murder in May 2000. Cullen's conviction was quashed in 2003 (see BBC News, 2004). The defence case at trial was that there could have been two attacks some time apart. Heath discounted the possibility. In his Summing Up His Honour Judge Watling said: 'The pathologist, Dr Heath, about whose evidence I shall remind you in due course, was clearly of the view that there was one sustained attack'.

Although Watling pointed out that the defence contested this view at trial, they did so in the absence of expert evidence. The question of how Heath was able to dismiss the possibility of a gap between attacks in spite of the absence of scientific certainty was never resolved. In fact, this would prove to be yet another example of Heath giving an opinion that went beyond his expertise. It is possible that there was only one sustained attack, but there was no credible scientific evidence that could rule out the possibility of a gap between attacks.

After the conviction, forensic pathologist Dr Iain Hill reviewed the pathology evidence and concluded that it was not possible to exclude the possibility that there had been a gap between attacks as medical science is not so precise. As it had been put to the jury that there had been no gap, the appeal judges concluded that if Dr Hill had given evidence Watling's Summing Up would have been different. He had excluded the possibility of a gap based on Heath's evidence. If the judge had heard Hill's opinion he would have been obliged to put it to the jury, which might have affected their verdict. It was enough to quash Cullen's conviction. Yet again Heath's opinion had been found wanting.

By this stage Heath's days were numbered. He made a complete mess of his post-mortem examination of Stuart Lubbock. It was a case that would not go away. Lubbock's father, Terry, doggedly pursued the truth about Stuart's death in the entertainer Michael Barrymore's swimming pool. Before long the flaws in Heath's pathology in this case had been exposed to the full glare of publicity. I do not propose to rehearse the facts of this case here as there is no shortage of material available on it. Suffice to say, there is no question that Heath's expertise was once again found wanting.

The Home Office Tribunal into Heath

Despite the forgoing, it was not until complaints by some of Heath's colleagues, who were deeply concerned about the quality of his work, resulted in him facing a Home Office Advisory Board Tribunal over the cases of Kenneth Fraser and Steven Puaca. In November 2005, the appeal court quashed the 2002 conviction of Steven Puaca for murdering his girlfriend Jacqueline Tindsley. Puaca was found guilty largely due to Heath's claim that Puaca had smothered Ms Tindsley. Dr Cary disagreed at trial. Five pathologists – including Professor Christopher Milroy – gave evidence at Puaca's appeal, disagreeing with Heath's opinion. They concluded that there was no pathological evidence to support Heath's conclusion that Tindsley had been smothered. Heath even suggested that Tindsley's face had been pressed into the bed – an opinion the appeal court found surprising. Tindsley had a history of alcohol and drug abuse. She had taken prescription drugs, including one of sufficient quantity to cause death. Far from killing Ms Tindsley, it appears probable that no crime occurred and that Puaca had raised the alarm. Puaca's solicitor, Chris Brown, said at the time: 'Our concern having dealt with this case is that there may be several other Steven Puacas out there' (quoted in Dyer, 2005).

Kenneth Fraser was acquitted of the murder of his girlfriend Mary Ann Moore in 2002 (see Lewis, 2006). He was accused of hitting her on the head with a wooden plank the previous year, causing her death. Three pathologists raised their concerns that Ms Moore's injuries were consistent with falling down the stairs and they wrote to the Home Office to express these concerns. They strongly criticized Heath's opinion that Moore had been battered to death. It was possible that she had been pushed down the stairs, but thanks to Heath this was not the Crown's case. The complaints made against Heath by the pathologists in these cases resulted in the Home Office Advisory Board Tribunal that Heath faced in 2006.

The Tribunal took place in June and July 2006. Charles Miskin QC represented the Home Office. Jean Ritchie QC represented Dr Heath. It was chaired by John McGuinness QC. The other members of the panel were Peter Ackerley, Dr Bob Bramley and Professor Thomas Krompecher:

> Dr Michael Heath is an extremely experienced consultant forensic pathologist who has been accredited by the Secretary of State on his Register for a long time, but it is the belief of the Home Office that Dr Heath has fallen short of the high standards required by the Secretary of State of forensic pathologists and it is the purpose of these proceedings to decide whether that view is correct or not.

These words were spoken by Charles Miskin QC when he opened the case against Heath on 19 June 2006. During the course of the tribunal Miskin cross-examined Heath about his practices and conduct in the cases of Fraser and Puaca. Miskin told the tribunal that 'in neither case was there any substantial evidence of unlawful killing save that of Dr Heath. It was his, so to speak, forensic pathological and scene reconstruction evidence which, on both occasions, on any reasonable view, must have persuaded the Crown Prosecution Service (CPS) to charge both Fraser and Puaca'.

On 22 August 2006, the Panel found that several charges against Heath relating to his performance and conduct in both cases had been proved and that they raised the question of whether he was fit to remain on the Home Secretary's Register. It was clear that he would lose his status as a Home Office pathologist. Just before the punishment was to be announced, Heath resigned from the Home Secretary's Register for Forensic Pathologists. He was thoroughly discredited; but was this sufficient?

The Tribunal focussed on Heath's performance and conduct in the cases of Kenneth Fraser and Steven Puaca. What about the other cases where Heath's abilities had been called into question? The tribunal had not considered them at all. The Attorney General announced that he was reviewing the tribunal findings to decide if it was necessary to review all of Heath's cases, but this review was limited to the tribunal cases alone.

Meanwhile, the CCRC decided to review 54 cases they had in which Heath had been involved. The review was conducted by one of its Commissioners, David Jessel, – erstwhile presenter of *Rough Justice* and *Trial And Error*. Perhaps Jessel was chosen to conduct the review because he had previous knowledge of Heath's limitations. In October 2006, the Attorney General announced that he would not review all of Heath's cases, arguing that the CCRC's review of him would suffice; but this approach was flawed from the outset, as it was limited to applications that had been made to the CCRC. As such, no review considered the issue of whether live investigations had been conducted properly by Heath.[3]

The CCRC's Review of Heath

On 31 October 2006, the CCRC announced that its review of the 54 cases in which Heath was involved had been completed. Jessel decided that three cases that were currently being considered by the CCRC should be subjected to further review and five cases that had been considered previously would also be investigated further. Jessel's review had special regard for cases in which medical evidence was critical to the conviction. The starting point of the CCRC's review was that Heath was thoroughly discredited.

But was the review thorough enough? Forty-six cases were not deemed worthy of further investigation. Does this mean that Heath's performance and conduct in these cases met the standard required of forensic pathologists by the Home Secretary? Ultimately, who is responsible for ensuring that forensic pathologists meet the minimum standard in all of their cases, both past and present? The Home Office Tribunal did not do so. The Attorney General abdicated his responsibility to ensure that this occurred, and the CCRC could only do so with respect to those cases where applications had been made to it. As such, it did not and could not resolve the issue of whether Heath had met the required standard in all of his cases. While the CCRC cannot and should not be expected to deliver a full investigation of Heath's cases, it can and must be held accountable for its investigation of the 54 cases that it considered. So, has the CCRC's review been of the quality that society is entitled to expect? I cannot speak with authority on the review of all of these cases. Nevertheless, the case of Neil Sayers is disturbing. It raises several points of importance regarding the thoroughness of the investigation of Heath's role in it.

Although Sayers's case is not currently at the CCRC, Jessel's review considered it. Sayers is now represented by leading solicitor Steven Bird. Jessel wrote to Bird about Heath's involvement in that case:

> In my review of those cases where Heath was the pathologist I have had special regard to those in which the medical evidence was critical to the conviction. Having revisited the Statement of Reasons in Mr Sayers' case I have not found this to be the case. Mr Sayers' defence was that the stab wounds had been inflicted by his co-accused, Mr Wallis, who pleaded guilty. I understand that the provenance, identity and ownership of the knife may have been an issue at trial, but I do not believe that this materially affected the case in terms of Dr Heath's evidence. I further note that in his submissions to the CCRC he argues that there was no forensic evidence which linked him with the commission of the crime in which case any challenge to the evidence of a forensic pathologist would appear to be misplaced. For those reasons I am not minded to re-open Mr Sayers' case. Please let me know if you think I have missed anything significant.

For reasons that will become abundantly clear below, I believe that the evidence clearly shows that the CCRC has slipped below the high standards of investigation that we have a right to expect from it. My experience of the CCRC suggests that this level of investigation has become the rule rather than the exception to it.

A wasted opportunity? The case of Neil Sayers

I have investigated Neil Sayers's case for more than five years. Albeit for different reasons, I find it as disquieting as that of the Lynette White Inquiry.[4] It offers a searing indictment, not only of the adversarial system of justice as practised in our jurisdiction, but of the mechanisms for correcting the inevitable mistakes that occur within that system. Sayers was let down badly at trial. His case should have been one in which forensic science played a very important part. His defence at trial did not secure the expertise that could potentially have proved his innocence. At the very least, it could have discredited the evidence that secured his conviction – the 'confession' of Graham Wallis – but this was more of an accusation against Sayers than an admission of Wallis's guilt, and it was not corroborated by forensic science when it could and should have been if the confession were true.

In fact, there were examples where forensic science comprehensively exposed Wallis as a liar regarding material issues, such as how and when mutilation occurred. And, this goes to the heart of the issue as to why the body of Russell Crookes was mutilated at all. Heath's statement clearly states that at least some mutilation occurred after the body was partially burned and implies that the other mutilation may have occurred after the fire as well. Yet, this is totally inconsistent with Wallis's account. When confronted with the suggestion, Wallis changed his account, but this too was implausible, as Wallis suggested that mutilation had occurred in a waterlogged grave. It would have been very difficult to obtain sufficient force to achieve mutilation there. There is no evidence of bone spicules or fat globules on the clothes that the Crown insist Sayers was wearing on the two nights when mutilation was alleged to have occurred. Heath gave evidence at Sayers's trial. He had previously said that no report would be complete without the results of forensic-science examinations. Heath was not called on to explain what kind of forensic-science examinations he had in mind.

Charles Miskin QC did not ask Heath for clarification of this issue. Arguably, it was not his responsibility to do so. Brian Higgs QC was defending Sayers. He did not resolve the mutilation issues either, even though it was a very important issue. Once Wallis's account was served on Sayers's defence they should have realized the importance of this potential evidence that could have proved Wallis's account false on this material issue. They could, and should, have sought clarification from the forensic pathologist that they had instructed.

Either Heath's pathology was so flawed that his evidence cannot be relied on against Sayers, in which case a review of his case is essential, or it can be relied on regarding the mutilation point, in which case Wallis's evidence cannot be relied on regarding a point of material significance. And, if Wallis has lied about this, can the rest of his evidence be accepted at face value in the absence of corroborative evidence?

It is unclear if the CCRC was aware of this when it conducted its review of Heath's involvement in Sayers's case. There were other examples of pathology-related issues in this case as well. It is also worth pointing out that Miskin relied on Heath's expertise during his prosecution of Sayers – expertise he robustly questioned during the Home Office Tribunal against Heath.

The maggot-infested remains of Russell Crookes was discovered in woods near Hadlow College in the morning of 26 May 1998. Heath was the forensic pathologist instructed by Kent Police. Medical issues were not integral to the conviction of Neil Sayers. Nevertheless, there is compelling evidence to suggest that the performance and conduct of Dr Heath caused severe problems in this inquiry – an inquiry that may have resulted in the wrongful conviction of Neil Sayers – and that it did so from the earliest stages of this inquiry. It was clear that Crookes had been dead for some time. Rigor mortis had long since passed. The best chance to obtain scientific evidence that could establish the post-mortem-interval was clearly forensic entomology, but like any science it cannot perform miracles. It relies on minimum levels of competence that appear to have been lacking in Heath's conduct in Sayers's case.

Before Heath began his post-mortem examination of the partially burned remains found in the woods, he had already compromised important evidence. Heath took maggots from the body, which he fixed, as was proper. He then took a live sample. Both were handed to a Scene of Crime Officer (SOCO). It is unclear if Heath even provided Kent Police with advice on what to do with the maggots. This was, however, far from his only failing in relation to the maggots. He failed to establish the temperature within the maggot mass. He failed to take the temperature under the remains. He did not establish the ambient temperature, and he failed to take samples from other areas of infestation at the scene. He did not establish if maggots had left the body. Nor did he establish if there was any other entomological evidence at the scene, such as 'casing', which would have established if any maggots had completed the final stage of development before emerging as flies.

Heath's conduct betrays little more than rudimentary knowledge of forensic entomology. It was possible that different species of insect had been present. The greater the area sampled the higher the chance that different species would be detected. The analysis of the life cycles of different species would have enabled a more accurate post-mortem-interval to be established. Dr Heath's failure to follow recommended procedure prevented this evidence – potentially vital evidence – from being established. Is this not a pathology-related issue? And, does it not raise questions about Heath's competence in this case?

Unfortunately, the consequences of Heath's conduct regarding the maggots would be dire. The maggots were taken away by a SOCO. It is still unclear if Heath even advised Kent Police to consult a forensic entomologist. Clearly, the police did not know what to do and extremely important evidence was lost as a result. The live sample was put in a container with some liver, which was then left in the fridge. They died there. The best chance to establish the post-mortem-interval had been lost. Even so, it need not have been disastrous. The fixed sample could still establish the post-mortem-interval. Data-logging experiments could have established a reliable estimate of the environmental conditions under which these maggots had developed. Neither Kent Police, nor Sayers's defence, instructed such experts. And worse was to follow.

After Sayers was convicted he made an application to the CCRC. It was not an application of the standard that Sayers had a right to expect. It did not include several scientific issues that ought to have been at the heart of Sayers's application. The CCRC cannot and should not be criticized for dismissing that application, but it is proof that the solicitor representing Sayers at that time had no understanding of the vital issues of his case. As with much else, the criminal justice system holds Sayers alone accountable for these failings. That solicitor refused to even ask Kent Police if any maggots still existed for examination. He laughed at the suggestion that they would still be available. He was wrong. Another solicitor not only established that they did exist, but had them examined by two independent forensic entomologists, Dr Mark Benecke and Dr Martin Hall. Outrageously, the fixed sample had been thrown away and the remaining maggots were in a very poor state. This decision to throw away evidence prevented the forensic entomologists from obtaining the evidence that the maggots could and should have been allowed to provide. Consequently, they could not confirm or refute Wallis's claims, but it would later emerge that Heath's failings on another pathology-related issue may have affected their conclusions.

Heath says that the body suffered extensive fire damage, but he does not clarify what this means. It implies a fire of great intensity and that, in turn, suggests that maggots could not have survived the partial burning of the body. The forensic entomologists, therefore, concluded that flies must have laid eggs after the fire had occurred and at a time when the remains had cooled down sufficiently for flies to lay their eggs. Photographs were taken of the post-mortem examination conducted by Heath. There is no question that fire damage has occurred, but some of those photographs establish that there are important pathology-related issues that need to be resolved, such as how extensive was the fire damage to the body of Russell Crookes. This is related to the issue of how intense the fire was that caused this damage. The post-mortem examination is also of significance in determining whether the fire damage sustained by the body was consistent with the manner in which it was alleged to have been burned. Establishing the precise extent of fire damage would have been essential to this task. Sadly, the fire expert instructed by Kent Police wrongly advised them that it was not possible to resolve this issue. This is not entirely Heath's fault, but more precise description could only have assisted in providing an answer to this important question. As such, this, too, is a pathology-related issue.

Some of the post-mortem photographs show that at the very least there were areas of the body that did not suffer 'extensive' fire damage. However, some of the photographs establish that not only was flesh raw, but that the fire did not generate sufficient heat to render body fat into the fire. In this context, it is impossible to eliminate the possibility that the maggots examined by Dr Benecke and Dr Hall had survived the fire by finding shelter from the heat within the body. That possibility could drastically affect the conclusions of the forensic entomologists as there would be no scientific evidence that could support Wallis's account of when the fire occurred in circumstances where there is plenty of evidence suggesting that it happened days after Wallis said it did. Consequently, Heath's performance and conduct in this case has adversely affected the ability of other forensic scientists to obtain evidence that could have been of vital importance in this case. While these are not medical issues, they are pathology-related issues. Are we not entitled to expect a thorough review by the CCRC of Dr Heath's involvement in Sayers's case to discover these issues and realize the importance of them?

As was shown previously, there are some cases other than Fraser and Puaca where either forensic pathologists, lawyers or judges rejected Heath's claims in circumstances that went beyond the disputes that would be expected of the adversarial system. One of them is of particular importance to Sayers's case. Despite requests for clarification of whether the facts of proven cases other than the tribunal cases were considered by the CCRC when considering which cases deserved further scrutiny, the CCRC showed it had learned nothing from the case of Gary Mills and Tony Poole (see Bowcott, 2003). Despite naming the cases, it claimed to be at a loss to understand the point being made. It was, in fact, a glaringly obvious one, and its obfuscation was disingenuous, to put it mildly.

It is at least possible that the facts of one of those proven cases will have greater similarity to the facts of a rejected case than that of Fraser or Puaca. In other words, the point is one of similar fact – a validated ground of appeal. The CCRC began its review from the standpoint that Heath was thoroughly discredited. This does not begin to address the issue of whether the facts of one of the rejected cases bears strong similarity to one of the other proven cases that was not considered by the tribunal – something that could constitute a ground of appeal on its own. It seems clear that the review has not looked into this possibility, which may or may not apply in any of those cases.

There is, however, one case that has enormous significance to Sayers's case, that of Craig Kerwin. Heath's pathology in that case was found sadly wanting. It is clear that, like Fraser and Puaca, the decision to prosecute Kerwin for the death of Jocelyn Strutt depended upon the opinion of Heath. There was no other evidence capable of justifying charging Kerwin. While Sayers's solicitor had access to knowledge of Heath's involvement in Kerwin's case, Sayers knew nothing of it and he had no reason to ask, but the criminal justice system holds Sayers alone responsible for the decision of his lawyers not to challenge Heath's involvement in his case – a decision reiterated by the CCRC's inability to see how a case that did not hinge on medical evidence, or raise complaints about the pathologist previously, could possibly have pathology-related issues that demand investigation.

If the CCRC investigated the possible impact of Kerwin's case when considering which cases should be looked into further, it failed to establish that a senior police officer and SOCO who were involved in Kerwin's case were also involved in Sayers's case. On its own it may not prove anything, but the professional relationship between Heath and them is important and in need of further investigation. To be sure, there are several pathology-related issues in this extraordinary case that have not been resolved by the CCRC's review of Heath's involvement and conduct in Sayers's case. And, this is not the only case to have important pathology-related issues awaiting resolution.

Justice denied

Among the cases that the CCRC considered in its review was Simon Hall's (BBC News, 2007). Dr Heath did not attend the crime scene. He was not obliged to do so, but it would have been desirable. Normal procedures were not followed, making it impossible to provide as accurate a range as would have been expected for the post-mortem-interval; but, while Heath cannot be blamed for this, there are other causes for concern over his pathology in this case.

The victim suffered 11 stab wounds. Heath claimed that 'considerable force' had been used in this case as well. Again, he fails to define what he means by this term. Was this the work of a crazed 'Ripper' or is this just emotive terminology designed to arouse the hostility of a jury? It appears to be a favoured phrase of Heath, but it raises other issues. If the stab wounds were forceful, are there bruises on the skin and underlying tissue? If the knife had a hilt this would be expected. There is no evidence of it. Perhaps the knife did not have a hilt. But, if it didn't, other pathology-related issues arise. Did the blade strike bone? If so, it would encounter resistance, and if force was used as Heath claims then the murderer's hand would slip down the blade causing bleeding. It is unclear if this occurred, but it does not appear that the possibility was considered by anyone. Either Heath's pathology was incorrect in his terminology, in which case his evidence is unreliable, or other lines of inquiry should have been investigated. It would appear that there are pathology-related issues that the CCRC's review has failed to resolve in this case as well.

As the CCRC's review was coming to an end, Michael Stone applied to it to consider his convictions for the 1996 murders of Lin and Megan Russell and the attempted murder of Josie Russell (BBC News, 2003). Stone was charged a year after the murders and subsequently convicted. His appeal was successful and resulted in a retrial, but he was convicted again in 2001. He appealed against those convictions unsuccessfully and applied to the CCRC in October 2006. He had already spent nine years in prison by then. This was his first application to the CCRC. It had taken several years to exhaust domestic remedy. Despite initial reports saying Stone's case was one of Heath's that would be subjected to further investigation, the CCRC decided that he must wait for a case worker to be appointed before it would be investigated at all.

This shows how little the CCRC has learned from the case of Mills and Poole. Stone had already suffered substantial delay in exhausting domestic remedy through no fault of his own. The CCRC responded by deciding that further delay was warranted. On any view, Heath's role in Stone's case will have to be investigated sooner or later. By not doing so then, it ensured that further delays will occur.

Either Heath's pathology was of the required standard or it was not in Stone's case. If it fell below the standard demanded of forensic pathologists, then Stone would, arguably, have a ground for appeal. And, if not, were there pathology-related issues to consider? Heath suggested that a bootlace discovered near the crime scene had been used as a ligature on Megan Russell. His account implied strong contact between the murderer and lace during the crimes. However, while Stone's DNA is not on that lace, the DNA of an as yet unidentified man is. It is unclear if the National DNA Database has been checked to see if that person can be identified now. Consequently, if Heath's opinion is correct, it strongly suggests that Stone is innocent. If not, then Heath's pathology is below the standard required in this case. Either way, it would appear that investigation of Heath's role in this case could only be beneficial to Stone if he is, in fact, innocent, and may even lead to the real perpetrator being brought to justice. Yet, the CCRC saw no reason to investigate it immediately. If justice delayed is justice denied, then the CCRC appear to be denying justice to Michael Stone and others.

Conclusion

There is no evidence that the CCRC's review considered any of the issues raised in this chapter regarding the cases of Neil Sayers and Simon Hall. It did not consider Michael Stone's case at all. Implicit in Jessel's decision that Sayers's case does not warrant further investigation is a blaming of Sayers for not raising these issues earlier – something for which Jessel had criticized the criminal justice system previously during his career as a journalist. The previous application to the CCRC is evidence of nothing more than the severe failings of the legal representation available to Sayers at trial and in his application to the CCRC. But, the CCRC did not understand the significance of the pathology-related evidence. The fact that Sayers did not raise the pathology-related issues earlier is entirely irrelevant. Why would a student at Hadlow Agricultural College know of them? How could a teenager of average intelligence be expected to not only be up to speed in the latest techniques in forensic pathology and, indeed, forensic science, but to be confident enough to demand lawyers to secure the necessary expertise and make submissions accordingly? And, would a fair and impartial system hold him responsible for not knowing it, when in reality the overwhelming majority would have known as little of this as Neil Sayers did? The CCRC had a chance to establish an important principle. However, it failed to do so, preferring the easy option of holding Sayers responsible for his own lack of expert knowledge. For most of us there are no consequences for not knowing of forensic pathology-related issues. For Neil Sayers it has cost nine years – and still counting.

Far from critically reviewing the performance and conduct of Heath in Sayers's case, the CCRC appears to have relied on the unrealistic and unfair expectations placed on Sayers that have dogged this inquiry from its inception. We are entitled to expect and demand better of the CCRC. And, if this has happened to Sayers, can we be certain that the review of the other cases has attained the standards that we expect and demand?

I can only comment with authority on Sayers's case, but the failure to investigate the pathology-related issues in this case suggests that it may have happened in other cases as well. The evidence suggests that the CCRC's review of Heath's involvement in Sayers's case betrays a fundamental lack of understanding of the consequences of Heath's conduct and knowledge of forensic pathology-related issues. One can only wonder if others have been as poorly served as Neil Sayers.

However, flawed as the CCRC's review of Heath undoubtedly was, it is important to remember that it was never capable of delivering anything more than a review of cases that had applied to it. David Jessel's review was not, and never could be, the definitive analysis of Michael Heath's pathology. The Attorney General abdicated his responsibility to order such a review – something the public still fully deserves. The CCRC cannot be held responsible for this, but it can and should be held fully accountable for trusting a review with serious ramifications on the lives of many people to the opinions of one of its Commissioners, who had no qualifications in forensic pathology, rather than to a qualified forensic pathologist. Sayers will not be alone in seeking the opinion of a reputed forensic pathologist rather than a CCRC Commissioner devoid of such qualifications, experience and expertise.

Notes

1. The references to expert reports, transcripts of the Home Office Tribunal into Michael Heath, personal correspondences relating to the case of Neil Sayers, and so on, that are cited in this chapter, which will not appear in the list of references at the end of the book, were obtained by the author by virtue of his role in working on the cases mentioned.
2. I dislike the term 'asylum seeker' as it places the burden on the individual to prove that he or she is fleeing persecution, rather than on the state to prove otherwise.
3. For example, Heath was the pathologist in the Child Adam case – the 'Torso in the Thames' (see BBC News, 2006). Was his work up to the required standard in that case? And there is the possibility that Heath missed something in cases that he did not label as homicides. Perhaps some of them were, in reality, homicides.
4. My book *Fitted In: The Cardiff 3 and the Lynette White Inquiry* provides a detailed rehearsal of the facts of that case (Sekar, 1997). Since it was published in 1998, the case was reopened again, resulting in the apprehension and conviction of the real murderer, Jeffrey Gafoor, in 2003.

Part III
Practitioner Perspectives

7
Historical Abuse Cases: Why They Expose the Inadequacy of the Real Possibility Test

Mark Newby

Introduction

In theory, the Criminal Cases Review Commission (CCRC) embodies a new and improved system of identifying and correcting miscarriages of justice. At times, however, it has become bogged down by its own institutional frameworks and operations, which have impacts upon its consistency as to how it conducts its reviews, as exemplified in its reviews of alleged claims of innocence in cases of historical sexual abuse.

This chapter takes the form of a case study of Anver Sheikh, a North Yorkshire care worker who was convicted of historical sexual abuse at York Crown Court in May 2002. Interestingly, it is a case the CCRC never had its hands on, yet it exposes, centrally, the deficiency of a system which relies on human beings deciding justice for other human beings. There is no doubt that had the CCRC been asked to consider referring the case of Sheikh in February 2005, it would have refused the application, and he would today still stand convicted of these offences. Had that been the case he would not be alone on the cutting-room floor of the CCRC.

The CCRC's failure to refer historical abuse cases

There has been considerable activity over recent years arising out of what are known as 'historical care home cases' or, as the title of Richard Webster's book termed it more eloquently, *The Great Children's Home Panic* (Webster, 1998). This arises out of the fact that, much in the same way that the issue of the justice system has become politicized, so the issue of child abuse has been even more so. As a result, the Chairman of the CCRC and its Commissioners have been called upon to speak publicly about the review of these cases and express general concerns over the dangers of such cases. However, it is arguable that these public statements have not been matched by the reviews that have taken place.

One of the real issues that has particularly challenged the CCRC is the inconsistency of approach in the application of the Real Possibility Test set out under s. 13 of the Criminal Appeal Act 1995. In the context of historical abuse cases, there has been a swift and rapid change of approach from the Court of Appeal (Criminal Division) (CACD) and it is a matter of concern that the CCRC seems to have fallen behind the pace in the approach it now takes. For the 'last hope' of justice, the CCRC's approach is clearly inadequate and we ought to explore the current shift of stance from the CACD more seriously.

The move first started in 2002 with the case of *R* v. *Williams-Rigby and Lawson*. This was followed by *R* v. *Mayberry* and latterly *R* v. *Burke*, *R* v. *Robson* and the two Sheikh cases (*R* v. *Sheikh* and *Sheikh* v. *The Crown*). At the same time, in Northern Ireland, the Court of Appeal in *The Queen* v. *Hewitt and Anderson* also demonstrated a different approach to the cases.

In order to assess why the CCRC's test is failing these cases, it is important to assess what these authorities have brought to historical abuse cases. Firstly, the cases demonstrate the deep-seated concerns of the CACD about these cases. The matter was well summarized by Lord Justice Latham in *R* v. *Mayberry*:

> The case therefore presented what is now unhappily a common problem for the courts, namely, a case of sexual abuse which of itself is always a potentially difficult offence for a jury to consider because of the usually private nature of the events surrounding the allegations, which is made the more difficult because of the very substantial delay which has occurred, in this case some thirty years. There is no doubt that much concern has been expressed about the ability of the courts to deal fairly with allegations which are of such antiquity. The Home Affairs Committee has produced a report in which it identifies a number of features which cause concern and those are features which have caused concern to the courts over the years and have been the subject matter of directions to the jury to seek to obviate the particular difficulties which old offences such as these create. The particular problems that were identified by the Home Affairs Committee, quite apart from the problems created by delay itself, relate to the fact that in many cases the evidence is produced by trawling for witnesses which carries with it the risk of instilling into those who are providing the information, in effect, the indication that certain answers may be expected by those who are making the inquiries. (Quoted in Webster, 2003)

In *R* v. *Robson*, the matter was further developed where the CACD, in criticizing the way in which the evidence was put at trial before the jury, stressed the need for a judge in such cases to adopt a rigorous approach as to whether a case should be left to the jury at all. *The Queen* v. *Hewitt and Anderson* brought an additional dimension with the court proceeding to scrutinize carefully the credibility of the accounts of the complainants and having them recalled to give evidence before them.

The English division of the CACD has in a number of cases ordered that the complainants be video interviewed and that evidence be considered not least in the case of Anver Sheikh and the more recent case of *R* v. *Foster* as well. On occasions this has led to the court receiving live evidence from complainants and them being cross-examined before the court. Whilst the cross-examination is usually limited to the fresh evidence or points raised in the appeal, it still demonstrates the willingness of the CACD to test the credibility of complainants when the case warrants it. This sceptical treatment of complainants in historical abuse cases by the CACD will be further examined in the analysis of the case of Anver Sheikh, although this remains a concept the CCRC seems to struggle to grasp.

The large pinch of common sense applied to these historical cases had of course started with the case of *R* v. *Bell* in 2003 (discussed further below). Although *R* v. *Bell* was not the 'get-out-of-prison' card which many appellants would have liked it to have been, it did establish the principle that in the final analysis it was more important that an injustice was not done to a defendant whilst balancing the interests of complainants as against defendants.

A clear illustration of the CACD's willingness to apply common sense started, however, in the case of *R* v. *Burke* where Lord Justice Hooper identified that, in respect of one complainant, the loss of documents which would have answered directly to whether the applicant had an opportunity to commit the offence one way or the other meant that he could not have a fair trial and stayed the counts. Other counts where documents might have given the defence good material would not lead to a stay as that was answering possibilities, rather than opportunities.

After *Burke*: the trial and retrial of Anver Sheikh

The CCRC at that time failed to recognize the significance of *Burke*, making a similar error to that which would be described as a serious error in the case of *Sheikh*, namely, to say that because appellants had been able to cross-examine the material they had obtained and had in fact made considerable progress, this in some way tempered the prejudice to the appellant caused by the missing documents. This was, of course, an entirely incorrect approach and in its application failed to appreciate that opportunity and lost documents was an entirely different assessment and one which was distinct from the classic assessment of serious prejudice (see, for instance, Attorney General's Reference (No. 1 of 1990)).

It was not simply the restatement of the principle set out in *Burke* which was to be the importance of *Sheikh*, but the way in which the CACD applied 'principles of common sense' – a concept which in the context of historical allegations the CCRC appears to grasp with some diffidence and difficulty. I will first set out how *Sheikh* supported and enhanced the argument in *Burke* from the specific facts.

Anver Sheikh was employed as a carer at the school in question between 1979 and August 1980. In fact, at the earlier trial leading to his conviction it was said he was employed between 1979 and 1982 – an incorrect establishment of his dates of employment and which contributed to the wrongful conviction. The Crown relied on the similar fact evidence of complainants, Boys 'A' and 'B'. Although the conviction also fell in relation to B, we are concerned here with Boy A's allegations.

Boy A had given evidence at the original trial that he arrived at the school in August 1980 and was subjected to abuse by Sheikh, including one episode where he claimed to have been buggered and virtually strangled by the appellant. His account was convincing because of the lengthy time period he alleged the abuse could have occurred and which was unchallenged in the first trial.

However, when Boy A's account was tested at appeal, serious questions arose over the case. The complainant alleged that the central serious episode of abuse upon him occurred after he was bullied by another boy in the school. However, it later became clear that this boy, whom the complainant referred to, was not in fact a student of the school until 1981, after Mr Sheikh had left. Complainant A also further embellished his evidence by referring to other individuals whom upon closer scrutiny could never fit into his account. As a result, the Crown did not oppose the appeal and the conviction was quashed. The Crown sought a retrial and the stage was set for a fresh look at the evidence of Boy A.

During the course of the retrial in January 2005, A's account was further narrowed down to just one possible weekend between 29 and 30 August 1980. It became clear from the evidence of other staff members and the headmaster of the school that the Day Book and the Staff Rota would have been central to demonstrating whether Mr Sheikh had an opportunity to commit the offence or not.

During the conclusion of the case, Sheikh's barrister, Mr Patrick Cosgrove QC, became aware of the then just released authority of *Burke* and made argument that the case ought to be stayed as a result. However, the trial judge declined the application, making the point that the appellant's legal team had made considerable headway, that they had obtained social service records not disclosed before and that they had effectively cross-examined the prosecution witnesses to the defence's considerable advantage.

With the applications declined, the matter went to the jury which, despite the weight of evidence in favour of the appellant, reconvicted him. The stage was, therefore, set for the case of Mr Sheikh to return unhappily once again to the appeal court. On appeal, the CACD decided that the trial judge had made a serious error in his approach to this case, quoting the following from the trial judge's Summing Up:

> *Burke.* The Court of Appeal Criminal Division this week quashed this conviction – essentially as I understand it, at Paragraph 40 they quashed it

because he was prevented from having a fair trial in the absence of crucial documents ... This case is factually in fact different from this one. There is an awful lot of evidence here which supports the Defence. They have been able to put forward an extremely good case before the Jury with the aid of the documents. There are a great deal more documents available in this case. It has already been to the Court of Appeal, the conviction quashed and been brought back because of some of the documents coming to light. All those documents are now available, such as they are, and I am still firmly of the view that if this Defendant is convicted, he will have received a fair trial. And although documents are missing, a lot of documents are there, and I do not think that the Defence have been so prejudiced in this case that they cannot get a fair trial. Mr Cosgrove, in relation to Boy A, has been able to show, from the documentation, that the offence, if it occurred, must have occurred on the last Friday, or possibly the Saturday of August 1980. <u>And even if the Defendant was off duty or on duty, it is a matter of agreement between the Defendant and the Crown that he had the keys available to him on or off duty, and he would have been able to visit the scene of this alleged crime at any time he wished to do.</u> And so I am quite satisfied about the case as it is at the moment, halfway through the Jury's consideration ... This Defendant, in my view, has received a fair trial, whatever the verdict. (*R* v. *Sheikh* (retrial), quoted in *Sheikh* v. *The Crown*; underline in original)

This extract is not only important in assessing the proper approach to loss of documents, it also exposes the importance of a common-sense approach to wrongful convictions. Why did the CACD underline the relevant phrase? The answer is clearly set out by them in their summary of this ruling by the trial judge and its inadequacy:

Prosecuting Counsel points to the sentence which we have underlined. That, he submits, is sufficient to cure the failure on the part of the judge to give proper reasons at the close of the prosecution's case. Prosecuting Counsel submits that the judge is there accepting his argument that the missing documents would not necessarily have assisted. The one sentence is not, in our view, an adequate way of dealing with a difficult issue. Furthermore, the balance of the ruling is in very similar terms to the earlier ruling (and we summarise) 'Mr Cosgrove has made extremely good progress, there is a great deal more evidence available to the defence and therefore the trial is fair'. In the circumstances of this case the use of this route to the conclusion that the trial was therefore fair *constitutes a serious error*. In our view the missing documents, in particular the staff rota and the personnel records, were likely to be highly relevant to two issues in this case. First, whether the appellant would have come into contact with Boy A so as to have the opportunity to win his trust as Boy A alleged that he had; secondly, whether the appellant had the opportunity to commit these offences against Boy A. In these circumstances, we have grave doubts whether a judge who properly analysed the consequences of the missing documents would conclude that the trial was fair. If we are wrong, we have no doubt that a judge who carried out such an analysis would not necessarily reach the conclusion that the trial was fair. (*Sheikh* v. *The Crown*; my emphasis)

Vitally, for the purpose of our later discussion, the Court said this:

We add that Prosecuting Counsel submitted that Boy A may have been wrong when he said that when he spoke to the appellant, the appellant was on duty. The substance of his argument was that, if the records had shown the appellant to be off duty, that would merely be one more inconsistency and given the number of inconsistencies in Boy A's evidence, the jury would have attached no weight to one more. This is an unattractive argument. (*Sheikh* v. *The Crown*)

The essence of the issue of opportunity was strongly supported by the court, that where a specific event or allegation would be answered one way or the other by missing documentation then the counts ought to be stayed. If the documents missing would not answer a specific allegation or event but merely assist the defence in building up their case, the case will not be stayed and the prejudice can be safeguarded by strong and careful directions from the trial judge.

The application of 'common sense' in historical abuse cases

There is another central matter raised in *Sheikh* which the CCRC remains yet to grasp and which is crucial to the fair review of historical convictions – the application of 'common sense'.

The prosecution in *Sheikh* argued the case against the appellant on the basis he may have had a master key and may have been able in some way to come and go as he pleased – a suggestion dismissed by the CACD in the second appeal as complete nonsense and which flew in the face of all reason and sense.

Sadly, it seems that the common sense approach adopted by the CACD is yet to trickle down to the CCRC's review of historical abuse cases, and I have so many cases where, although allegations of abuse simply could not have happened based on the facts of the case, they will not be met with a referral from the CCRC.[1]

One might ask: is the case in any way safer simply because a jury (with the prejudices a jury brings to such a case) was prepared to accept the case no matter how fanciful the allegation was when the facts did not stand up to any common-sense scrutiny? Although the answer is, evidently, not at all, the constraints of the Real Possibility Test mean that there is little or no prospect of the CCRC making referrals in such cases.

This begs the further question as to why the CCRC finds it so very difficult to refer historical cases back to the court of appeal. The answer seems to be that, when one looks at many of the cases the CCRC refers, it approaches the task from a 'forensic point of view' – for example, it is perhaps much more straightforward for the CCRC to find support in expert opinion to refer the 'cot-death' cases of Sally Clark (see Batt, 2005) and Angela Cannings (see Cannings and Davies, 2006); to find expert opinion which challenges the reliability of the gynaecological examination of the complainant at trial in the indecent assault case of *R* v. *Fulton*; or, indeed, the safety of the firearms discharge evidence in the case of Barry George (see CCRC, 2007b) to name a few.

These are the flagship cases for the CCRC which they should rightly be proud of for having referred back to the CACD. However, it remains clear that for the majority of possible wrongful convictions where there are no forensic quick hits but, rather, the requirement for a realistic and common-sense approach, the CCRC remains ill equipped to tackle them.

For example, the CCRC, it appears, suffers from a complete mental block in referring historical care-home abuse cases on the basis of police malpractice even when cogent evidence has been presented to it. From a common-sense point of view, if a complainant is told the name of a suspect and what he or she is claimed to have done before a statement is taken, it might be considered that this is a matter which may cast substantial doubt on the reliability of that evidence. Indeed, my experience of the CCRC's persistent refusal to refer such cases to the appeal courts appears questionable and certainly at odds with the fact that it was created in the aftermath of some of the most notorious police malpractice cases the country has ever seen.

One of the problems with the current Real Possibility Test is that it is a 'one test fits all' assessment and the construction of it necessarily favours referral of cases that hinge on forensic science evidence – it is certainly far easier to address a gunshot residue case and reach a conclusion whether or not the CACD would quash the conviction than a conviction based on an allegation where it is one person's word against another's, with no other physical evidence to prove or disprove the allegation.

However, where the issues in the case turn upon interpretation of evidence and the application of common sense, the Real Possibility Test places the appellant in a wholly disadvantageous position. In attempting to second-guess what the CACD will do, it is in fact seeking to second-guess the approach the court will take to matters of individual interpretation. It is that difficulty that has on a number of occasions placed the CCRC completely out of sync with the approach of the CACD. As a result, our 'independent last hope of justice' is *reactive* in its approach – it reacts to the actions of the appeal court. As such, it is the appeal court which is left to make inroads into miscarriages of justice, but if cases are not referred by the CCRC those inroads will be limited.

Aligning the CCRC's test with the CACD?

The CCRC argues that its hands are tied, that it must operate within the limitations of the Criminal Appeal Act 1995, which is clearly true. However, it has a voice and one which will be heard: if it considers there are limitations to the current test it should express those views, just as it should express concerns with common areas of concern which should be available to it from a trend analysis of past cases. There is little public evidence that the CCRC has carried out that public duty.

Moreover, the CCRC has in the past argued that the notion of having two divergent and 'asymmetrical' tests between the CACD and the CCRC is both confusing and absurd as follows:

> Whatever statutory test Parliament ... imposed it has to be one that articulates with the test that the Court of Appeal itself has to apply. If you break that link and you establish an asymmetry between the two tests, you will be creating an absurd situation. It would create tension between the Court of Appeal and the Commission, it would raise expectations, it would cause confusion, and it is difficult to see what possible public interest could be served by referring cases on a basis that had no relation to the test employed by the court itself. (The then Chair of the CCRC, Professor Graham Zellick, 2004, quoted in par. 55, *R* v. *Cottrell and Fletcher*)

Although one initially could see the sense of the point being made, however, it does not really stand up to closer scrutiny. A test that there had been a miscarriage of justice should, in reality, bring with it no real change to the assessment process of the CCRC in determining whether a case should be referred or not. The test for the CACD is one of 'safety' and not about a 'real possibility of the conviction not being upheld'. In that context, the CCRC is already operating out of sync with the CACD.

The CACD has visited the issue of miscarriage of justice and assessed the safety of convictions in the light of that principle in *R* v. *Bell*. Briefly, Bell, who denied all of the allegations, was convicted of ten counts of indecent assault on a female under 16 years old, between September 1968 and September 1972. Before the start of the trial the defendant made an application for a stay for 'abuse of process' based on the delay of 30 years between the alleged incidents and the complaint being made. The judge rejected the application, although it was recognized that the delay could cause difficulties for the defendant in that it would be hard to gather witnesses or evidence so long after the alleged incidents had happened. The judge considered that any possible unfairness to the defendant, however, could be dealt with within the trial process. Bell was, nonetheless, convicted and appealed on the ground that the conviction was unsafe as the evidence relied on was unreliable and unsupported by any independent evidence.

In quashing Bell's conviction, the judgment of Lord Woolf stressed that because of the delay that had occurred the appellant was put in an impossible position to defend himself at trial. He was not able to conduct any proper cross-examination of the complainant; there was no material he could put to the complainant to suggest that she had said something had happened on one occasion which could be established to be incorrect; and there was no material in the form of notes that were given to the doctors which showed that she had changed her account. Given the effect of delay, all he could do was to say he had not done anything. Saying that to a jury amounted to virtually no defence at all. Moreover, Lord Woolf noted that in all the circumstances this was a case where in the interests of justice the court had to interfere and set aside the conviction. It was accepted that the judgment could mean that an injustice was done to the complainant and also to the public because a man who was possibly guilty had been let free. However, it was asserted that it was the CACD's duty to allow the appeal, having regard to the lapse of time and very limited evidence that was available (see Keogh, 2008: 4).

R v. *Bell*, then, illustrates the limits of the CCRC's working rationale and its argument that the CACD has confined itself exclusively to a stringent test in every appeal case. To be sure, the CACD appears adaptive to the assessment of cases to correct possible miscarriages of justice in a way that embraces a common-sense approach, which the CCRC fails to grasp.

If the CCRC test were to be amended from 'a real possibility' to one aligned with the CACD's wider notion of a 'miscarriage of justice', it would empower and bring to those charged with reviewing convictions the significance that they should command. It would enable the CCRC to assess whether a miscarriage of justice has occurred, rather than an unrealistic forensic examination of the evidence leading to a second-guessing exercise. If both the CACD and CCRC's tests need realigning then this is what should happen. What cannot continue is for one of the largest user groups of the CCRC to find itself in large part left on the cutting-room floor of the Commission because of the limited forensic test which the Commission applies to its reviews.

Conclusion

If the CCRC is, ultimately, to develop as a strong, independent body for assessing miscarriages of justice, it must raise its game. It must ensure its consistency of approach in all of its reviews and apply itself in considering the facts of the case in a common-sense approach. More significantly, the CCRC ought to be alive to the considerable shifts in the approach undertaken by the CACD, which has been prepared on a number of occasions, not only to apply common sense in assessing alleged miscarriages of justice, but to test rigorously the reliability of complainant evidence in historical abuse cases.

This is not to say that the whole basis of the appeals system (including the operations of the CCRC) should be radically transformed from one of *review* to a fresh hearing altogether. Rather, it is to highlight the need for the CCRC to be able to identify cases where the unreliability of the conviction is so evident (and, consequently, the possibility that an innocent individual has been wrongly convicted is so real) that, with common sense, it has to take the step forward to say that such cases represent a potential miscarriage of justice which ought to be assessed by the appeal court.

Note

1. For confidentiality reasons, this discussion is confined to cases in the public domain.

8
Only the Freshest Will Do

Campbell Malone

Introduction

If there is one category of case that most frustrates the practitioner in appeals against convictions for serious crimes it is in relation to whether the Court of Appeal (Criminal Division) (CACD) will receive 'fresh evidence' and, in particular, fresh expert evidence. By comparing the approach of the CACD and the Criminal Cases Review Commission (CCRC) in specific cases it is apparent that the CCRC frequently either misunderstands or overlooks the circumstances in which the CACD will exercise its discretion to receive evidence, even though all the criteria set out in s. 23 of the Criminal Appeal Act 1968 may not have been met, i.e. it may not actually be 'fresh' evidence that was not or could not have been made available at the time of the original trial. The result can be that a prisoner will remain a convicted person, and not just because he or she has been convicted for a crime committed by another but perhaps, even, because no crime may ever have been committed (see Naughton, 2005a).

Against this background, I will argue that whilst the CACD will, and often does, receive evidence in appeals that was available at the time of the original trial as it operates in the 'interests of justice', it takes a far stricter approach to its interpretation of the 'fresh evidence' and the relevant case law, as it seeks only to refer cases that have a 'real possibility' of success. First I will set out the 'fresh evidence' test of the CACD. Then, I will critically assesses three cases, *R* v. *Rhee*, *R* v. *Huckerby and Power* and *R* v. *Harris*, to illustrate the different views that can be taken by the CCRC and the CACD when faced with cases that display deep-rooted differences between forensic-science expert witnesses. I conclude that the CCRC could take a far less cautious approach to its case referral decisions, which would help to reduce the devastating and damaging experiences of victims of wrongful conviction.

The fresh evidence test

In giving to the CCRC the power to refer cases back to the CACD, Parliament set the parameters of the legislative test that was to be applied, linking the

CCRC thought process to the approach likely to be taken by the CACD. As other chapters have shown, the CCRC can only refer a case back to the CACD if it believes that there is a 'real possibility' that on such a referral the conviction will not be upheld (s. 13(1) Criminal Appeal Act 1995). It is, therefore, on a statutory basis that the CCRC has to anticipate what the CACD will make of the referral. Those of us who deal with the CCRC on a regular basis believe that, on too many occasions, it is more cautious than the CACD. This is, I believe, particularly so in cases involving fresh evidence where I would argue that the CCRC tends to misunderstand or ignore the approach likely to be adopted by the CACD.

Under s. 23(1) of the Criminal Appeal Act 1968, the CACD has very clearly an overriding discretion to act in the 'interests of justice', expressed as follows:

> The Court of Appeal may, if they think it necessary or expedient in the interests of justice: (a) order the production of any document, exhibit or other thing connected with the proceedings, the production of which appears to them necessary for the determination of the case; (b) order any witness who would have been a compellable witness in the proceedings from which the appeal lies to attend for examination and be examined before the court, whether or not he was called in those proceedings; and (c) receive any evidence which was not adduced in the proceedings from which the appeal lies.

Yet, the CCRC too often seems to apply the criteria on a narrow basis, which is particularly apparent when it is asked to consider fresh expert evidence. To assist in an analysis of the way in which the CCRC interprets applications that offer fresh evidence, it is instructive to consider two key judgments from the CACD that it is fond of referring to. The first has been a particular favourite case that the CCRC has relied on in its decisions, making regular appearances in their Statement of Reasons justifying the non-referral of a case. In *R v. Jones*, Lord Bingham commented that:

> expert witnesses, although inevitably varying in standing and experience, are interchangeable in a way in which factual witnesses are not. It would clearly subvert the trial process if the defendant, convicted at trial, were to be generally free to mount on appeal an expert case which, if sound, could and should have been advanced before the jury. (Cited in *R v. Jones* [1997] 1 Cr App 86)

More recently the CCRC has often relied on comments in *R v. Kai-Whitewind* that:

> where expert evidence has been given and apparently rejected by the jury, it could only be in the rarest of circumstances that the Court would permit

a repetition, or near repetition of evidence of the same effect by some other expert to provide the basis of a successful appeal. If it were otherwise the trial process would represent no more, or not very much more than what we shall colloquially describe as a 'dry run' for one or more of the experts on the basis that if the evidence failed to attract the jury at trial, an application could be made for the issue to be revisited in this Court. That is not the purpose of the Court's jurisdiction to receive evidence on appeal. (*R* v. *Kai-Whitewind* [2005] EWCA Crim 1092)

These two cases, and those particular comments on them, are used time and time again by the CCRC to justify not referring a case back to the CACD where either expert evidence was given at trial or could have been given at trial if the appropriate decision to obtain an expert report had been taken. The Statement of Reasons from the CCRC that outline its disinclination to refer a case back to appeal will say that in applying those two cases the CACD would not receive the fresh evidence. In fact, what the CCRC fails to acknowledge is that in both *R* v. *Jones* and *R* v. *Kai-Whitewind* the CACD, notwithstanding its remarks, actually did listen to the fresh evidence – though in the end felt itself not persuaded by it.

In a case rarely mentioned by the CCRC, *R* v. *Cairns*, the CACD *was* prepared to admit 'fresh' expert evidence despite the absence of any reasonable explanation for the failure to call such evidence at trial, as normally required by s. 23(2)(d) of the Criminal Appeal Act 1968. The CACD adopted the approach that as the 'fresh' evidence indicated that the conviction was unsafe, the interests of justice required that it be admitted. That approach was consistent with the wording of s. 23 of the 1968 Act, which makes it clear that the interests of justice are the overriding consideration. It is also consistent with the clear position in law, i.e. the overriding test for the CACD to apply is its view of the safety of the conviction.[1]

The remainder of this chapter will critically consider three cases to further illustrate the different approaches between the CCRC and the CACD from the perspective of the interests of justice.

R v. *Rhee*

Jong Rhee was convicted at the Crown Court in Chester of the murder of his wife (see Woffinden, 1999a). At the trial, the prosecution alleged that he had murdered his wife by setting fire to the bed and breakfast accommodation where they were both staying. Briefly, the prosecution evidence included the following:

1. There was considerable forensic evidence regarding the fire. This evidence included that of experts intended to describe the causes of the fire, but it

was far from conclusive and none of the experts were able to say for certain how the fire was started or whether it had been started deliberately.

2. The landlady of the bed and breakfast accommodation gave evidence that Rhee had failed to make efforts to rescue his wife.

3. There was circumstantial evidence pointing towards Rhee's possible guilt: for example, evidence of a petrol can in the back of his car and the fact that he had taken out a large insurance policy shortly before his wife's death.

4. The prosecution called a Mr Hughes, who was an Investigating Fire Brigade Officer. He concluded that there were two seats of fire. His evidence was based on his examination of the scene of the fire and the damage that had been done to the building.

5. The Crown also called Mr Sheen, a Forensic Engineer, who also concluded that there were two seats of fire. His evidence was based in part upon the damage that had been done to the building and in part upon the description of the fire given by witnesses.

6. A Fire Examiner, Mr Jones, gave evidence to the effect that it was impossible to identify the cause of the fire. He based his evidence on the damage to the building as well as a description of the fire given by the witnesses.

One of the defence expert witnesses endeavoured to express a view on the effects of fumes etc., but the judge would not allow that evidence to be given as it was outside the witness's area of expertise.

At trial, the prosecution case was that fires had started both downstairs in the living area and upstairs in the bedroom of Mr and Mrs Rhee. The defence case was that there was only one seat of fire, which was downstairs and which must have been accidental in cause, and that the deceased had been overcome by fumes. To demonstrate how central it was, the trial judge Justice Ebsworth said in her Summing Up: 'In this case the Crown must prove that the defendant set a fire in reality in the bedroom as well as the lounge' (*R v Rhee* [1998] [unreported]). The fact that Rhee had managed to escape from the fire while his wife had not crucial for the prosecution. It was suggested by the Crown that both the defendant and his wife would have been able to escape the fire had the fire been an accident.

Ebsworth further commented in her Summing Up that:

> Now what do the Crown say over circumstances that you in broad outline have to look at ... [the victim] who was 5' 5"/5' 6" and a healthy sensible girl not given to panic failed to escape from a window 9 [feet] from the ground; whereas the defendant got out. (*R v Rhee* [1998] [unreported])

The prosecution did not call any evidence to explain how the victim might have died and her husband escape, but they did call a Dr Benfield to give evidence that carbon monoxide poisoning can take minutes (although he did not say precisely how many). That would certainly have left the jury with the impression that she could have escaped.

We have battled with the CCRC over a number of years and have put before it the following reports:[2]

1. A report from Professor Chris Milroy, a highly regarded Home Office Pathologist. His opinion was that the deceased had died from inhalation of smoke and fire gases and there was no medical evidence that she had been incapacitated before the fire had started and that 'the pathological findings do provide support for the defendants contention that Natalie Rhee died in an accidental fire'. No pathological evidence was put before the jury at trial on behalf of the defendant.

2. A report from leading fire expert Dr Roger Berrett concluded that there was only one seat of fire which had started in the lounge and had developed into a 'flash over' spreading to the roof space and from there to the bedroom where Mrs Rhee's body was found. Dr Berrett, for the first time, identified and highlighted breaches of the Home Office guidelines on fire investigations and was critical of the experts called on behalf of the Crown in relation to their methodology as well as their conclusions. His opinion was that the investigation by the prosecution witnesses had fallen well short of the standard required. He said there was no meaningful scientific evidence to suggest that the fire had been started deliberately.

3. Finally, I submitted on behalf of Mr Rhee an interim report from Professor David Purser. David Purser has been a leading expert in fire safety and has made a particular study as to the circumstances and mechanisms in which people become incapacitated and killed in fires. Studying physiology, toxicology and predictive model developments, he has been involved in an analysis of many of the leading fire disasters in the world and the CCRC accepted that he was a highly qualified expert. Whilst I considered that it was arguable that the CCRC might find that the evidence of Professor Milroy and Dr Berrett could have been given at trial, I considered that it was unlikely that it would have come to the same conclusions regarding Professor Purser and, certainly, there was nobody who gave evidence at trial either for the Crown or defence who had anything approaching his level of particularly relevant expertise. Sadly, I was wrong.

Professor Purser's Report concluded that the high level of carbon monoxide in Mrs Rhee's blood would have indicated a long exposure to a slow burning fire, the seat of which would probably have been in another room. He confirmed that it was extremely unlikely that she would have survived the heat exposure from a fire, the seat of which had been in the bedroom, long enough to have obtained a carbon monoxide level of the reading actually recorded. This clearly confirmed the defence case at trial.

His report also provides an explanation as to how it could have been that Mr Rhee managed to escape the bedroom but Mrs Rhee did not (i.e. she had been overcome by fumes) and confirmed that not only was there likely to have been one seat of the fire, but that fire was likely to have started accidentally.

Before finalizing the decision, the CCRC decided to go back to one of the principal prosecution witnesses to see if his views were changed by the fresh evidence submitted on behalf of Mr Rhee. Not entirely surprisingly, the prosecution witness confirmed his preference for his own evidence.[3] Comforted by this opinion, the CCRC expressed the view that the CACD would not receive the evidence submitted on behalf of Mr Rhee and accordingly rejected his application.

At the time of writing, further work is being carried out in connection with Mr Rhee's case with a view to another application being submitted to the CCRC. But should his case have already have been referred? How would the CACD, in practice, deal with such a case? I have already pointed out that in both *R v. Jones* and *R v. Kai Whitewind*, notwithstanding what was said by the CACD, the evidence was actually heard by the court, and that is a frequent experience. Whilst I can remember the distinguished but now retired pathologist Professor Bernard Knight (the expert involved in *Jones*) complaining bitterly outside the CACD that he too often sat there waiting not to be called, the truth of the matter is that in appropriate cases the CACD has shown itself ready to exercise its discretion and admit evidence even though all of the criteria of s. 23 are not met.

In *R v. Hanratty*, for instance, Lord Chief Justice Woolf stated that:

> It is clear that the overriding consideration for this Court in deciding whether fresh evidence should be admitted on the hearing of an appeal is whether the evidence will assist the Court to achieve justice. Justice can be equally achieved by upholding a conviction if it is safe or setting aside if it is unsafe. (*R v. Hanratty* [2002] CR App R 419)

Moreover, in *R v. Richardson* the appellant had been convicted of murder. At trial he had refused to give evidence and agreed with trial lawyers that witnesses who might have helped him should not be called. It was acknowledged that he had not been honest with his trial lawyers. In the CACD dealing with an application to call fresh evidence, Lord Justice McCowan said:

> On the one hand this is a case of a man who has advanced an admittedly lying defence and it having failed now wants to try another one. The Court is extremely reluctant to lend any assistance to that sort of purpose. Indeed it can only be in an exceptional case that it would do so. On the other hand, we have to consider whether there is a risk that by reason of his own stupid lies a miscarriage of justice may have occurred ... Having

weighed the matter up and after a great deal of hesitation, we have come to the conclusion that there is a possibility – we put it no higher at this stage – that there may have been a miscarriage of justice caused entirely by the appellant's fault. In those circumstances, we have come to the conclusion that we should exercise our discretion under Section 23 [1][C] to receive the evidence of the witnesses. (*R* v. *Richardson* [1991] [unreported])

The judgment in *R* v. *Criminal Cases Review Commission, ex parte Pearson* is quoted in probably every Statement of Reasons issued by the CCRC because, in it, Lord Justice Bingham spelt out the power of the CCRC to refer and its obligation to make a judgment on the case's prospects of success, including, to be fair, the likelihood or otherwise of the CACD receiving 'fresh evidence'. Rarely quoted, however, is that part of the judgment where Lord Bingham quoted *Richardson* and said:

It seems clear that by 1991 the Court had come to recognise, even in an extreme case of this kind, the paramount need to ensure that a conviction was safe...The overriding discretion conferred on the Court, enables it to ensure that, in the last resort, defendants are sentenced for the crimes they have committed and not for the psychological failings to which he may be subject. (*R* v. *Criminal Cases Review Commission, ex parte Pearson* [2000] 1 Cr App R 141)

R v. *Huckerby and Power*

In the case of *R* v. *Huckerby and Power* the CACD dealt with an application in relation to an appeal against a conviction for conspiracy to rob, with Graham Huckerby seeking leave to call fresh evidence that his apparent cooperation in the robbery could be explained by the fact that at the time of the robbery he had been suffering from post-traumatic stress disorder (PTSD) which had caused him to panic.

The Crown opposed the application and included in the reasons for objection the fact that the appellant had made a conscious decision not to rely on the evidence which was available at the trial and could not, therefore, ask for the verdict to be set aside on the basis of evidence which he had made a previously informed decision not to use.

Briefly, Huckerby, it was suggested by the prosecution, had been the 'inside man' in an armed robbery. He had, some years earlier whilst working for Securicor, been the subject of a knife-point robbery. On the advice of trial counsel, a report was obtained from a forensic psychiatrist on the issue of PTSD but, again, on the advice of counsel, it was decided not to call that evidence which it was believed would not assist. After Huckerby's conviction, further reports were obtained from appropriate experts, psychiatrists and psychologists, which confirmed that he had unresolved symptoms from the first incident which were likely to have been reactivated at the time of the second robbery and which, therefore, might have affected his response.

In my experience, there is little doubt that had Huckerby's appeal been unsuccessful, and he then made an application to the CCRC, his application would have been refused on a similar basis as the refusal of the application of Jong Rhee, with the usual reference made to *R* v. *Jones* and *R* v. *Kai-Whitewind* – but he was not in that position.

Nevertheless, the CACD in its judgment acknowledged that the admissibility of the evidence was difficult: 'we have found much more difficult the question whether the evidence should be admitted on this appeal (Lord Justice Potter in *R* v. *Huckerby and Power* [2004] EWCA Crim 3251). However, the CACD dealt with the matter as follows:

> Mr Kamlish [counsel for Mr Huckerby] acknowledges that the failure of the appellant to make clear the position to his advisers, coupled with the intervention of this girlfriend were the principal reasons for the non-availability of such evidence. However, he submits that in the overall interests of justice that evidence should be admitted now...after careful thought we accede to that submission in the particular circumstances of the case namely that we have overall doubts as to the safety of the conviction. (*R* v. *Huckerby and Power* [2004] EWCA Crim 3251, para. 112)

The CACD concluded as follows:

> We consider it necessary in the interests of justice to admit the evidence of Dr Green and Mr Ragel for the purposes of this appeal. Having done so, we are not satisfied as to the safety of the conviction of Huckerby and his appeal against conviction will be allowed. (*R* v. *Huckerby and Power* [2004] EWCA Crim 3251)

These cases demonstrate, clearly, that the CACD will apply common sense when considering an application and above all will be guided by its sense of justice and what is right and will not prevent a wrongful conviction from being overturned simply on the basis that the evidence which undermines the safety of that conviction could have conceivably been called at an earlier stage. Contrary to this, I believe the CCRC have frequently been out of step with the approach taken by the CACD and have been overly cautious in their approach to fresh-evidence cases, particularly those involving expert witnesses.

Having said this, it would be wrong to suggest that the CCRC is always timid. For instance, the CCRC did refer the case of *R* v. *Solomon* where convictions for serious sexual offences were quashed on the basis of a video which showed that the sexual acts complained of were consensual. At trial, the defendant had shown a video which had been edited and tried to escape conviction on the basis that nothing untoward had occurred. While it was clear that he had deliberately withheld the genuine video for tactical reasons, the CACD were prepared to admit it as it clearly demonstrated he had been wrongly convicted. This shows that the CCRC can weigh up such applications and correctly assess the likely approach of the CACD. Regrettably, such examples are rare, with non-referral in such cases being the norm, which also demonstrates an underlying problem of inconsistency still unaddressed by the CCRC more than ten years after its inception.

R v. *Harris*

In describing the general approach of the CCRC and its reluctance to refer cases where the evidence was, or could have been, available at trial, I referred to the decision to refer the new evidence from Professor Purser to one of the prosecution witnesses at the trial of Jong Rhee. At the time, it raised no more than mild surprise with me and I found it predictable that a prosecution expert would not be affected by the views of a new expert, but in the context of the CCRC's general approach it did not seem to be a major factor.

However, in a more recent case, the CCRC have done a similar thing. The debate amongst experts regarding head injuries amongst infants is a controversial one. For many years the concept of what has been described as Shaken Baby Syndrome (SBS) was accepted without question by experts, but in the last decade this has certainly not been the case.

In the case of *R* v. *Harris*, for instance, the CACD dealt with four separate convictions involving infants and found itself involved in controversial issues where eminent medical experts could not agree amongst themselves on the likely causes of injury or death. Of the four cases, two convictions were overturned completely, a conviction for murder was reduced to manslaughter and the conviction of Alan Cherry was upheld. Reports from two American experts in bio-mechanics were submitted to the appeal, one for Mr Cherry and one for the Crown. Because of pressures on court time, the CACD were not able to actually hear that evidence and at that stage concluded that the evidence of bio-mechanics was complex, developing and (as yet) necessarily uncertain.

However, since that judgment was given the expert instructed by me on behalf of the appellant has continued to do more work and has given evidence not only in the United States but, also, on several occasions in courts in both England and in Scotland. Having had the opportunity of doing further specific tests, a report from him was submitted as being central to an application to the CCRC for a reference back to the CACD. It not only provided far more information than had been available at the time of the first appeal, to explain why Cherry's explanation for the fatal injuries may well have been right, but also demonstrated the flaws in the prosecution's response at the CACD.

It was certainly our reading of the judgment that the CACD anticipated that in the appropriate circumstances it was likely that the issue of bio-mechanics would come back to them. We were all, therefore, stunned when in declining to refer Mr Cherry's case back to the CACD, the CCRC disclosed that it had sought to have the bio-mechanical evidence evaluated by two of the prosecution experts who gave evidence for the Crown in the CACD – experts who acknowledged their lack of experience and understanding of bio-mechanical issues. The response of those experts was, perhaps, predictable, and the CCRC declined to refer the application on that basis.

It is, of course, entirely reasonable that if an applicant invites the CCRC to refer a case back to the CACD it should have any expert evidence forming the basis of the application independently assessed. The important word here is 'independently'. There can be little point in having that evidence assessed by experts who have largely committed themselves to a contrary review. In any event, as the case of *R* v. *Harris* made clear, the mere fact that experts disagree is not going to be fatal for an appellant, indeed, the reverse may very well be the case. As the CACD said: 'even on the interpretation of objective evidence there can be two views expressed by highly experienced and distinguished experts' (*R* v. *Harris* (2005) EWCA Crim 1980). Again, the CCRC decision not to refer the application of Cherry shows that it may misunderstand the way the CACD actually works and how it may deal with such appeals in practice.

Conclusion

The approach of the CCRC is worryingly inconsistent, and that is something that should have been addressed after more than a decade of referring cases and evaluating the CACD's judgments in relation to those references.

Moreover, when the CACD dispose of appeals that it receives following a reference from the CCRC, it is, effectively, auditing and reviewing the CCRC's reasoning and decisions, but there is no such audit for those cases that have not been referred. Whilst it may be open to an applicant to try and challenge the decision of the CCRC by way of an application to the Administrative Court for Judicial Review, the reality is that the court has made it abundantly clear that it is very reluctant to interfere in a process delegated by Parliament to the CCRC. It will certainly not interfere, even if the view of the Court is that the CCRC's decision is wrong, as it is only able to review the decision if it is irrational or unlawful.

Finally, I believe that it would be a useful process, and beneficial to the CCRC, for there to be a random-sample audit of a small number of cases which have been considered by a panel of three Commission members but not referred.[4] Such a review could be carried out by independent Leading

Counsel or a retired High Court Judge. Such a process might expose weaknesses of a kind that I have tried to highlight. It may help to eliminate the inconsistencies and bad decisions. It could assist in the overturning of wrongful convictions that currently go uncorrected, which ratchets up the harm to the victims and their families on the receiving end of the CCRC's poor judgment, especially cruel when such victims are let down by the official body that exists to help them.

Notes

1. In the cases I use to illustrate the problem with the CCRC the clients concerned have confirmed their consent to their cases being ventilated in this way.
2. The following quotations from the various reports that have been submitted to the CCRC are in the author's possession by virtue of being the solicitor in the case.
3. The strategy of the CCRC of going back and seeking an opinion from one of the prosecution experts at trial has recently been repeated in another case that I have been dealing with in circumstances which are even more surprising, and it is a point to which I will briefly return below.
4. If a Case Review Manager (CRM) believes that a case should not be referred it has to be confirmed by a single Commissioner. Alternatively, if a CRM believes that a case should be referred, it has to be confirmed by a panel of three Commissioners. It has been suggested that this introduces a structural barrier to referral as the hurdle is higher.

9
Applicant Solicitors: Friends or Foes?
Glyn Maddocks and Gabe Tan

Introduction

Over the last decade, the operations of the Criminal Cases Review Commission (CCRC) and its case review process have continually evolved in response to an increasing need for greater consistency and transparency. Despite this, the precise nature of the 'working' relationship between Commissioners and/or Case Review Managers (CRMs), and defence solicitors representing applicants (applicant solicitors), appears to be highly elusive: investigative and case review methodology employed in the case review process seem to differ significantly between CRMs. Some tend to take a more proactive approach in their case investigations and are much more receptive and communicative with applicant solicitors. At the same time, there are also CRMs who view their investigative role and their relationship with applicant solicitors quite differently – they appear to be far less dynamic and rarely or never engage with applicants or their solicitors.

It seems, therefore, that it is very much the luck of the draw as to which CRM is assigned to a case, and it is arguable that both the quality of the investigation and, more significantly, the ultimate outcome, that is, whether or not the case is referred to the Court of Appeal (Criminal Division) (CACD), may be significantly affected by the randomness of the allocation process within the CCRC. Put simply, if an applicant is allocated a very proactive CRM who is able and willing to engage in a positive relationship with an experienced solicitor, the chances of a successful referral in a case with merit appear likely to increase.

In this context, we will examine the relationship between the CCRC and applicant solicitors, and how the way in which individual CRMs undertake their investigative role appears to vary. Noting that the investigative approach of CRMs may be a significant determining factor in whether or not a case is going to be referred to the CACD, greater consistency and dynamism is called for in case investigations, and CCRC Commissioners and/or CRMs need to be more receptive towards the constructive role and assistance that experienced solicitors representing applicants can offer in the case review process.

We will first discuss the methodology that underpins the chapter. Next, we will look at the CCRC's case review process and will explore the role that applicant solicitors can and do play at the various stages, particularly in identifying key lines of investigation and clarifying the essential factual matrix of a case. Further, drawing from a discussion that we had with members of the CCRC, we will critically examine the reasons why communication and engagement between Commissioners/CRMs[1] and applicant solicitors is relatively infrequent and the significant implications of this. Finally, we will attempt to suggest constructive ways in which the CCRC can build a more positive working relationship with applicant solicitors which will serve to improve the facilitation of its case review process, and promote thoroughness and greater uniformity in the way in which it reviews and investigates its cases.

Methodology

This chapter is primarily based on the experiences of Glyn Maddocks, a practising criminal appeal solicitor with over 15 years of working in this specialized area. Although it is to be acknowledged that his personal views may not be representative of criminal defence solicitors *per se*, the purpose of this chapter is not to present a definitive account but, rather, to initiate a discussion on the CCRC's working relationship with applicant solicitors, drawing from around 25 CCRC applications he has made, out of which a number have led to subsequent successful appeals, including the case of Paul Blackburn who, after spending nearly 25 years in prison for attempted murder, had his conviction quashed in May 2005 following more than 12 years of pro bono legal work on the case.

In addition, to obtain a qualitative insight into the existing working relationship between Commissioners/CRMs and applicant solicitors, we conducted a 'focus-group' meeting with members of the CCRC in February 2008, consisting of two Commissioners, three CRMs and other CCRC officials. The circumstances in which CRMs meet solicitors and applicants; the various difficulties the CCRC had referred to as arising in working with applicant solicitors; and some of the benefits for applicants in having legal representation, based on the CCRC's experience to date, were discussed in some depth. Selected parts of the recorded discussions are quoted in this chapter.

Unfortunately at present, the CCRC does not hold any information on the number of cases referred to the CACD by individual CRMs. The lack of availability of specific data on the investigative practices of its caseworkers and CRMs, to support its contention opposing the suggestion that there is no uniformity of approach and methodology in its case review process, is regrettable. Our original intention was to devise a questionnaire for both Commissioners and CRMs, to allow those who participated in the meeting (and those who did not) an opportunity to clarify the points they raised in writing and after reflection, and to obtain quantitative data on the number of referrals and the differing practices of individual CRMs and Commissioners. Although the CCRC did not initially reject this request when first informed of the questionnaire research, and accepted our questionnaires during the meeting, this was subsequently declined on the grounds that they:

> already have a number of formal research projects in progress, one of which is looking at the impact of legal representation on cases coming to the CCRC, and includes interviewing defence lawyers and CCRC staff ... [and it] ha[s] to take into account the time demands that such projects make on [its] staff.

As a result, we have only been able to base our research on our meeting with the CCRC. We recognize that several methodological limitations arise from this narrow approach: the accounts of our research participants cannot be generalized or taken as a 'definitive individual view', but rather are articulated in a specific context within a specific organizational culture (see Gibb, 1997: 4). Positional and power differences between Commissioners and CRMs present at the meeting will also, inevitably, influence their responses. However, it is hoped that the findings from the meeting can offer some insights into the CCRC's position, the realities Commissioners and CRMs face in conducting case reviews, and open up an important debate into an essential issue which has, hitherto, been largely overlooked.

Reviewing a possible miscarriage of justice: a thorough investigation or a multiple-guessing game?

As an independent public body established to investigate possible miscarriages of justice, the CCRC's stated aims, as set out on its website, are:

* to investigate cases as quickly as possible and with thoroughness and care;
* to work constructively with our stakeholders and to the highest standards of quality;
* to treat applicants, and anyone affected by our work, with courtesy, respect and consideration; and,
* to promote public understanding of the Commission's role. (CCRC, 2008g)

However, our research suggests that these laudable objectives are only fulfilled to a fairly limited extent (see also Chapter 5). Whilst it is acknowledged that aims such as these have to be adequately balanced against the background of the practical difficulties and the realities that the CCRC faces, and that this is rarely a straightforward process, there is, arguably, much scope for improvement in all aspects, as will be critically examined in this section.

Thoroughness, care and a proactive investigation

Subjective inferences in the CCRC's case review process not only have to be made in attempting to second-guess the CACD, but also inevitably at various stages of the investigation. For instance, at the initial stage of processing the application and allocating it a level of priority and complexity, guesswork is often involved in trying to gain a clear understanding of the applicant's assertions and his or her potential grounds of appeal. Further clarification is often also required to establish significant details of his or her case and what, if any, important and relevant developments have occurred since conviction. To achieve a truly thorough investigation approached in an inquisitorial manner, a proactive approach by CRMs is essential. This is to ensure that the extent of any such 'guesswork' can be limited as far as possible, and that the outcome of the review is grounded on high quality, objective and thorough case investigation at all stages. No stone should be left unturned and superficial assessments, which may well be attractive, will always be subjected to intense critical examination before a final conclusion is reached.

Despite acknowledging that high illiteracy rates amongst convicted prisoners mean that very often applications received by the CCRC may be unclear, some solely consisting of a simple statement, such as 'please look at my case', it was revealed during the course of our discussion that out of the one thousand or so applications received each year, CRMs and/or Commissioners only arrange to meet applicants in a handful of cases. Indeed, little utility is seen in a face-to-face meeting with an applicant, and such meetings are often declined, even after multiple requests have been made by the applicant or his or her solicitor.

For instance, during our discussion, one case was brought up involving an applicant (who was represented by Glyn Maddocks) who had suffered serious brain damage at the age of four, was convicted of a murder for which he has consistently maintained his innocence of a crime for which another person had admitted his guilt and confirmed that the applicant was not involved. During the application's passage through the CCRC, multiple requests were made for the CRM to visit the applicant personally, to gain an insight into the character of the applicant and, more importantly, to form a view as to the nature of his disability – all of which were denied.

Although it is highly debatable whether a personal visit by the CRM may have had a significant bearing on the way in which the case progressed through the CACD and, ultimately, on its decision not to refer the case back to the CACD, it was argued by the CCRC that the CRM could not be regarded as an 'expert' and would not be able to assess whether the various expert assessments on that particular applicant were correct or not. Perhaps, more interestingly, as a CRM commented:

> Do you think the reverse could also be true? An applicant of mine whose case was referred ... when we [the Commissioner and the CRM] saw him,

we knew exactly why he was convicted. He came across as a really, really peculiar man.

Whilst this 'character assessment' of the applicant was viewed by the CRM and the Commissioner as entirely negative and even detrimental to the applicant, what was overlooked, however, was how the meeting may have provided a first-hand insight and understanding into how the applicant's personality, the way he or she presented him or herself (which can, at times, be attributed to some form of personality disorder or disability), may have contributed to a possible wrongful conviction. Albeit somewhat speculative, arguably, a meeting between a CRM and an applicant in a case such as the one described earlier would perhaps have been far more valuable and instructive than reading scores of pages of documents and reports. Such a meeting, and the insight that can only be gained at first hand, could perhaps provide the tipping point in a closely balanced case, possibly even leading to a decision being made to refer rather than to reject.

Instead, both CRMs and Commissioners appear rather settled in the current, some would say cosy, practices where meeting applicants seems to be at the very bottom of, if not completely excluded from, its list of priorities in conducting a case review. One Commissioner, who was previously a criminal practitioner, expressed the current thinking:

> When I first got here, all my legal training up till then is that you always go and see a client first. It is how you start a case, that is the first thing one does in a case, and I had difficulty with it when I arrived. But now, I think I'm happily convinced that ... the system works pretty well. Unless you want to sort things out ... maybe it's a particularly complex area and we still can't understand how [the applicant] reconciles this matter ... if there is a good reason to see him, we would ... You have to accept that we don't come to it with the same approach as most lawyers who would start with their client's evidence first.

On asking whether this reluctance to meet applicants was more to do with the CCRC's well publicized lack of resources than with a policy decision, rather unconvincingly the response by the same commissioner was:

> It is not really about resources...We will go and see the applicant if we think it would be useful...If we don't think there is any objective justification, we won't do it.

This, however, appears to be at odds with the CCRC's official written replies to applicants requesting to meet the CRMs assigned to their cases. In one such case involving an applicant whose CCRC application had recently failed, the applicant had requested to see the CRM. Being barely literate he felt he could not adequately express himself in his written CCRC application. The applicant's request was denied (although he was encouraged to contact the CCRC by telephone despite the fact that he is in prison) on the grounds that such a meeting cannot be arranged due to the CCRC's 'very limited resources'.[2]

Perhaps more significantly, it appears that both CRMs and Commissioners take a very narrow view as to what is considered an 'objective justification' to meet an applicant. Meetings with applicants and/or their solicitors rarely occur, even in the most complex cases. In fact, it seems that meetings are initiated by CRMs only in highly exceptional circumstances, for instance where the applicant is of a different nationality and requires a translator.

Although how precisely this apparent reluctance to communicate and meet with applicants impacts on the thoroughness of the CRM's investigation remains a highly debatable issue, this approach appears to result in applicants or their solicitors (if instructed) having little or no opportunity to input into the CCRC's review process, despite their often detailed and valuable knowledge acquired from sometimes years of work on the case. This lack of communication frequently leaves applicants and their solicitors completely in the dark as to the progress of the cases and at times having to speculate about what the CRM's view of their case is. This to some extent seems incongruous with the spirit of the CCRC's stated aim 'to treat applicants, and anyone affected by [its] work, with courtesy, respect and consideration'.

Highest standards of quality and a respectful treatment? Only if you are lucky!

Although, increasingly, some efforts have been made to systemize the investigative approach of CRMs, it is perhaps surprising that more than ten years into the life of the CCRC, CRMs are yet to undergo any formal skills training or courses on case review or investigation techniques. Instead, it was claimed that regular specialist talks and/or workshops are provided on different areas of criminal law, such as forensic science, the criminal appeals system, etc., but no information was provided as to how regular such talks or workshops occur. Although the CCRC remains largely reliant on the previous review and investigative experiences of individual CRMs (which presumably have been built up from a very low base point in 1997), CRMs come from a wide range of different occupational and academic backgrounds (including academic psychiatrists, criminal practitioners, the police, probation officers and law graduates), some with previous investigative experience and others with none.

This diversity is one of the obvious strengths of the CCRC, as different angles will be considered, but, inevitably, this must result in an inconsistency in the ways in which CRMs approach their investigative roles. As acknowledged during our meeting: 'We have a framework within which we operate [but], clearly within that, people will have slightly different styles and approaches.'

Whilst it is recognized that CRMs' investigative approaches and case review methodology must vary with the nature and complexity of each case, it appears that differences in CRMs are not limited to stylistic variations but to attitude and thoroughness as well – some CRMs may be more detailed and meticulous in the fact-finding process of the investigation, and may be more proactive in liaising with applicant solicitors in examining possible fresh lines of inquiry. On the other hand, others seem to take a more neutral approach and deal with cases allocated to them in what appears to be a less inquisitorial and a much more 'mechanistic' way, where case investigation seems to be a question of 'going through the motions'. Such CRMs are by and large either unwilling or unable to respond to any prompting by the applicant solicitor to pursue possible lines of further enquiry or investigation and do not see their role as participating in a collegiate approach with an applicant solicitor to establish the precise merits of a case. Indeed, it was conceded by one Commissioner that:

> undoubtedly, there are some CRMs who are less comfortable in talking to solicitors and communicating with them ... Some will find it a little more difficult but they have more resources [and] more chance now to get some advice on how to do it.

Although it was not explained during the meeting, why training and 'advice' would be required for some CRMs, when often all that applicant solicitors expect is an honest and open update and discussion as to how the case review is progressing, it was emphasized that efforts have been made to improve the uniformity and consistency of the case review approach by CRMs by initiating a new 'group system'. CRMs now have an appointed group leader (who is an experienced CRM) to oversee and provide case investigation advice. While this is to be greatly welcomed and presumably has been introduced in recognition that the previous system needed to be improved to ensure greater consistency in the case review process, unfortunately the CCRC seems to be of the view that this is the best it can do:

> The new system of group leaders is about as good as we are going to get in terms of trying to control consistency, along with a lot of training and memorandums etc. that we have internally.

Perhaps more significantly, as the next section will explore, responsibility for any apparent communication breakdown has been largely attributed (correctly or otherwise) to procedural and structural factors and, more so, to the lack of understanding and knowledge of how the CCRC operates amongst many applicant solicitors, without any suggestion being made as to how this can be improved.

Who needs applicant solicitors anyway?

It is perhaps in light of the complexities involved in this intrinsically inquisitorial process that the potentially crucial role of applicant solicitors emerges. Although the official position of the CCRC maintains that the use of a solicitor when making an application is not necessary, it also highlights a number of functions that applicant solicitors can play in facilitating its case investigation process. As the CCRC's 'Notes for Legal Representatives' issued by the Legal Services Commission (LSC) states:

> Some investigation may be necessary on behalf of the convicted defendant before any application is made...If an application is made to the CCRC, then the solicitor will be involved in gathering and rationalising the material, preparing a chronology of events, and preparing the submission of any legal arguments required. The solicitor is also likely to need to advise and assist the convicted defendant after the application is submitted to the CCRC by assisting the CCRC with specific queries, making further submissions ... *liaising with the CCRC as to its approach and progress and advising the client in relation to any decisions made by the CCRC in the case. It may be necessary for the solicitor to meet the CCRC's representatives on more than one occasion in a complex case.* (CCRC, 2008k; our emphasis)

Despite these various crucial roles that applicant solicitors may undertake, the existing working relations between the CCRC and applicant solicitors appears to be somewhat different from the constructive model described by the LSC. The reason for why communicative breakdown often occurs was discussed in detail by Commissioners and CRMs present in the meeting, and will be outlined and critically evaluated below.

The distinction between trial and applicant solicitors

It is right to point out that, as a general rule, defence solicitors who have acted for a CCRC applicant during his or her trial or previous appeal(s) will be more likely to assist CRMs in clarifying the essential facts of a case and providing details of what happened at trial than would solicitors who have only been engaged at the application stage. Both CRMs and Commissioners at the meeting felt that:

> There is a distinction between solicitors who acted for the client at trial ... and those who come in at the CCRC stage. [The former] would have greater and more in depth knowledge of the case and therefore would be more likely to help us in clarifying what happened during the trial, pre-trial, etc.

Further, as one CRM commented:

> Quite often, regardless of whether [the applicant] is represented or who they are represented by, sometimes we need insight into a particular aspect

of the evidence, it's very helpful to go back to the trial solicitor ... sometimes one has to because there is a question that needs an answer, and they can provide an insight into something that might have been difficult to appreciate unless you were there during the trial.

A major obstacle, however, is that it is quite common that an applicant has had a number of solicitors and trial counsel, who are, more frequently than not, alleged by the applicant (rightly or wrongly) of having provided him or her with an inadequate service which they claim contributed to or directly led to their alleged wrongful convictions. There is, therefore, frequently a conflict between trial solicitor(s) and the applicant, at times making it almost impossible for CRMs to gain from the trial representatives any constructive or accurate insight and knowledge into the case and what happened at trial.

It is acknowledged that a far more in-depth study is required to gain a thorough understanding of the difficulties in investigating and overturning miscarriages of justice where poor defence is alleged (see also Chapter 4). However, it does raise worrying concerns as to how the thoroughness and fairness of the CCRC's case review process in such cases may be seriously compromised, and it highlights an urgent need for the CCRC to address openly its limitations in this respect.

Applicant's solicitor or 'application solicitor'?

An important issue raised at the meeting is that just as proficiency, dynamism and thoroughness may vary between CRMs, from the CCRC's point of view, the level of engagement and the attitude of applicant solicitors also varies significantly. In fact, very often, applicant solicitors are reluctant or simply too busy to answer requests and queries that CRMs may have. One Commissioner said:

> There are equally as many stories and complaints ... from CRMs saying [they] can't get an answer out of [a] solicitor ... and they are in a stalemate until they hear from them. The frustration works both ways ... In the final analysis, [the CRM] may have to progress and submit the case to the Commissioner on the basis that [he or she] cannot get an answer [from the solicitor].

Indeed, it is frequently the case that solicitors are unwilling to put in too much work on the case, other than writing a covering letter for the CCRC application, due to limited or inadequate funding. Therefore, an applicant solicitor may often just be a named legal representative put down by the applicant for the purpose of the application only, and may not in fact be keen to communicate or liaise with the CRM:

> You can tell from the quality of the application whether a solicitor has been involved in the case and in fact whether they want to have any

ongoing dialogue with you during the course of the review. If it is just a solicitor's name by the applicant as someone who has got the case papers, or someone who is acting for [him/her] now, and there is no letter from the solicitor, or the application doesn't arrive together with the submission from the solicitor, then it is less likely that a solicitor is engaged in the case.

Perhaps more disconcertingly, as one CRM recounted, there are occasions when the applicant solicitor, despite having drafted a submission to the CCRC on behalf of the applicant, does not even possess the trial files or case papers, and has no knowledge whatsoever of the client's case:

> I have even dealt with cases where you have submissions at the outset, you work on the submissions ... and six months later, the same solicitor writes back saying 'well actually, we have no case papers at all ... We don't know very much about the case except for what you've told us', and then they seek from us, at that stage, disclosure of the entire CPS [Crown Prosecution Service] file.

This graphically highlights that the present limits to legal-aid funding in relation to post-conviction cases can have a detrimental effect on potentially innocent individuals trying to make an application to the CCRC. At present, the only public funding that is available to assist criminal appeal solicitors in preparing CCRC cases is that which is provided under the LSC's Advice and Assistance scheme which enables a franchised solicitor to undertake an initial amount of work (currently £300 at the economically impractical rate of £49.70 per hour) (LSC, 2008). Extensions to the cost limit are available, but it does not require a great deal of financial acumen to understand that very few competent and experienced solicitors are able or willing to take on and pursue complex appeal cases, often over many years, at that rate of remuneration (for a fuller discussion, see Chapter 10). Of course, if the Commission ultimately refers the case to the CACD, it will as a general rule grant a Representation Order for the applicant's solicitor. But bearing in mind that only 3.8 per cent of the CCRC cases are referred on average each year,[3] the vast majority of cases are to all intents and purposes dealt with by the solicitors on what is, in effect, a pro bono basis.

A conceptual problem?

However, even when applicant solicitors are actively engaged in a case, their 'assistance' is not always helpful. For instance, it is very often the case that applicant solicitors have no knowledge whatsoever of the CCRC or how it operates (see also Chapter 13). One Commissioner, who from time to time answers telephone queries from members of the public and solicitors, described his experience:

> Some of us are on an 'advice call rota' ... In one of these calls, the solicitor hadn't got a clue what we are about ... she had seen in a judgment,

reference to the CCRC, and the applicant had been told that if his case has any merit, he could then make a further application to the CCRC ... so she calls and asks 'who are you', and 'what are you all about'.

Whilst it was emphasized that the CCRC is 'quite happy' to answer these 'low-level' queries, a perhaps more serious but related problem is the frequent lack of conceptual understanding amongst solicitors of the independent position that the CCRC is required to take: CRMs must adopt a position of non-partisan alignment separated from the applicant or his or her defence team – a position which both Commissioners and CRMs claim applicant solicitors who have to work in the best interests of their clients cannot easily grasp:

> [for] some solicitors ... their mindset is that you are either with them or you are on the side of the prosecution. [Sometimes solicitors think that] we are an extension of their solicitor's firm, and somehow we will carry out their instructions. I think there are conceptual problems and lack of understanding that we are in fact a very different organisation compared to the other parts of the criminal justice system, in one respect, we are gatekeepers for the Court of Appeal.

Significantly, it was also highlighted that solicitors' lack of knowledge of how the CCRC's case review process operates often means that applicant solicitors are unable to provide any constructive assistance to either their clients and/or the CRM:

> The reality is that for the vast majority of applicants to the CCRC, the solicitors actually do very little, or if they do, it is to provide a mad [sic] piece confusing all of the legal and factual arguments ... so even though they have theoretically 'assisted', it is fairly often the case that the assistance has no tangible benefit to anybody.

Further, the CCRC revealed that the inability of solicitors to appreciate the impartial and independent position that both CRMs and the CCRC must take often leads to a breakdown in the working relationship between both parties and can give rise to significant tension (see also Leigh, 2000: 373). Interestingly, a Commissioner and a CRM disclosed that previous hostile experiences, not with solicitors but with certain campaign groups and organizations, have led certain CCRC applications, which were made on behalf of applicants by such campaign groups or organizations, to have been informally 'blacklisted'.

No specific campaign group or organization was named, and the question of how such applications are treated to ensure that the applicant receives a 'fair' and 'impartial' review of his or her case was not addressed. But perhaps more importantly, this, to some extent, strengthens our contention that an applicant represented by a good and experienced solicitor who has an understanding of the CCRC's referral criteria and case review process is on balance likely to be in a much more advantageous position than those who are not represented, or rely on lay representation or miscarriages-of-justice campaign groups and organizations to assist them with their applications. There is, of course, no hard evidence or data to support this contention, but on the face of it this would seem to be a logically sustainable proposition.

Interestingly, when the concern was raised that (the large majority of) applicants who may not be able to afford to pay privately for, or to obtain public funding to engage, such proactive solicitors may be disadvantaged, one CRM suggested it could be the case that applicants who are really innocent may be more likely to engage a solicitor than those who are just 'trying it on':

> It may be that an innocent person would, perhaps, be that much keener to use a solicitor to get himself out of prison rather than trying to do it by himself, so it may be that cases with more merit, will automatically be in the hands of a solicitor.

There is no evidence to support such a view but, perhaps more problematically, it appears to reflect that – although the inquisitorial approach of the CCRC means that legal representation at the CCRC stage is not theoretically necessary, in reality – whether or not the applicant has a solicitor representing her or him will have a fundamental bearing on the case review process and its ultimate outcome, as even CRMs will tend to see applications that are not actively supported by a solicitor as more likely to be unmeritorious.

Further, it is hard to square the CCRC's official stance of 'independence' and 'impartiality' with the occasions where having conducted a detailed and painstaking analysis and investigation with an applicant solicitor for a number of months, or even years, an individual CRM may have formed a clear and unambiguous view that 'something has gone wrong' and a miscarriage of justice has occurred and the case ought to be referred to the CACD (see, for instance, Lewis, 2004). To this end, the question of how that individual CRM is going to prevent his or her strong conviction that an injustice has been suffered (based upon an often unrivalled knowledge of the case) from conflicting with the CCRC's official position of impartiality on such occasions remains yet to be resolved.

We suggest that there is at the heart of the CCRC a conflict. On the one hand, the CCRC argues perfectly validly that it must be independent and impartial and that its job is merely to review alleged miscarriages of justice, so that if a case passes the appropriate test, a referral is made to the CACD. On the other hand, when comprehensive investigations have been conducted on an alleged miscarriage of justice, and detailed grounds supporting a referral have been produced, it is intrinsically difficult for the CCRC to retain its independence (or impartiality) which ought (in our view), at that stage, be put to one side in order to assist in the best way the potentially innocent applicant in overturning his or her potential wrongful conviction. In practice, this often appears to be the case.

Building a constructive working relationship: the way ahead?

An important point emphasized in this chapter is that, in cases where there are apparent communication difficulties between the CCRC and applicant solicitors, a double-edged problem is identified. On the one hand, there is a general lack of understanding of the way in which the CCRC operates within the legal community; on the other hand, there is the scepticism and reluctance of Commissioners and CRMs to liaise with and engage in an inclusive and more transparent way with applicant solicitors during the case review process. This is, no doubt, a self-perpetuating conundrum in that the unwillingness to engage with criminal practitioners will undoubtedly accentuate the ignorance and misunderstanding of its role and function amongst lawyers (and vice versa). On this note, we would like to put forward some (very modest and tentative) suggestions which the CCRC may wish to consider to enable it to build a more positive and mutually beneficial relationship with applicants and those who represent them.

Accredited training sessions and a specialist group of solicitors for CCRC applications

A common consensus that emerged during our discussion is that a good, proactive solicitor with the necessary knowledge and expertise to represent clients during the application's passage through the CCRC will evidently benefit its case review process. Whilst it was maintained by those present at the meeting that the CCRC's governing statutes do not provide for training solicitors, as the only gateway for applicants who have exhausted the normal appeals process to have their cases referred back to the CACD we would suggest that the onus should nevertheless be on the CCRC to 'reach out' to criminal practitioners to promote a greater understanding of its role and operations within the legal community. We are aware that it has been suggested that individual Commissioners should more frequently venture out from the relative sanctuary of Alpha Tower and play a far more ambassadorial role in seeking out and communicating with criminal practitioners (both solicitors and counsel), with the academic community and with the media. We feel that this suggestion should be pursued vigorously and with genuine commitment.

Initiatives were taken by the CCRC in the first years of its establishment, where Commissioners gave accredited talks and lectures to criminal practitioners around the country. Although these were an effective means of fostering a constructive working relationship with practitioners, they seem unfortunately to have been one-off events, which were perhaps concluded too prematurely. However, with continual changes to the 'jurisprudence of the Court of Appeal' to which it is subordinate (cf. Kyle, 2003: 666), and with new batches of criminal practitioners entering the criminal justice system each year, promoting an understanding of the CCRC's role and function and raising awareness of its work ought to be a continual, ongoing task, which would also enable the CCRC to obtain valuable feedback from those who practise at the sharp end of the criminal justice system.

Representatives from the CCRC do give occasional talks to universities and participate in a number of academic conferences and events. This is perhaps an area which can be developed and extended to criminal practitioners through routine accredited training sessions in basic areas, particularly, how to make a CCRC application, the availability of public funding, its statutory powers, remit and functions, and what applicant solicitors can do to assist with the case review process.

It is to be acknowledged that, in light of the shrinking list of solicitors willing to take up post-appeal cases, a possibility that the CCRC is presently exploring, which we believe to be in conjunction with the Solicitors Regulation Authority (SRA) and the Law Society, is to establish an accreditation system for practitioners with specialist expertise in making CCRC applications. We believe that this is a very positive initiative and should be pursued with all possible haste. When such a panel of accredited specialist solicitors has been formed, the CCRC and the professional bodies should publicize this amongst potential CCRC applicants to ensure that they are aware that their cases will in all probability benefit from the involvement of a practitioner who has knowledge and experience of the CCRC.

Encouraging a culture of feedback

Although the CCRC does send out feedback questionnaires to all its applicants each year, yielding a response rate of slightly over a third, or 390 replies in the year 2006–07, its Annual Report contains no analysis on the feedback received except for reporting the positive response it achieved in terms of its accessibility to prisoners and applicants (see CCRC, 2007a: 36). With no publicly available information on what its feedback questionnaire asked, who responded and the findings from their responses, it is unclear how meaningful the existing system of feedback currently in place is.

No doubt, it is acknowledged that applicants' responses may not provide a representative picture of the reality of the CCRC's operations and working practices, and may be strongly influenced and prejudiced by referral decisions. However, particularly in cases which have been successfully referred and quashed by the CACD, feedback from applicants (and their solicitors) on their specific experiences with an individual CRM, their views on some of the key positives and limitations of the CCRC's case review process, is perhaps fundamental for providing transparency and improving the quality and standards of case review for future applicants. We would, therefore, suggest that the CCRC should look again at both the manner and the purpose of its feedback exercise. There seems to be a lack of clarity in what it hopes to achieve and it is difficult to understand how the feedback process as it presently operates would influence the way in which future applications to the CCRC would be dealt with.

Conclusion

Pulling together all of these various strands, a number of themes appear to emerge. The first, and perhaps most important, is the fact that at present there is, undoubtedly, a lack of uniformity and consistency in the way in which individual CRMs undertake the case review process. Given that the CCRC is still a relatively new organization, and that, apart from the rather poor example provided by the now defunct C3 Division of the Home Office, it has developed its culture, ethos and working methods effectively from scratch, these operational limitations are perhaps not surprising. Added to this is the fact that CRMs are recruited from a wide variety of different backgrounds and with a wide range of pre-CCRC experience, and that there exists no formal training programme or pre-employment study scheme to equip CRMs better with the skills and expertise to undertake their case review work.

The end result is that the very randomness of the selection of a CRM will, potentially, have a profound impact upon the ultimate outcome of a case. If a good, committed and experienced CRM is allocated to a case with merit but which requires considerable investigative input, and what could be called a dogged determination to get to the heart of a case, the chances of a referral are exponentially increased. We argue that this gives rise to a worrying cause for concern and should be addressed far more effectively and openly by the CCRC.

The second theme is the apparent reluctance at least up until now for the CCRC to openly recognize and encourage the important part to be played by experienced and knowledgeable solicitors representing an applicant during the passage of his or her case through the CCRC. Although there now appear to be signs that the CCRC is developing a more inclusive attitude towards practitioners, and in some cases is working during the case review process with the applicant solicitor, these relationships on the whole are rare and informal, and in our view they should be encouraged and developed in the interests of justice. Indeed, the fact that a majority of successful applicants to the CCRC are represented by the same few solicitors is, perhaps, indicative of a strong case to be made that proper legal representation of CCRC applicants by an experienced practitioner can contribute positively to the case review process and is, on balance, likely to increase the applicant's chances of having his or her case thoroughly investigated and establishing strong grounds for a referral to the CACD.

Finally, and leading on from this, there seems to be a clear need for the early establishment of a professional accreditation scheme to be created by the SRA and the Law Society in conjunction with the CCRC and the LSC. This would mean that only those solicitors who are members of the panel will be able to access public funding (private fee-paying applicants would of course be able to use any solicitor of their choice), but more importantly the applicant will know in advance that he or she will be represented by a specialist appeal lawyer experienced at dealing with the CCRC. From the CCRC's point of view, such an initiative can, undoubtedly, reduce the various problems with applicant solicitors that they have identified in the course of this research.

We are aware that the CCRC is a constantly evolving organization. As we write, interviews are being held to appoint the present Chairman's successor. There is no doubt that the Chair of the CCRC plays an influential role in driving through changes and influencing the culture and ethos of the organization. There was, undoubtedly, a significant change of both style, content of policy priorities and performance between the first and second Chair. We would urge the third Chair, when appointed, to critically examine all of the preconceptions that currently operate within the CCRC. He or she should look objectively at what its primary purpose has been and what it should be, namely, to identify possible wrongful convictions and reach a conclusion (one way or another) as to whether a case should be referred to the appeal courts after carrying out an inquisitorial, detailed and thorough examination of all the evidence and the information relating to the case. The quality of the investigation by the CRM and how it affects the ultimate outcome of whether a referral does or does not take place is self-evident.

Applicants who are wrongly convicted and whose convictions should be quashed look to the CCRC to ensure that justice will prevail. The CCRC must, therefore, do everything in its power to ensure that this objective is achieved. As the only gateway to the CACD for an individual applicant who may, in fact, be innocent, the stakes are high and the standard and quality of case review cannot and must not be a matter of chance or luck.

Notes

1. 'Commissioners/CRM' is combined in reference to the overseeing role that Commissioners play in the CRMs' reviews and/or investigations of cases. However, the main object of this chapter remains the relationship between CRMs and applicant solicitors.
2. Information provided by INUK's Database of Cases.
3. Figure drawn from CCRC's Case Statistics (see CCRC, 2008c).

10
The Inadequacy of Legal Aid

Steven Bird

Introduction

The Royal Commission on Criminal Justice (RCCJ) (1993) was clear on the need for there 'to be adequate arrangements for granting legal aid to convicted persons who have lost their appeals so that they may obtain advice and assistance in making representations' to the new body that it recommended should be set up to investigate alleged miscarriages of justice, the Criminal Cases Review Commission (CCRC) (RCCJ, 1993: 187).

In light of this, this chapter outlines the available funding for an application to the CCRC under the Advice and Assistance scheme administered by the Legal Services Commission (LSC). In order for any firm of solicitors to provide advice under this scheme they must have signed either a General Criminal Contract (GCC) or an Appeals only contract with the LSC. The scheme allows solicitors and counsel to provide advice to people who are seeking advice either to appeal against sentence or conviction out of time or to make an application to the CCRC (usually in circumstances where that legal team did not represent the client at trial). Once a case is referred, funding comes from the Ministry of Justice via the Court of Appeal. A judicial review of the decision not to refer a case is funded via the LSC but under civil legal representation.

It should be said at the outset that the Advice and Assistance scheme is about as poorly paid as any legal aid scheme. As a direct consequence of this, there are very few firms who take on a significant number of such cases. A relentless onslaught of cost cutting by the current Government has so reduced the profitability of any criminal legally aided work that more and more firms are withdrawing from criminal defence work altogether.

The new payment structures introduced over the last few years and the lack of any rises in the rates of pay for legal aid, generally, inevitably put cost and time pressures on solicitors' firms dealing with trial work. This applies from the police station to the Crown Court and is likely to lead to a reduction in quality of that work and an increase in potential miscarriages of justice, however they are defined. It also means that more convicted persons seeking Advice and Assistance for an application to the CCRC will find it more and more difficult to obtain such advice of any quality.

In this eminently practical chapter, I will firstly consider how the current regime works in terms of Advice and Assistance – the Means Test and the Sufficient Benefit Test – before turning to the use of experts/transcripts/counsel, the payment structure, limitations and rates, and some miscellaneous points. Following this, I look at problems with the current system, such as the audit process, financial limits and extensions, the Sufficient Benefit Test, delays, and rates of pay. Finally, I conclude with suggestions for improvement, including a proposed panel system of providers, a need for a system of individual case assessment of costs, enhanced rates of pay and a binding authority for extension requests.

The current regime

The Advice and Assistance scheme is available only to those persons who satisfy the two tests for eligibility – the Means Test and the Sufficient Benefit Test. If either test is failed the only way to fund an application to the CCRC is for clients to pay for it themselves or through friends and family. Alternatively, applicants can make their own applications to the CCRC.

The Means Test

The Advice and Assistance scheme is strictly means tested. The limits are changed each April. From April 2008, the limits are as follows:

Weekly income

The applicant's 'disposable income' must not exceed £99 per week. This is aggregated with the income of the applicant's partner, and is income after tax, but not taking into account rent or other outgoings. A weekly allowance is deducted for dependants such that £33.65 is deducted for a dependant partner and £47.45 for each dependant child.

If the applicant is in receipt of Income Support, Income Based Job Seekers' Allowance, Guarantee State Pension Credit, Working Tax Credit plus Child Tax Credit or Working Tax Credit with a disability element he or she is automatically eligible for the scheme. However, if in receipt of Working Tax Credit plus Child Tax Credit or Working Tax Credit with a disability element his or her gross annual income must not exceed £14,213.

Capital

There is a limit to the capital that an applicant can have, such that advice under the scheme is not available to an applicant with capital of £1,000 for those with no dependants, £1,335 for those with one dependant and £1,535 for those with two dependants, with an increase of £100 for each extra dependant. Capital must be assessed in all cases. Capital also includes equity in the applicant's home above £100,000 after taking account of a mortgage up to a maximum of £100,000.

Of course, many people seeking such advice will qualify financially, not least because they are often in custody with no income and no capital. However, there will be a significant number of people seeking such advice who will fall outside these very strict financial limits. For those people, advice can only be obtained by paying for it themselves.

The Sufficient Benefit Test

The Sufficient Benefit Test is set out in the GCC specification at Part B para. 2.5 as:

> Advice and Assistance may only be provided on legal issues concerning English law and where there is sufficient benefit to the Client, having regard to the circumstances of the Matter, including the personal circumstances of the Client, to justify work or further work being carried out.

This is a rather vague test and is, therefore, open to various interpretations. However, what it means in essence is that before advice can be given under this scheme, the solicitor has to consider, subjectively, whether the case merits public funding. If the case passes the Sufficient Benefit Test at the start it must continue to do so throughout the life of the case.

Quite often, the solicitor will have to provide some initial Advice and Assistance in order to work out whether he or she believes that there is likely to be any benefit to the client. However, once it is apparent that the test is no longer satisfied, the solicitor should stop working on the case and tell the client immediately.

In practice, the LSC believes that the test should weed out cases which do not merit public funding, understood in the very narrow sense of the ability of the solicitor to find grounds for a possible appeal as opposed to the wider notion of the interests of justice. At the most basic level, the test is intended to prevent a solicitor starting or continuing work where there is no real legal issue in relation to which the client will benefit from the provision of Advice and Assistance.

However, it is specifically not intended to prevent the solicitor from providing any Advice and Assistance merely because the client's case is not very strong. A client may be entitled to advice about appealing his or her conviction out of time, even if it soon becomes clear that there are no legal grounds for pursuing such an appeal. In general terms, no work should be done under the scheme, beyond taking initial instructions and advising the client of his or her options, unless, on the evidence available at the time, the client's case involves a legal issue worthy of investigation.

Perhaps, most crucially, then, legal aid for CCRC applications works entirely within the scope of the legal system and does not consider that there may be innocent people who can exhaust the aid provided by the LSC and remain an innocent in prison; the test is not about whether the client may be innocent but, rather, if there is fresh evidence or new argument that may constitute grounds for appeal.

Often, a problem arises when a client has received negative advice and wishes a second (or sometimes third or fourth) opinion. The solicitor should consider how long it was since the first opinion was given. If it was recent and it appears that all issues have been considered, no further work should normally be undertaken. This is more clear-cut where the previous advice was given under the Advice and Assistance scheme, and one can see the rationale behind this restriction as it is meant to prevent convicted persons going from one solicitor to another, shopping around for a positive advice and using up scarce public funds in the process.

However, it is not so clear-cut when the client is seeking advice having received negative advice on appeal from his or her trial lawyers. Very often clients do not accept the advice given by their trial lawyers and may feel that errors were made in the trial process for which those lawyers may in some way be culpable (see Chapter 4). Generally, it is easier to justify a re-examination of the case in these circumstances than if previous advice had been given under the Advice and Assistance scheme. However, the solicitor is always open to an adverse finding by the LSC on any subsequent audit of the file (discussed further below) with the result that all of the work could be considered outside of the scope of the scheme and, therefore, no payment would be made, which also acts against the interests of potentially innocent victims of wrongful convictions and/or imprisonment, as they may struggle to find a solicitor who is prepared to take on their case. However, the LSC does accept that where there is new evidence, or the solicitor can point to some defect in the original opinion or the proceedings, then work will be justified for a further opinion, regardless of when the first opinion was obtained.

Rules on claiming

Solicitors are paid on an hourly rate for the work done, with letters written and telephone calls made or received remunerated at a fixed rate. In London, the rates are £49.70 per hour and £3.85 for each letter written or phone call. Out of London, the rates are slightly lower at £46.90 and £3.70 respectively. Travel and waiting is remunerated at an hourly rate of £26.30 throughout the country. It should perhaps be noted that these rates have not changed since the introduction of the GCC in 2001. Therefore, year-on-year this work becomes even less profitable as inflation eats into the rate paid.

When one considers that many cases are serious and involve complex legal issues, it would be generally appropriate to have a senior solicitor conducting the case. However, senior solicitors cannot generally work at such a level of payment. This is, of course, not money that goes to the solicitor but money which goes to the firm. Normal expenses such as the solicitor's salary, a proportion of the rent, practising certificate fees, tax and national insurance, a proportion of other overheads (e.g. telephone, computers, stationery, printing, postage) have to be deducted. It is felt that a solicitor working full-time on these cases will only make a loss for the firm.

Not only is the rate of payment extremely poor, the way these matters are actually paid militates against a firm taking on too many such cases. A single claim must be submitted for all work in relation to advice on the appeal or CCRC application.

As a rule, this means that no claim for payment can be made until the matter has concluded. For an application to the CCRC, the end of the case is either after the CCRC has referred the case to the appropriate appeal court or has finally refused to refer the case. As a result of the time it can take the CCRC to reach either of these points files can remain open for many years with no payment due to the firm.[1] However, during that time the firm will have incurred considerable expenses, including paying money out on disbursements such as transcript costs, the costs of experts or counsel.

Firms doing a lot of this work will, therefore, carry expenses on these files for a considerable time, routinely running to several years, without any reimbursement. Indeed, when the case is concluded no extra payment is received from the LSC, but the final costs are reconciled against the firm's standard monthly payment for all criminal work.

Financial limits on the scheme

Advice is initially limited to £300 on appeal matters and £500 on CCRC matters. Given the hourly rates applicable this roughly equates to six and ten hours' work respectively. In order to exceed this limit an application must be made to the LSC using a form CDS5 to increase the financial limit. Any such application must be made and agreed in advance of the work being undertaken. The Sufficient Benefit Test must be reapplied before any extension is sought. If authority is granted to exceed the limit the solicitor may claim at the appropriate payment rate for the work actually and reasonably carried out up to a maximum of the amount authorized by the LSC in the particular case. If the LSC refuse to grant an extension to the upper limit, a right of review arises to the Funding Review Committee.

The cost of Advice and Assistance includes:

1. The fees which the solicitor can claim in respect of the Advice and Assistance under the terms of the GCC;
2. Any disbursements, including counsel's fees, properly incurred by the solicitor in connection with the giving of Advice and Assistance (VAT is not included).

If authority is granted, the LSC will set a new upper limit on the matter, above which payment will not be made unless the solicitor has applied for and been granted a further extension. In general, authority will not be granted unless the work carried out to date and the further work proposed is reasonable and satisfies the Sufficient Benefit Test. For example, it would not be reasonable to include any work which has to be undertaken as a result of the solicitor's obvious error or omission, and any such work should not be included as part of a claim for costs. Extensions cannot be granted retrospectively and do not operate retrospectively. The solicitor will not be paid for any work undertaken in excess of the upper limit if an extension has not been obtained. This introduces an inevitable element *of pro bono* to criminal appeal work, as not all of the work undertaken will be paid for.

Commonly, when applying for an extension the solicitor will set out what work is required and how long that work is likely to take. The LSC may disallow payment for work if it does not fall within the scope of the extension granted, unless there are circumstances which justify the unanticipated work as 'reasonable'. Experience suggests that as cases are fluid in their development, the LSC is unlikely to disallow work done by the solicitor under an extension if the work actually done is reasonable and properly undertaken. However, a solicitor would be well advised not to use funds to cover his or her own work where those funds have been obtained on the basis of paying for a disbursement which is no longer required. Indeed, if it becomes clear that the disbursement requested is no longer required but another one becomes necessary, it is advisable to reapply to the LSC for an 'extension' to cover that new disbursement, even if no further funds are actually required because the deduction of the disbursement which is no longer required compensates for the one which is now required.

Steps in making an application to the CCRC

The LSC sets out in the GCC certain steps which it considers necessary in the making of an application to the CCRC. The LSC accepts that, in most cases, the solicitor considering making the application to the CCRC will not be the solicitor who handled the defence at trial. Therefore, in order that the convicted defendant can be given advice on the possibility and merits of the application, it will be necessary for the new solicitor to obtain and consider a transcript of the judge's Summing Up (in Crown Court cases) and the defence solicitor's file of papers. The LSC reminds solicitors that when first taking on the case, the solicitor should take instructions from the client to establish whether the case is one which the CCRC could consider, i.e. it falls within the CCRC's remit. If the client is able to satisfy the CCRC criteria, the solicitor must then go on to consider whether the case may be able to meet the referral criteria applied by the CCRC, i.e. whether it has a 'real possibility' of succeeding if it is given a further hearing in an appeal court (Criminal Appeal

Act 1995, s. 13). Once the basic information has been obtained by way of a statement from the client, the LSC advises that the solicitor should carry out an initial screening of the case to determine whether an application to the CCRC should be made. This process should enable the solicitor to screen out weak claims which would not meet the CCRC's referral criteria.[2] However, the information available at such an early stage may be very limited. The decision as to whether the costs of further investigation are justified must be made by the solicitor in the light of information available and using the solicitor's professional skill and common sense.

If a client qualifies for Advice and Assistance, the LSC states that initial case screening will normally be carried out within two hours. They accept that it may not be possible to complete case screening within this time if the client is located at a distant prison. However, such a time limit is patent nonsense. The vast majority of cases will take considerably longer than two hours to consider, even at this stage, given that the initial case screening should include taking instructions, considering any relevant papers or records (such as are available at that stage) and the provision of initial advice as to law and procedure. On only the most basic of cases will it be practically possible to do this within the suggested two hours. This is guidance only and will not prevent the solicitor from being paid if more time is spent on the case at this stage.

The solicitor should reject a case following initial screening if there is no reasonable prospect that it will meet the CCRC referral criteria. Clearly, uncertainty over the merits at the initial screening stage would not necessarily result in the solicitor refusing to take forward an application, particularly where the solicitor considers that further investigations are necessary to establish whether the referral criteria are met. These cases will often involve novel or unusual kinds of evidence. Very often a degree of investigation is necessary on behalf of the convicted defendant before any application to the CCRC can be made. Such investigations may include further forensic testing, the obtaining of witness statements and seeking counsel's opinion. The LSC states that if an application is to be made to the CCRC, then the solicitor will be involved in gathering and rationalizing the material, preparing a chronology of events and preparing the submission of any legal arguments required. This will not be the only work which will be necessary and not the only work which will be paid for under the scheme.

Transcripts

A full trial transcript is rarely necessary to support a CCRC application. It is a necessary first step in virtually all cases to obtain a transcript of the judge's Summing Up. However, whether further transcripts of parts of the case, such as parts of the evidence at trial, are necessary will depend on the facts of the case and the issues which it throws up. If the solicitor is seeking a transcript of part or all of the evidence, then a specific justification should be provided to the LSC.

Counsel

As far as the LSC is concerned it would be unusual for a solicitor to instruct counsel prior to the lodging of an application to the CCRC. However, in some cases specialist advice is required which may fall outside the solicitor's own expertise, especially if the solicitor does not undertake a lot of appellate work. The LSC gives an example of where it might be reasonable to seek an opinion from counsel as specialist advice on whether the judge properly directed the trial jury in his or her Summing Up. This example seems a little odd as one would expect such considerations to be within the normal range of expertise of a solicitor. The expense of any disbursement or counsel's advice will count towards costs for the purposes of calculating whether an extension to the upper limit is necessary.

Fee rates for counsel are not set out anywhere in the GCC. It is for the solicitor to negotiate the fees with counsel and have the fees agreed with the LSC. Sometimes, counsel may work on a fixed fee for advice at a certain stage or on an hourly rate, normally in the range of £70 to £100 per hour depending on the complexity of the matter and the seniority of counsel. It may be possible to negotiate a higher rate if a QC is required.

The rate agreed should not be reduced by the LSC on audit once agreed, but the number of hours worked by counsel could be the subject of later reduction if the LSC felt that the time spent was unreasonable, even if the number of hours for the task was agreed by the LSC in advance. This approach should be challenged by the solicitor following any audit, particularly as by that time counsel will have been paid in full and in the expectation of no subsequent difficulties with the payment.

Advice under the scheme does not stop once an application is submitted to the CCRC. Inevitably, further advice will be required by assisting the CCRC with specific queries, making further submissions (if appropriate) arising from the material disclosed by the CCRC in the course of the review and investigation, liaising with the CCRC as to its approach and progress, and advising the client in relation to any decisions made by the CCRC in the case. It may be necessary for the solicitor to meet the CCRC's representatives on more than one occasion in a complex case. There is no other form of public funding available for this type of work, although the CCRC will, in considering the application, make what further enquiries it considers appropriate to enable it to investigate the case and reach a decision.

Miscellaneous points

Postal applications

The solicitor may exercise a 'Devolved Power' to accept an application for Advice and Assistance by post from a client where there is good reason to do so. This is not possible where the client is resident outside England and Wales and either (i) his or her residence abroad is temporary and he or she can, without serious disadvantage, delay the application until he or she has returned to England and Wales; or (ii) the Advice and Assistance could be applied for on the same matter by a person resident in England and Wales; or (iii) it is otherwise unreasonable to accept the application. An example of the latter may be where the client has absconded from custody and is living abroad but wants to apply to have his or her conviction reviewed. It would not be reasonable to accept a postal application on behalf of a person resident abroad if he or she could be expected to attend personally in any event, for example because he or she undertakes regular visits to England and Wales.

Attendance on the client's behalf

Where there is good reason for a client not to be able to see the solicitor personally, he or she may authorize another person ('the authorized person') to attend the meeting on his or her behalf. The authorized person must provide the solicitor with the information, and satisfactory evidence in support, that is necessary to assess whether the client meets the financial criteria. The authorized person must see the solicitor personally to make the application and sign the form on behalf of the client. As stated above, the solicitor cannot accept an application for Advice and Assistance from an authorized person on behalf of a client who is not resident in England and Wales. The reason as to why the client could not attend personally must always be noted by the solicitor and kept on the file. If the client provides written authority, a copy should be kept by the solicitor. If the authorization was by telephone, an attendance note should be made and retained on file. The form should be signed by the authorized person on the client's behalf and should be annotated indicating the full name of the person signing, to make it clear that the application signed was in accordance with the appropriate rule in the GCC.

Telephone advice

The solicitor may claim payment for advice given to a client over the telephone before that client has signed the application form, where he or she cannot for good reason attend the solicitor's office, and where he or she meets the Qualifying Criteria for the provision of Advice and Assistance (including the financial criteria) and has subsequently signed the application form. The reason for giving the initial telephone advice should be noted by the solicitor and kept on the file. The client does not have to attend the solicitor's office to sign the application form after having been given the telephone advice. Instead, the solicitor may send the form to the client after the advice for signature and return.

Outward travel

The solicitor may claim for the mileage or cost of public transport for outward travel to visit a client away from the solicitor's office, before the application form is signed, where the visit is justified for good reason, the client meets the Qualifying Criteria for the provision of Advice and Assistance (including financial criteria) and has subsequently signed the application form. Where the solicitor is visiting the client in detention, prison or hospital then the solicitor may also claim the travelling time at the appropriate rate. Costs must be reasonably incurred, taking account of all the circumstances, including, for example, the distances involved as against the availability of advice from a more local solicitor with a GCC and the justification for travelling to attend on the client at all, bearing in mind that telephone advice can be given and applications accepted by post. It is of course commonplace for clients in such cases to be in prison. Sometimes they are at a considerable distance from the solicitor's office. It is probably a good general practice to make use of the postal application or have a family member bring any material to the office and sign the form on the client's behalf, unless the client is in a reasonably local prison.

Problems with the current funding regime

There are a number of problems with the current funding regime, quite apart from the dismal rates payable.

The audit process

Most of the problems become apparent when one considers the audit procedure. It would appear that the LSC auditors are uncomfortable with auditing appeal files, as they come across them very rarely. Audits only take place on closed files and the audit can take a considerable time after the close of the case. The main concern is that, by assessing the files at this late stage, the amount payable may be reduced by the auditors. This may include amounts already paid out on disbursements, such as counsel's fees. Audit results can also result in a reduction on a large appeal file, which could lead to a claim by the LSC to claw back money from the solicitor or even lead to the loss of the GCC and, therefore, the ability to continue legally aided work.

Auditors apply the benefit of hindsight to the files they audit. They do not always appear to understand the nature of these cases. As an example, on one audit the LSC disallowed time spent instructing counsel because counsel was not 'assigned'. This is a provision which only applies in the preparation of Magistrates' Court work and has no relevance or implication to appeal cases or CCRC applications. The LSC subsequently admitted their error. It would be beneficial to all concerned if such files were removed from the audit process.

CDS5 applications

An extension granted by the LSC on a CDS5 does not guarantee payment for the work done or the disbursement incurred if the file is selected for a subsequent audit. The work still needs to be reasonably carried out both in terms of the amount of time spent and the rate applied. This is most starkly illustrated with counsel's fees. Often the LSC will agree an extension of counsel's fees for a certain task for a certain number of hours at a certain rate of pay. However, on audit the LSC has considered both the amount of hours spent by counsel and the hourly rate (albeit previously agreed by the LSC) to be excessive. This means that the firm may have paid counsel, e.g. 12 hours at £100 but are only allowed on assessment 6 hours at £70.

This uncertainty is very unnerving for firms dealing with a lot of these types of cases. One may more easily understand the rationale behind the auditing of the hours spent by counsel than reducing the previously agreed hourly rate. In the above mentioned example the firm concerned has stopped all appeal work. Criminal Appeal Lawyers Association (CALA) has raised the issue with the LSC who seemed surprised that such a situation had arisen.

Sufficient Benefit Test

One must be very careful about the application of the Sufficient Benefit Test. Of particular concern is the provision whereby one should consider when previous negative advice was given. It is, of course, a very frequent occurrence that a client wishes to seek advice from the solicitor in relation to an appeal where he or she has been given negative advice rather recently by trial counsel. Whether or not the client is seeking to criticize previous counsel, there have been many cases which have been overturned on appeal where the trial counsel has advised against appeal. If the LSC is not satisfied on audit that there was sufficient benefit in giving any advice at all, the entire claim could be disallowed with potentially disastrous financial consequences. This is unlikely to be a problem in a case where representations are subsequently made to the CCRC or grounds of appeal lodged out of time, but it may well be in a case where considerable time is spent before the client is given negative advice.

Rates of pay

The current rates of £49.70 in London are extremely poor for the complexity of this work and the level of experience of the fee earner who ought to be conducting the bulk of it. Many firms who do have a commitment to such work are finding it increasingly difficult to justify doing such work when the remuneration is so poor. A large number of potential clients are turned away as firms cut back on such work and many alleged victims of wrongful conviction and prisoners maintaining their innocence are finding it almost impossible to get any advice at all.

Conclusion

From the forgoing analysis, at least eight suggestions for improvement of the current regime arise. To conclude, these will be considered in turn.

A panel system

If the LSC had any will at all to meet with practitioners who undertake this work, it may be that a dialogue could be opened towards obtaining more appropriate rates of pay by the introduction of a system whereby a firm has to belong to an accredited panel in order to deal with the work. Thus far, the LSC has been singularly unwilling to engage in such dialogue, despite efforts particularly by CALA. The chances of increased rates of pay on any legal aid work at present are vanishingly small. As a basic suggestion, if a firm wishes to apply to join the panel they should demonstrate that the solicitor supervising the work has the requisite experience. For instance, that he or she has advised on and conducted a certain number of appeals or CCRC applications within a certain period of time.

Assessment of individual cases on completion

In order to deal with the potential problems on audit, it may be that each case should be assessed at its end (in the same way that more complex magistrates' court cases are if they escape the fixed-fee structure). There could be a limit on the costs before individual audit applies. A reasonable amount might be £1,500. This system would have the advantage of the firm knowing that there can be no nasty surprise at audit and no chance of any recoupment across the annual payments. Payment to counsel and expert witnesses could be delayed until the assessed amounts were known, although the chances of most experts agreeing to such a delay in CCRC cases is minimal, bearing in mind the time taken to reach decisions. However, it would also mean that most appeal cases would be subject to assessment, though this would increase the exposure of the LSC to assessing such files.

Enhanced rates

With individual assessment of cases, it should be possible to apply the principle of enhancement to the more difficult cases. This is particularly so if a panel system is introduced.

Interim billing

At present the case can only be billed on completion, which can take several years. A system whereby a bill can be submitted at various stages of the case would improve cash flow immeasurably for firms doing a substantial amount of this work. For example, submission of a bill once the representations have been sent to the CCRC is a logical option, with a further claim being made for any subsequent work undertaken before the case is either rejected or referred. Alternatively, one could envisage a system whereby work in progress was submitted to the LSC for payment at a specified time (e.g. every six months) on all ongoing appeals and reviews class cases.

'Prior authority' or binding status of CDS5 disbursement applications

It would be of great assistance if, for disbursements such as counsel's fees and experts, the LSC were to honour the hourly rates and the number of hours allowed on a CDS5 application. It is grossly unfair to have a rate allowed on prior application on a CDS5 and then have another lower rate applied on audit. The LSC could ask for more information at CDS5 stage in order to properly address the issues concerned. The London CDS5 team, apparently, do not just rubber stamp CDS5 applications but scrutinize them, both in terms of the hours requested and the rates claimed. If that is so there can be no justification for a reduction on audit.

Pay counsel separately

It may be that counsel should be paid directly by the LSC as is the case for 'assigned counsel' in magistrates' courts. This would mean that solicitors would not be penalized for claims made by counsel which the LSC subsequently consider to have been unreasonably made. It may be that fixed hourly rates should be set down for counsel rather than a rate being agreed with the LSC on a case-by-case basis (and then reduced on audit). There may need to be a few different rates depending on the nature of the case (although this equally applies to solicitors).

Trial counsel's advice

It should never be a bar to giving advice that trial counsel has recently advised negatively. Advice should be allowed at least until an assessment can be made as to any merits of an appeal.

Once the case has been referred

Legal aid is available by application to the Court of Appeal once a case has been referred. Again, legal-aid cost cutting means that the paid work of the solicitor is often limited, for instance merely to instructing counsel. If further work is required, counsel should so advise and an application made to the court for the wording of the Representation Order to be amended. It is imperative to keep the wording of the Representation Order in mind as the solicitor will not be paid for any work which is done outside the scope of the wording on the Order. The Costs Department at the Court of Appeal have their own interpretation of the wording on some orders, so if the solicitor is in any doubt as to whether the work he or she has to undertake is covered by the Representation Order then he or she should check with the Court of Appeal and make a note of any positive response.

Overall, then, the existing framework that governs the funding for criminal appeals contains far-reaching limitations that can act to deter firms from taking on such work. It also has significant impacts on the quality of any work undertaken under the present arrangements. Perhaps even more importantly, the present scheme addresses the problem of the wrongful convictions from a strict legal standpoint that gives insufficient consideration that grounds of appeal are seldom readily apparent. On the contrary, the complexities of criminal appeal cases require the LSC to be more fluid in its approach, embracing a proactive approach to assisting in overturning wrongful convictions by providing more adequate funds to enable cases to be fully investigated and to unearth potential grounds for appeal. As things stand, it is possible that innocent victims of wrongful conviction and imprisonment may fall outside of the parameters of the funding stream and may, therefore, be denied access to justice.

Notes

1. See, for instance, Chapter 5, which explores the ten years that it took for the cases of Michael Attwooll and John Roden to be referred to the CACD.
2. This means that cases where there is clear evidence of innocence but the evidence has either already been put before the trial court or could have been put before the trial court may not qualify and may be closed by their solicitors under the rules of the LSC funding system.

Part IV
Academic Perspectives

11
After Ten Years: An Investment in Justice?

Richard Nobles and David Schiff

Introduction

The Criminal Cases Review Commission (CCRC) replaced a division at the Home Office, C3, which consisted of 21 staff, plus three staff at the Northern Ireland Office. The division received between 700 and 800 applications a year, of which around 10 per year were referred to the Court of Appeal (Criminal Division) (CACD). This division was accused of being slow, inefficient, reactive rather than proactive, and of showing too great a deference to the CACD. The Royal Commission on Criminal Justice's (RCCJ's) diagnosis of the perceived reluctance of C3 to refer cases to the CACD was that it reflected a constitutional problem: C3 was part of a Government department and, as such, was handicapped in making referrals by the doctrine of separation of powers, which requires the executive not to interfere with the judicial system (RCCJ, 1993: ch. 11).[1]

By creating a non-departmental public body, the expectation was that it would not be handicapped in this way. Thus, even if the rate of referral remained the same, decisions not to refer could be expected to have more credibility. However, as well as a change in institutional framework, the creation of the CCRC represented a major increase in the level of public resources devoted to the rectification of miscarriages of justice. The annual staff costs of C3 in 1991 were £357,000. If one uses Retail Price Index tables, this translates into a staff cost budget for, as an example, 2006 of £530,290. In contrast, the staff budget for the CCRC for 2005–06 was £4,930,439. So we have a ninefold increase in expenditure.

What, following the 10th anniversary of the launch of the CCRC's operation, has been achieved from this increased investment in the processes of remedying miscarriages of justice? This chapter explores three criteria by which one might wish to measure that achievement, and how successful the CCRC has been or could be: by reference to all possible miscarriages; by reference to the CCRC's relationship with the CACD; and by reference to lurking doubt and exceptionality.

By reference to all possible miscarriages

If one regards the CCRC as a body with responsibility for remedying miscarriages of justice, and if this responsibility is interpreted to include (after the normal processes of appeal have been completed, or time to appeal has passed, or leave not granted) quashing the convictions of those who are not factually guilty of the crimes charged, as well as those who have been convicted after errors in the procedures of their trial or serious errors in processes pre-trial, and those whose sentences are unfair or inappropriate, then how large is this task? How can we know the unknown? There are no methods for extrapolating from the mistakes which have been discovered, through normal appeals and those following CCRC referral, to those which remain unidentified, without already knowing the ratio of the one to the other. Metaphors about icebergs and their tips, commonly used in media reporting about miscarriages, are quite misleading – we always have the potential to know the exact percentage of floating ice in relation to that which is submerged, but all one can surmise with miscarriages of justice is to identify the level of error acknowledged by the legal system and consider whether this amounts to a likely percentage. Thus, at best, all one can do is take the number of convictions and sentences and consider whether the number changed on appeal (with or without the CCRC) represents a likely percentage of error (Naughton, 2007b: 37–78).

For example, it may be possible to extrapolate from the Department of Constitutional Affairs's 'Judicial Statistics' to get some indication of the acknowledged rate of error for cases tried on indictment (Department for Constitutional Affairs, 2006a). The year-on-year figures roughly take the following form: there are over 80,000 committals for trial in the Crown Court each year, out of which roughly 58 per cent plead guilty. Of the remaining 42 per cent who plead not guilty, about two-thirds are found not guilty.[2] Thus, of the around 80,000 committals for Crown Court trial, an approximate of over 57,000 of them are found guilty and sentenced. The annual number of successful appeals against conviction is in the region of less than 300 (0.53 per cent), and of successful appeals against sentence, less than 1,700 (2.99 per cent). Thus, following the leave and appeal processes, the CACD admit to a level of mistake in relation to conviction and/or sentence of around 3.5 per cent. This reflects those who appeal and the outcome of those appeals, but simply ignores the undisclosed figure of those who might be subject to miscarriages of justice but do not appeal.[3]

If 3.5 per cent, admittedly a very rough figure, represents the level of mistake that the CACD can remedy by itself, what difference has the CCRC made? What does the CCRC contribute to this level of acknowledged mistakes? Whilst, of course, every non-remedied miscarriage of justice is an individual tragedy, the contribution of the CCRC,[4] taking the 2006/07 figure, is some 33 (close to three-quarters of which were conviction appeals) of the

2,000 successful appeals each year, or just over 0.058 per cent of the annual conviction rate. Is 3.5 per cent anywhere close to the number of miscarriages of justice that the CACD need to remedy annually? Is 0.53 per cent (of which the CCRC contributes 0.058 per cent) anywhere close to the number of conviction miscarriages of justice that the CACD needs to remedy annually?

Graham Zellick, the outgoing Chairman of the CCRC, in giving evidence to the House of Commons Home Affairs Select Committee, admitted that 'it is quite impossible to say' (Zellick, 2006: q. 41). He pointed out that satisfaction with the CCRC's contribution to the elimination of miscarriages of justice depended quite crucially on one's assumption as to what the background level of miscarriages of justice might be:

> If you start from the premise that lots more cases than we refer should end up in the Court of Appeal, of course you are going to feel that there is something wrong with the test, or something wrong with the Commission, or something defective and deficient in the Commissioners, but that is a bit of *ex post facto* rationalisation. It depends where you start from. (Ibid.: q. 40)

In the absence of any method for providing objective statistics on the number of unidentified miscarriages of justice, Zellick is undoubtedly correct – it depends on the assumptions made. But the CCRC's ability to claim success, which it regularly does in its annual reports (cf. Nobles and Schiff, 2001: 280), with only a 0.058 per cent additional annual contribution towards remedying wrongful conviction and sentence, is somewhat surprising when one recalls the assumptions that were being made during the period which led to the CCRC's creation. By 1992, media reporting on miscarriages of justice was accompanied by a theme of loss of public confidence in the criminal justice system. Part of this reporting included a willingness to assume that the high profile cases (such as those of the Birmingham Six, Maguire Seven and Guildford Four, for example) were evidence of a much greater number of undisclosed miscarriages of justice. We have carried out a study of media reporting in which we identified the manner in which numbers (the implication that those miscarriages of justice identified pointed to the existence of more yet undiscovered) became a regular feature of media reporting at this time. This has been published elsewhere and need not be reproduced here (see Nobles and Schiff, 2000: 92–170). But some examples will give a flavour of this media opinion. There was David Rose's (1996) *In the Name of the Law: The Collapse of Criminal Justice*, the book behind the BBC television series *The Verdict*. There was an article on the Pinfold case published in *The Observer* (1992) which talked of well-publicized cases representing only 'the tip of an iceberg: waiting in the wings of the Court of Appeal is a legion of further, less notorious but equally shocking miscarriages'. Similarly, following Judith

Ward's successful appeal, Margarette Driscoll made similar arguments in *The Sunday Times*:

> Those who watched Judith Ward walk free from the Court of Appeal last week hoping it would mark the final page in an ugly chapter of judicial history should brace themselves. The legal establishment will barely have time to draw breath before the next wave of appeals washes before it. (Driscoll, 1992)

If this kind of media reporting had continued to this day, then Zellick might have found it less 'impossible' to answer the question of whether the CCRC was doing an adequate job (Zellick, 2006). Media willingness to publish articles about individual miscarriages of justice in terms of further large numbers of non-remedied miscarriages would have made it very difficult to present the CCRC's 0.058 per cent annual contribution to solving the problem as an adequate one.

While media reporting on the legal system and miscarriages of justice has changed since 1992 (see Chapter 2), there are groups who continue to assume that the level of error is far higher than the judicial statistics' acknowledgement of error would suggest. Such groups cannot be dismissed as ill-informed or prejudiced. Some of those who protest their innocence of crimes for which they have been convicted have their claims taken up by solicitors, innocence projects and investigative journalists, where their claims will be subjected to extensive scrutiny. Indeed, some of these claims will be investigated by CCRC staff who themselves may become convinced on occasion of the applicant's factual innocence.[5] And, while it would be naïve to believe that all of those who claim wrongful conviction are actually innocent, it would be equally naïve to believe that at least 96 per cent of those that claim innocence in these circumstances are actually lying.[6] There are significant penalties within our prison system for those who fail to accept their guilt, as acceptance of guilt is regarded as a sign of rehabilitation and a condition for admission onto many of the training programmes through which prisoners progress to a less secure environment and an earlier release date (see Naughton, 2005a; James, 2003). But if the assumption that all those protesting innocence after conviction were factually guilty is naïve, is 4 per cent (the percentage of applications referred by the CCRC to the CACD) still a high enough figure?

If there is no statistic for the size of the problem that needs to be solved, can one nevertheless compare the performance of the CCRC with other similar bodies in order to see whether it could perform better? Certainly the National Health Service generates statistics about the relative performance of different hospitals with a view to identifying those that might be expected to do better. Can one do something similar with the CCRC, using the performance of the Scottish Criminal Cases Review Commission (SCCRC) as a comparator?

In Scotland, against a background of a lower number of annual applications[7] there is an annual referral rate of over 8 per cent, namely double that of the CCRC. The success rate of Scottish referred appeals is below (but only just below) that of the CCRC's referrals at just under 65 per cent compared to the figure of approximately 70 per cent. So, on the basis of these crude figures, the SCCRC would seem to be adding more in identifying miscarriages to the Scottish system than its counterpart adds to its system. When this argument was put to Zellick, his reply was fourfold. He pointed out that the relatively smaller number of cases going to the SCCRC meant that their referral and success rate could be significantly altered by only a small number of additional cases. He was also able to point to variations in the regional rates of referral and success within his own caseload, by referring to the example of Northern Ireland. Between 1997 and 2007 the CCRC received 131 applications pertaining to Northern Ireland, completed a review of 113 and referred 16, which is a referral rate of 14 per cent, with 13, namely 87 per cent, being quashed (CCRC, 2006a: 19–20). This higher rate of success, if it is statistically significant, cannot obviously be traced to anything other than factors relating to the kinds of cases the CCRC were being sent, rather than the powers or efforts of the CCRC itself. A further argument went to the characteristics of the SCCRC, claiming that the different powers of the SCCRC and the Scottish High Court (to which it refers cases) make comparisons difficult. And, his last response was to suggest that it might, for unidentified reasons, simply be easier to overturn convictions in Scotland (Zellick, 2006: q. 32; see also s. 194C of the Criminal Procedure (Scotland) Act 1995).

The smallness of the numbers involved does, indeed, make it difficult to claim that the SCCRC is achieving more than its counterpart, though the longer the two organizations are in existence the greater the numbers each of them will have processed, and the harder it will be for the CCRC to deny that a higher rate of referral has any statistical significance. The use of the Northern Irish figures is a weaker argument. The fact that a different caseload might lead to different results is actually one reason for excluding the Northern Ireland figures from an assessment of the CCRC's performance, and without these the CCRC's performance would dip still further, albeit only slightly given their low overall numbers. The history of the Northern Ireland troubles, including the so-called 'dirty war', and the suspension of trial by jury for terrorist cases during this period, could well be expected to give rise to more examples of material irregularities than an English and Welsh caseload. In these circumstances, the regional differences between different caseloads could be expected, whilst it is less clear how the investigation and trial of crimes in Scotland would produce such a different caseload.

What of the argument that the different statutory powers of the two Commissions and their respective appeal courts undermine comparisons of their performances? The Scottish High Court have to consider whether there has been a 'miscarriage of justice', though a referral only requires the SCCRC to decide that a miscarriage of justice 'may' have occurred.[8] The CACD has to consider whether a conviction is 'unsafe', with the CCRC unable (unless there are exceptional circumstances) to make a referral unless there is a 'real possibility' of the conviction not being upheld (s. 13(1)(a) of the Criminal Appeal Act 1995). The suggestion that the SCCRC's higher rate of success might be due to its statutory powers, and those of the Scottish High Court, invites the suggestion that the powers of the CCRC should be brought into line with those of the SCCRC. There are a number of possible reforms here. For example, the Real Possibility Test might be lowered to something closer to 'may', such as an 'arguable case' on appeal, or the 'unsafe' test might be changed to the Scottish test of 'miscarriage of justice'. But, whilst such changes might increase the number of successful referrals, there is reason to expect that they would also undermine the ability of the CACD to carry out its normal role (see also Chapter 12). To put this in numerical terms, attempts to increase the annual figure of 0.058 per cent successful conviction appeals following referral by changing the referral powers of the CCRC might undermine the CACD's ability to identify the 0.53 per cent of conviction mistakes that it remedies without help from the CCRC. To understand the reason for this, we must leave the question of how the achievement of the CCRC might be assessed in terms of its contribution towards solving an unknowable level of mistakes and consider, instead, how its achievement might be understood in terms of its relationship to the CACD.

By reference to the CCRC's relationship with the CACD

Only the CACD can quash an unsafe conviction, and, in forming the view that a conviction is unsafe, the CACD operates as a court of review, not a court of rehearing.[9] This distinction is crucial to understanding the manner of the CACD's operation and, in turn, the ability of the CCRC to refer cases to it with any prospect of success. As a court of review, the CACD does not retry the case. Instead, it reviews the original trial to see if there is any reason why the verdict should be disturbed. The assumption brought to this task is that a criminal trial, properly conducted, should lead to a correct decision. This assumption creates a relationship of deference between the CACD and the jury, as the fact finding body within a Crown Court trial.[10] The CACD has often been accused of showing undue or excessive deference towards the jury, and for reversing the burden of proof by requiring appellants to show that there was something wrong with their trial (Nobles and Schiff, 2000: 71–91; RCCJ, 1993: ch.10). But, it is simply not possible to abandon this assumption, without the CACD becoming a court of rehearing, expected to redecide any contested decision for itself, on the basis of all the evidence.[11]

Acting as a court of review, and applying this assumption, the CACD approaches an appeal to see if there is anything that indicates that the trial in question was not correctly conducted, or that, even though properly conducted, it might not have reached the correct result. An improperly conducted trial is one where important rules of procedure were not properly followed, with breaches of rules being examined by reference to whether those breaches could have made a difference to the result (see Naughton, 2005b). Where there was a properly conducted trial, and applying the usual assumption, the only other routine way in which the decision might still be incorrect is where evidence is discovered that was not available at trial, for even the most perfectly conducted trial can still come to a wrong decision in these circumstances. Alongside these two approaches to appeals lies a third which must, given the CACD's role as a court of review, operate only exceptionally. This is where the CACD forms the view, without reference to any significant mistake of procedure or new evidence, that the jury reached the wrong decision. The exceptionality of this last approach, and the assumption that juries generally make correct decisions, can be justified by differences between the CACD and the trial court: one sees all the evidence, the other only reviews what is brought to its attention in the appeal; one actually hears all the witnesses, the other reads the transcript of the trial and hears oral testimony only where this amounts to new evidence; one has a cross-section of the community to assess the credibility of witnesses, the other has a narrow professional group; etc. These factors all play their part, but the consideration which operates alongside them, and would continue to operate whatever the particular characteristics of the trial and a court of review, is that a court of review cannot routinely overturn the decisions of a properly conducted trial without becoming that legal system's de facto trial court. To put this in simple terms, if the CACD routinely overturned jury verdicts without reference to incorrect procedures or new evidence, then most convicted prisoners could be expected to appeal their convictions, or that, at least, is the spectre.

Once one appreciates the self-imposed limitations that the CACD must necessarily adopt in order to maintain its role as a court of review rather than a second trial court, one can understand why statutory reformulations of the grounds of appeal do not lead to radical change in its practices. The CACD began life as the Criminal Court of Appeal in 1907 with a power to quash convictions if the court felt that 'on any ground there was a miscarriage of justice'. It was the Court's interpretation of its role as a court of review which led to a reformulation of its statutory powers in the 1960s, and again in 1995. With this history, there is no reason to expect a change in the powers of the CACD to bring them into line with those of the Scottish High Court (a return to the standard of 'miscarriage of justice') to result in a significant increase in the numbers or nature of successful appeals (see also Schiff and Nobles, 1996: 573–81).

The CACD is locked into practices which follow inevitably from its adopted role as a court of review, and the CCRC is similarly constrained when deciding how to go about its role of referring cases to the CACD. Even without a statutory duty to refer only where there is a 'real possibility' of success, the CCRC would not be acting responsibly if it failed to consider the likely outcome when choosing which cases to refer. Sending cases that had no hope of success would raise false hopes for appellants and delay the CACD's hearing of cases which were going to succeed, resulting in longer periods of imprisonment for wrongfully convicted prisoners. For Zellick, the necessity for the CCRC to approach the issue of miscarriages of justice in the same manner as the CACD is an objective reality that cannot be ignored:

> If you start from a wholly objective standpoint, one would not find the arguments for a new test cogent or compelling unless you simply want to see our role eliminated and far more cases fall on the Court of Appeal itself ... There has to be a basis for [impugning a conviction], otherwise every criminal conviction is necessarily open and there are thousands every year and the task would be impossible. (Zellick, 2006: q. 41)

The full difficulties facing the CCRC are only apparent when one remembers that, outside of exceptional circumstances, a referral by the CCRC only occurs if applicants have already exhausted their normal rights to appeal either by appealing during the time limit, or appealing out of time following leave to appeal, or having such an application for leave refused. This raises, in effect, a further layer of assumption. Alongside the assumption that a properly conducted trial can be expected to reach a correct decision, one finds the assumption that a properly conducted appeal (or application for leave to appeal) is capable of assessing an applicant's grounds for appeal and reaching a correct decision. And, as with the assumption about trial, this is a necessary assumption within the legal system. It justifies denying applicants the right to make the same appeal over and over again, until some particular sitting of the CACD accepts their argument, just as the assumption about trial justifies denying them the right to be tried over and over again until such time as a jury reaches a different verdict. This assumption about appeal processes is built into the powers of the CCRC as, in the absence of exceptional circumstances, a referral to the CACD must be based on evidence or arguments not already raised, and rejected, on an earlier appeal or application for leave (s.13 of the Criminal Appeal Act 1995). But, even if the CACD were not so limited, there would be good reason to expect the CACD to resist referrals that simply repeated the same grounds already raised, and rejected, in an earlier appeal or application for leave, because the CACD would be expected to reject (with criticism) any referral that took this form.[12]

The CCRC has accepted the constraints imposed by its relationship with the CACD, warning applicants of its inability to refer cases without new evidence or arguments not previously raised at trial or on an earlier appeal (CCRC, 2008j). It has even tended to view its 'rate of success' (the percentage of referrals which succeed) as evidence as to whether it is getting this relationship right. Referrals that do not succeed are, with hindsight, appeals which have reduced the ability of the CACD to cope with its 'normal' appeals without correcting a miscarriage of justice. And the CCRC has accepted that it cannot have too many of these. Conversely, if the CCRC was successful in all of its referrals, this would indicate that there might be further cases that met the criteria of the CACD, but were not being referred. A successful relationship lies between these extremes, as acknowledged by the first chairman of the CCRC, Sir Frederick Crawford, when the rate of success was around 75 per cent, who said: 'It would not worry us if it dropped to 50 per cent but we would be very worried if it was 10' (Crawford, 2000: q. 73).

With this relationship with the CACD, the CCRC is never going to make a substantial numerical contribution to the number of recognized miscarriages of justice. The increased resources which it has received, compared with C3, represent not a change of approach but an increased ability to investigate: to read transcripts, interview witnesses, commission tests; with a view to identifying the kind of mistake to which the CACD will respond. The benefits of this, in terms of media confidence in the ability of the legal system to identify its own mistakes, should not be underestimated. One only needs to look at a couple of the iconic cases that led to the CCRC's creation to understand the importance of this. Consider the successful appeals of the Maguire Seven and the Birmingham Six. Both of these appeals were, eventually, successful as a result of commissioning new scientific tests which cast doubt on the reliability of the evidence given at trial. In the case of the Birmingham Six this involved repeating the most reliable of the tests that had been used to ascertain whether the appellants had been in contact with explosives and producing an unexplained false positive, which allowed the CACD to conclude that a similar error might have occurred when the appellants were originally tested. This, together with the new Electronic Static Document Analysis tests which cast doubt on the police claim to have made contemporaneous notes of their interviews with the appellants, allowed the CACD to reach the conclusion that the convictions were unsafe or unsatisfactory.[13] With the Maguire Seven appeal, new tests on the possibilities for traces of explosive to be passed between persons (so called 'innocent contamination') led the CACD to conclude that, whilst the Maguire Seven were all in contact with, directly or indirectly (e.g. through a towel), someone who had handled explosives, the evidence did not establish that any one of them had actually handled the explosives themselves (see Nobles and Schiff, 2000: ch. 5). In each case, the evidence generated by these new tests was not what had created a widespread belief that the appellants were factually innocent of the crimes for which they had been committed. These beliefs preceded these tests. But in each case the tests provided new grounds for appeal. They generated a means by which the CACD would be able to reconsider the verdicts and might (and then did) reach a conclusion that the convictions were unsafe or unsatisfactory.

The importance of new evidence as a means of gaining access to a new review of a conviction that is questionable for other reasons has been acknowledged by Gareth Peirce (House of Commons Select Committee on Home Affairs, 1999: q. 26):

> Every case involves some form of investigative thought. Very rarely, it can involve rereading all of the papers and seeing a point that was not there. Most cases involve finding witnesses, finding documents, finding evidence which is a purely investigative task, and then beyond that trying to systematize that and analyse it into some form of legalistic format that provides an appeal, because what produces one is not necessarily the other. You have to define what you have into a formula that the Court of Appeal will understand and recognize as a point of appeal. Therefore, sometimes the difficulty is raised that this was available at trial. That is a common feature. If something was available either as evidence or as a tactic to use evidence or not, then there is an inhibition against reopening a case because that is available but not used; but yet that can have been the cause of the wrongful conviction in the first place.

By reference to lurking doubt and exceptionality

The challenge to provide new evidence cannot always be met. This means that there remain cases where the original conviction is unsafe, but there is no basis for challenging it which does not also question the reliability of the jury as a fact finding body, or the reliability of a prior CACD as a mechanism for reviewing that conviction. The CACD has a means for responding to such cases, known as the doctrine of lurking doubt.[14] This doctrine can only operate on an exceptional basis. It simply represents an acceptance that juries and courts of appeal *can* reach incorrect decisions and, where the CACD becomes convinced of this, even in the absence of a procedural error or new evidence, it can quash the conviction. The need for this approach to be exceptional follows from what we have said about the nature of a court of review. The reviewing court cannot routinely substitute its verdict for that of the trial court without turning the trial into some kind of preliminary hearing. Indeed, not only must a court of review not routinely act in this manner, it must discourage appellants from entertaining any hope that their case will be treated in this manner. If they do not do so, too many appellants may be encouraged to appeal without grounds.

There are always going to be some persons who are convicted who are factually innocent who cannot point to any significant error at their trial or produce new evidence or arguments, and for these persons the doctrine of lurking doubt offers their only hope. But, the CCRC goes out of its way to deter such persons from applying. This message is given on the CCRC's website, where the CCRC insists that they operate within a 'strict legal frame-work', which prevents them from putting a case to the CACD simply because they have doubts as to the accuracy of the jury's verdict and which requires them to identify an argument or evidence that was not put to the jury:

> Our legal role means that we are not allowed to perform a 're-run' of your trial just because your evidence was not accepted by the jury and the evidence of the prosecution was. We have to be able to identify convincing fresh evidence or issues if we are to have a chance of referring cases back to the Court of Appeal. If evidence was put before the jury from which they could properly reach conclusions, it is of no help that we might reach a different view – what we will need is new evidence or arguments ... So the Court of Appeal is not going to be interested in whether we at the Commission would have convicted you if we had been on the jury. Instead, we have to be able to say to the Court, 'Look, here is a new piece of evidence, or a new legal argument that hadn't been identified at the time of the trial, that the jury never got the chance to consider. It could have changed the whole outcome of the trial.' Only then will the Court of Appeal be able to ask itself whether the conviction was unsafe. (CCRC, 2008d)

Are the CCRC justified in excluding all 'lurking doubt' cases in this way? The answer is probably 'yes', and their claim to be prevented by a 'strict legal framework' is correct, though the point needs some explanation. The requirement of a real possibility of success, and the need to produce new arguments or evidence, are, like the need for applicants to have exhausted their ordinary rights to appeal, stated to be unnecessary where there are 'exceptional circumstances'. At first glance, this might seem to provide a route whereby, albeit exceptionally, the CCRC might be able to refer cases to the CACD, which did not meet the normal requirements of new evidence or arguments, and invite the CACD to quash the conviction solely on the basis that, after a review of the evidence, it was left with a 'lurking doubt' as to guilt. But a right to refer in exceptional circumstances is not the same thing as lurking doubt. Referring in exceptional circumstances forces the CCRC to indicate what, exactly, is exceptional (or different) about the case in question. A statement that the CCRC were simply unhappy with the verdict is not going to be treated by the CACD as exceptional circumstances. And, whilst the CACD cannot refuse to hear an appeal, even if it disagrees with the reason for the referral, it can be expected to express its disapproval. Such a referral would also open the CCRC to the risk of an application for judicial review by the prosecuting authorities.

So the CCRC appears to be correct in refusing to accept lurking doubt cases, even though the CACD has power, when appeals reach it through the normal route, to quash a conviction solely on the basis of lurking doubt. Which raises the question as to whether the powers of the CCRC should be altered so that its referrals need not always involve new evidence or argument, but could also include cases where they are simply unhappy with the jury's verdict, and invite the CACD to share their concerns? This, according to the SCCRC, is the position which it currently enjoys. It has interpreted its power to refer cases which 'may' involve a miscarriage of justice as allowing it 'to identify, in the public interest and as a last resort, real concerns about a conviction which, under existing jurisprudence or under existing rules of evidence and procedure, might not necessarily be recognised in the context of an appeal'.[15] The Scottish CCRC has welcomed this additional discretion and regards it as part of its ability to operate as a 'truth-seeking' body and not one rigidly limited to finding conventional grounds for appeal.

Power to refer lurking doubt cases could never operate other than on an exceptional basis. If every case which might have been decided differently was referred to the CACD, the CACD would, for reasons we have described, be unable to process its 'normal' appeals. So the exercise of such a power would need to be restricted to a small number of cases. And, it would be difficult to signal this to potential applicants. The likelihood is that, if the CCRC had, and advertised, the potential to refer cases which raised lurking doubt, it would have to consider a large number of cases in order to identify an extremely small number where its reconsideration of the evidence allowed it simply to question the original jury's verdict. It would also have to face criticism from the CACD, since it could not expect its judgment of when lurking doubt might be present always, or even mostly, to match that of the CACD. Would the benefits of such a power exceed the costs? Not if one is looking for a significant further increase in the number of miscarriages of justice likely to be remedied through the CCRC. Nor if the hope is that the CCRC could become a body which abandoned the CACD's routine approach to what constitutes an unsafe conviction, in all, most or even many of its cases. But, as the example of the SCCRC demonstrates, the ability to refer cases solely on the basis of a concern that a person may be factually innocent, even in the absence of conventional grounds of appeal, could allow the CCRC to present itself publicly, to a higher degree, as a 'truth-seeking' body. And, in terms of its responsibility to maintain public confidence in the criminal justice system, this might prove an advantage that outweighs the costs in terms of any increase to the number of applications that would need to be investigated.

Conclusion

The relationship between the three criteria we have explored to assess the achievement of the CCRC following ten years of its operation are not the only criteria that would need to considered for any overall assessment. Many other criteria can be found in the pages of this book. But the ones that we have explored raise particularly problematic issues. Without any direct knowledge of the size of the problem, namely the actual number of miscarriages of justice, claims to a successful operation by the CCRC (acting as a safety net to eradicate those miscarriages of justice produced and then not remedied through the normal appeal processes) are speculative. The figures produced by the operations of the CCRC when matched against the general figures for annual conviction can be described as reinforcing the idea that one should have confidence in the overall accuracy of the outcomes of the criminal justice system, even while each individual successful referral has the possibility of challenging that assumption. In that sense, the CCRC has been 'successful', namely it has helped to re-establish confidence in the criminal justice system as a whole to various constituencies, especially the media, who were readily willing to claim a lack of confidence in the period leading up to the CCRC's establishment.

The relationship that has had to be established, and then managed, throughout these ten years has not only been with the media and various political constituencies (especially those who hold its purse strings), and applicants and the support groups that always emerge in the support of their campaigns, but crucially its relationship to the CACD. It is certainly less easy for the CCRC to hide behind issues of constitutional propriety to camouflage the limitations of its operations, as the previous arrangements with referrals from the Secretary of State allowed. However, constitutional propriety was not the only reason for the weaknesses of the earlier arrangements, and one can find a number of cases in which the CACD has been particularly critical of the CCRC, for example the recent case of *R* v. *Gore*.[16] The CACD has demonstrated a clear concern to rein in the CCRC to a set of operations that mirror its own sense of appropriate appeal mechanisms. But this concern is a double-edged sword. Throughout the 100 years of operations of the CACD it has been criticized for its narrow interpretation of its statutory powers, and there is no reason to believe that such criticisms will end with the setting up of a more independent referral body, or that the Court's 'unliberality' will somehow reduce. The reason for this we have briefly explored by considering our third criterion, that relating to lurking doubt and exceptionality. Although these two concepts do not reflect the same ideas, they combine operationally to enable each of the bodies institutionally responsible for identifying and remedying miscarriages of justice both to uphold the routine practices of the criminal justice system and reinforce them, and at the same time create the practically necessary safety valves for it. We find the CACD willing to allow itself a certain leeway on occasion with the concept of lurking doubt, but unwilling to encourage the CCRC to feel that it also has such leeway. Whereas the statutory powers on which the CCRC operates give scope to using exceptionality, it is an exceptionality that the CACD views as something whose use must be made accountable to it. Those who believe that the criminal justice system has the potential to, and does in practice, produce more erroneous findings than it admits, will want the CACD to operate as more than a court of review and the CCRC to adopt an approach to its operations which is less restricted by its relationship with that Court and its approach to its own powers.

Notes

1. The Report, in particular, recognizes these criticisms as having been established by Sir John May's various reports into the Maguire Seven case (May, 1990, 1992, 1994; for a summary, see also House of Commons Select Committee on Home Affairs, 1999; CCRC, 2008b).
2. These statistics do not include all the complications of multiple charges, guilty pleas to some charges but not others, etc.
3. Also, it only considers appeals from Crown Court trials, rather than appeals from all criminal convictions, including those from magistrates' courts. This analysis, then, includes what Naughton (2007b: 40) terms 'exceptional' miscarriages of justice overturned by the CACD following a referral by the CCRC and 'routine' miscarriages of justice quashed by the CACD at first instance from conviction given in the Crown Court, simply excluding what he refers to as 'mundane' miscarriages of justice, namely appeals allowed by the Crown Court from the decisions of magistrates' courts, nearly an average of 4,500 per year. Naughton's analysis offers a very different perspective on the overall figure or, as he might put it, the relation between the official iceberg and its tip in relation to miscarriages.
4. The CCRC's annual number of applications is over 900 and it has a referral rate of around 4 per cent, with nearly 70 per cent of referred convictions quashed and over 80 per cent of sentences varied. These figures are extracted from the CCRC's annual reports (CCRC, 1998, 1999, 2000, 2001, 2002, 2003, 2004, 2005a, 2006a, 2007a, 2008a).
5. This was described by Graham Zellick in the following terms: 'If in any case we have a feeling, as one does in this kind of work, that an innocent man or woman has been convicted we will struggle with that case until there is literally nothing else that can be done to correct the errors. There usually is something because there is usually some basis for our supposition that something here has gone wrong' (Zellick, 2006: q. 58).
6. As admitted by Commissioner Weedon in his evidence to the Select Committee, when asked if there are 'innocent men in the twilight of their lives still rotting in prisons for crimes they did not commit': 'I cannot answer that. As a matter of statistics generally, I am sure there are lots of people charged with lots of offences who remain in prison, who are innocent' (Weedon, 2006: q. 58). See also Naughton (2008a) for a 'typology' of the various reasons for why those convicted of criminal offences claim to be innocent.
7. An average of around 100 per year, thus just above 10 per cent of the CCRC rate of applications for England, Wales and Northern Ireland, although there was a large increase to 165 in 2005–06 (SCCRC, 2006: 6–10).
8. As amended by s. 25 of the Crime and Punishment (Scotland) Act 1997.
9. There are a range of possible appeal mechanisms which take different forms, including the distinction between review and rehearing, which itself is distinct from the possibilities for judicial review of Crown Court proceedings (for what is, and what is not judicially reviewable, see Taylor, 2000: ch. 4). However, this

distinction between review and rehearing is fundamental to so much of the organization of the respective roles of the Crown Court – as first instance decision-maker in relation to criminal conviction and sentence – and the appeal machinery available. (For the technical grounds of appeal against conviction from Crown Court Trial, see Taylor, 2000: ch. 8). However, this distinction does not apply in relation to decisions in magistrates' courts, since the relevant appeal machinery involves a rehearing in the Crown Court. The latter arrangements have come under sustained criticism, especially from the Review of the Criminal Courts undertaken by Lord Justice Auld in 2001 (Auld, 2001). With the CACD as the main appeal body from the decisions of the Crown Court, the lack of willingness to step over the threshold of review and engage in rehearing has also been the subject of considerable criticism for most of the 100 years of its operation. See, for instance, Pattenden (1996), whose analysis of conviction appeals included many of these potential criticisms, which she summarized at the end of Chapter 5 in terms of the ensuing inconsistencies and confusions that an organizing of appeal mechanisms around the distinction between review and rehearing could easily be seen to precipitate. See, also, in relation to both appeal systems, Roberts and Malleson (2002: 272–82). In addition, the inconsistency between the appeal mechanisms from the different first-instance criminal courts have themselves been subjected to criticism (Spencer, 2006: 677–94). The overall consequence of Spencer's analysis suggests that the appeal mechanisms currently available have developed parochially, rather than logically or consistently.

10. Such deference also necessarily operates in the way that the CCRC investigates (see Duff, 2001: 341).

11. We would surmise that few, if any, of those who criticize the CACD's deference towards the jury would wish to replace this system of trial with another, such as trial by judges; hence the establishment of the possibility of quashing a conviction and ordering a retrial in the Crown Court by the Criminal Appeal Act 1964.

12. This requirement for new evidence or arguments, and associated requirements such as the definition of 'new' to exclude anything available at trial, are justified by reference to the need for finality. The point can be put somewhat more strongly: what these restrictions seek to avoid is a system in which no institution has authority to decide on a person's guilt, except temporarily, until the next hearing (see Nobles and Schiff, 2002: 679–84).

13. The statutory test (s. 2(1)(a) of the Criminal Appeal Act 1968) for overturning convictions operating at the time.

14. Classically formulated by Lord Widgery in *R* v. *Cooper*. There were and have been other formulations of this conception before and after this judgment and none have achieved a permanent or clear status (see Leigh 2006: 809).

15. Claim made by counsel for the SCCRC in *BM, KK and DP(Petitioners) v Scottish Criminal Cases Review Commission* (para. 15). It is, however, unclear whether the SCCRC does in fact have this residual power, given the criticisms of this and other claims to act as a 'truth-seeking body' made by the Court in that case (see Nobles and Schiff, 2008: 466).

16. 'We are surprised that the Commission should have seen fit to refer this case to us. This is not a case where the system failed a distressed defendant ... She never wanted to resurrect this matter and it is unfortunate that, given there can be no benefit whatsoever to her, her parents' expectations have been raised only to be dashed' (*per* Lady Justice Hallett (para. 42)).

12
Real Possibility or Fat Chance?

Kevin Kerrigan

Introduction

For the 96 per cent of applicants to the Criminal Cases Review Commission (CCRC) whose cases are rejected without being referred to an appeal court the answer to the question in the chapter heading is clear. For them, and an increasing number of campaigners, lawyers and academics, the CCRC has come to be seen not as a solution, but as a contributor to systemic injustice in criminal law. Initially high expectations among prisoners, families and their representatives have developed into cynical rejection of the CCRC as a maintainer of the status quo and a means of taking the political sting out of the continuing reality of wrongful convictions.

A definitive figure for the number of people that are convicted each year of offences that they did not actually commit is not possible. Yet, research has shown that if miscarriages of justice are evidenced by the official statistics on successful appeals against criminal conviction, then they can be said to be 'mundane' and 'routine' features of the criminal justice system, amounting to an annual average of almost 5,000 a year, or approximately 20 each day (Naughton, 2007b: chs 2–3). Similarly, many receive sentences or other orders that are excessive or otherwise inappropriate. If they seek to challenge their conviction or sentence there are a number of possible routes depending on their circumstances (ibid.: 37–42; Spencer, 2006: 677–94). Those seeking to challenge Crown Court convictions must seek leave to appeal in the Court of Appeal (Criminal Division) (CACD). If leave is refused or if a full appeal is unsuccessful then that is normally the end of the matter.[1] Since 1997, the CCRC has provided a remedy of last resort, replacing and expanding the functions previously performed (unsatisfactorily) by the Home Office. It does not decide appeals itself, but has powers to investigate applicants' claims and may refer cases back to the appeal courts.

A common target for criticism is the nature and operation of the CCRC's test for referring cases to the CACD: it may refer a conviction back to the relevant appeal court only where there is a 'real possibility' of an appeal succeeding. The real possibility must (in the absence of exceptional circumstances) arise due to some new evidence or argument not previously advanced at trial or at the first appeal. This is a major limitation on the CCRC's power to refer cases to the CACD and has been criticized on numerous occasions as encouraging a deferential or dependent approach towards its statutory role, in that it must always second-guess the likely approach of the appeal court (see for example Naughton, 2006; Nobles and Schiff, 2001: 280–99). This risks replicating rather than challenging endemic injustice within the system.

Nevertheless, the CCRC has repeatedly expressed itself satisfied with the current test. This test is realistically grounded in the test that is subsequently adopted by the CACD if a referral is made; it is correct in principle and has been shown to work well in practice; moreover, a more permissive test would risk emasculating the role of the CCRC and overwhelming the CACD (see, for instance, Zellick, 2005: 561–2).

This chapter revisits this debate by focusing on the nature and interpretation of the Real Possibility Test. It will be seen that the CCRC currently performs a predictive, not a normative, role, meaning that it has very limited capacity to challenge failings in the appeal regime. It considers how changes to the threshold for referral may impact on applicants' cases. Examination of the consequences of various reform proposals will show there are significant problems with alternatives to the Real Possibility Test. It is concluded that much of the criticism of the test is misplaced and that prisoners' rights would not be significantly enhanced by reform of the test. Indeed, focus on the test applied by the CCRC may serve to obscure the real obstacles to a meaningful review of miscarriages of justice.

Thresholds in the criminal justice system

There are various threshold tests in the criminal justice system where differing levels of proof are required to justify interference with the rights of a person accused or convicted of a crime:

- Arrest threshold: is there reasonable suspicion that an offence has been committed? (s. 24, Police and Criminal Evidence Act 1984 (PACE));
- Charge threshold: is there a realistic prospect of conviction? (CPS, 2004: para. 5);[2]
- Committal threshold: is there sufficient evidence to put the accused on trial for the offence (s. 6(1), Magistrates' Courts Act 1980), i.e., is there a case to answer?
- No-case-to-answer threshold: could a properly directed jury properly convict on the evidence? (see *R* v. *Galbraith*);
- Jury (or magistrates') verdict threshold: has the prosecution proved the accused guilty beyond reasonable doubt? (see *Woolmington* v. *DPP*);

- CACD conviction threshold: is the conviction unsafe? (s.1, Criminal Appeal Act 1968);
- CACD sentence threshold: is the sentence manifestly excessive? (see *R v. Waddington*); and,
- CCRC referral threshold: is there a 'real possibility' that the Court of Appeal may find the conviction to be unsafe? (s.13(1), Criminal Appeal Act 1995).

The test in each case differs depending on the decision at stake. Thus, the temporary deprivation of liberty by arrest has a relatively low threshold with no requirement for admissible evidence at all, whereas the trial verdict requires a high threshold so that the jury are sure of guilt on the basis of admissible evidence.

The Real Possibility Test

Where does the CCRC test fit into this framework? The Real Possibility Test is a unique threshold in the criminal process. It is the last resort of the aggrieved alleged victim of a miscarriage of justice and normally comes after all other appeal routes have been exhausted. In cases where the applicant was convicted on indictment[3] it is linked directly to the unsafety test applied by the CACD.

Thus, when Commissioners come to consider whether an applicant's case should be referred to the CACD they must predict the potential outcome in the CACD. This requires them to anticipate the application of the deceptively simple legal test for quashing a conviction: whether the conviction is unsafe in law.

'Real possibility' is not defined in the statute. In *R v. Criminal Cases Review Commission, ex parte Pearson* the Divisional Court stated:

> The 'real possibility' test ... is imprecise but plainly denotes a contingency which, in the Commission's judgment, is more than an outside chance or a bare possibility, but which may be less than a probability or a likelihood or a racing certainty. The Commission must judge that there is at least a reasonable prospect of a conviction, if referred, not being upheld. (p. 149)

When the Home Affairs Select Committee first examined the operation of the CCRC it thought there were potential problems with the phrase:

> [Real possibility] is a phrase which could mean something different to the ordinary public from how it might be understood by a court. This gives rise to there being a range of possible interpretations by the Commission. (House of Commons Select Committee on Home Affairs, 1999, para. 21)

The Select Committee thought it was:

> important that proper opportunities for referral are available in all cases, and accordingly that the statutory test for referral is as effective as possible in allowing justified cases to be referred ... we think it is worth noting, even at this early stage, that there may be problems with the statutory test laid down in the Criminal Appeal Act 1995. (Ibid., para. 24)

The Real Possibility Test has been variously described as 'deferential', 'subordinate', 'second-guessing', 'restrictive' and 'legalistic'. The first Chairman of the CCRC tellingly explained the limits on the CCRC's task: 'The question is not in the true sense "Is a person in jail who should not be?"' (Crawford, 2000).[4] This leads to criticisms that the CCRC is not actually concerned with resolving miscarriages of justice (Zellick, 2005: 33–4) or is helpless to refer the cases of innocent convicts who do not fit the real possibility criteria (see Chapter 2).

The approach of the CCRC before the Home Affairs Select Committee was to argue that there was no realistic alternative. There was a need to avoid cases being referred by the CCRC on one set of criteria only to be rejected by the CACD using a different set (House of Commons Select Committee on Home Affairs, 1999: Appendix 13). In addition, the Select Committee believed that it was inappropriate at that stage to consider changing the statutory test after so few referrals had been considered. The Committee recommended that a formal review of wording of the test be conducted after the CCRC had been in operation for five years. In 1999, the government accepted that such a review should take place.

Although the review should have begun some time after April 2002, there is no indication that a formal review ever took place, either in the CCRC or in the Home Office. There is no mention of the Select Committee's recommendation in either of the Annual reports for 2001–02 or 2002–03. The closest the CCRC came to analysing the statutory test was as follows:

> During the period 2000–03, the Commission's case committees have referred to the relevant courts of appeal about 55% of the 331 cases that they have considered ... of the 133 appeals that have been heard to 31 March 2003, 65% have succeeded ... *This suggests that the Commission's interpretation of 'real possibility' is reasonably generous, both in considering plausible referrals, and in the decisions made on them by case committees.* (CCRC, 2003: 25; my emphasis)

This is exactly the same conclusion as was reached the previous year (CCRC, 2002: 22).

More recently, the CCRC's Chairman stated:

> I have no objection to a review. We will simply restate the arguments that I have attempted to state here this morning, and as I did on the last

occasion, and alternative formulations can be considered. It is our view, it is certainly the view of the Court of Appeal, that the current test has worked satisfactorily. (Zellick, 2006)

Moreover,

> we are of the view that the present test is not only correct in principle but actually it has been shown over the last decade to work extremely satisfactorily ... [T]here is no point at all, and considerable dangers, in our applying a test which is different from that which is applied by the courts to which we send the cases. (Ibid.)[5]

Alternatives to the current test for referral?

There appear to be two variables within the current test for referral. First, there is what may be described as the *probability* value (currently 'real possibility') which dictates the degree of certainty required before a referral may be made. Second, there is what I shall refer to as the *consequence* value (currently 'unsafety') which dictates the outcome anticipated by the referral. These are not the only ways of describing the probability and consequence values. There are a large number of potential alternatives[6] including:

- Arguable case [probability value] of wrongful conviction [consequence value].[7]
- A miscarriage of justice [consequence value] may have occurred [probability value].[8]
- A possibility [probability value] of innocence [consequence value].[9]

A coherent critique of the CCRC's current approach must address the implications of changing the probability and/or consequence values.

Increasing referrals by relaxing the probability value?

It would be possible to alter the statutory test so as to enable more referrals to be made. Rather than the current Real Possibility Test a lower threshold of certainty could be imposed. The three values set out above are possible examples, but there are others such as 'potential' or 'suspicion'. At least in theory, the lower the threshold of certainty required the higher the applicant's chances of persuading the CCRC to refer. The judgment to be made by the CCRC would become less onerous because it would be able to refer cases with fewer chances of success.[10]

This confirms that liberalizing the test for referral by adjusting the probability value would not itself achieve anything apart from a larger number of referrals. Each of the cases referred would still have to meet the exacting standards required in the appeal courts. The appellant would need to satisfy the CACD, for instance, that the conviction was unsafe or the sentence excessive. In reality, relaxing the threshold for referral would only make a tangible difference if there were a significant number of cases that were not currently being referred that would succeed *under the existing safety test* if they were referred. It is not possible to make any clear assessment of whether this is likely to be the case.

An alternative to altering the statutory test is to reconsider the way in which the CCRC currently interprets the real possibility criteria. 'Success' rates in the CACD following CCRC referrals have remained consistently high at around 70 per cent. The 1999 Home Affairs Select Committee report reviewed the interpretation of the test and considered that the success rate (then 10 out of 13 referrals) 'suggests that the Commission has perhaps been cautious in its interpretation' (House of Commons Select Committee on Home Affairs, 1999).

As we have seen, the CCRC itself rejects the accusation of being over-cautious, describing its approach as 'reasonably generous'. Nevertheless, equating real possibility with a 70 per cent chance of success does seem counter-intuitive. The civil standard of proof (balance of probabilities) is often characterized as a 51 per cent or higher threshold. By contrast, 'real possibility' appears to be conceptually lower in terms of probability, so it might be expected to have a success rate of less than a half. In other words, the statutory language would appear to support the CCRC referring applications even though it thinks they will be likely to fail.[11] It is acknowledged that it is very difficult and perhaps inappropriate to reduce serious arguments in complex criminal cases down to crude probability grades. The overall point, though, is that the 70 per cent success rate could be much lower (indeed it could be reversed) while still fitting comfortably within the existing statutory test.

Ironically, the high rate of success in referred cases leads some to question the CCRC's commitment to challenging unsafe convictions. Arguably, if more cases were referred then the CACD would have a more realistic view of the number and causes of post-appeal grievances by alleged victims of miscarriages of justice and, perhaps, a better insight into the practices within the criminal justice system, including those of the CACD itself, that may contribute to enduring injustice. Thus, a more liberal interpretation of the probability variable within the statutory test may have a beneficial educative effect on the CACD. Whether this is something that would be welcomed by the Court is another matter. There have been a number of occasions even under the current fairly conservative referral approach where the CACD has taken it upon itself to express surprise or concern at the decision to refer a case and urge the CCRC to take account of its resource limitations.[12]

The then Chairman of the CCRC pointed out recently in his evidence to the Select Committee that a change to the probability value would potentially change fundamentally the nature of the CCRC itself:

When the Commission was established it was not established simply to be an investigative body. [Commissioners] are charged with the vital duty of deciding whether the new evidence, or the new argument, as the case may be, raises a real possibility that there should be another appeal. So, if you introduced an arguable case test, you are totally emasculating the Commission, you are giving it a completely different role ... In fact, you would not need Commissioners. You would, however, be giving a great deal of extra work to the Court of Appeal, in my judgment, for no particular purpose and with considerable disadvantages. (Zellick, 2006)

If changing the nature of the CCRC in this way would improve the chances of miscarriages of justice being resolved then clearly it ought to be supported. However, it seems that the logjam would simply move further down the river. Appeals referred by the CCRC as arguably unsafe might routinely be upheld by the CACD as safe; having an argument is not the same thing as winning it.

Increasing referrals by relaxing the consequence value?

As we have seen, the current consequence value is unsafety, the same as that applied by the CACD when considering whether to allow an appeal.[13] The CCRC's approach would clearly be less subordinate if it adopted a different test to that applied by the appeal courts. The three alternatives stipulated above (wrongful conviction, miscarriage of justice and innocence) would arguably free the CCRC from the shackles of the appeal court and enable it to fulfil a more holistic and creative approach to the grievances of convicted people.

The alternative formulations are not without their definitional difficulties and it is not certain that they would all lead to increased referrals being made, but it is certainly the case that the CCRC would be less concerned with anticipating the legal intricacies of the safety test and may be more able to conform to the popular notion of a last resort Commission as being concerned to uphold concepts like justice or innocence.

However, it must be recognized that if the CCRC's approach ceased to be anchored to the test applied by the CACD, it would no longer have any concern with the likelihood of an appeal succeeding. If the approach of the CCRC were divorced from that of the CACD, then applicants could be referred to the appropriate appeal court despite them having no prospects of success at all. Whichever alternative to the consequence value is formulated, the problem remains that each case will ultimately be considered by the CACD on the basis of the safety test.[14] Referring on a basis other than the safety test would mean the CACD would not have the power to quash the conviction. For example, if the CCRC referred a case to the CACD on the basis that the applicant may be innocent, the CACD would still not be able to quash the conviction unless it found that the conviction was unsafe. To the extent that there is a difference between the safety of a conviction and innocence, the court would be obliged to follow the safety test.

Is there a Scottish solution?

Scotland has its own CCRC, established following the recommendations of the Sutherland Committee Report (Sutherland Committee, 1996). The approach of the Scottish Criminal Case Review Commission (SCCRC) differs somewhat from the CCRC in that it may refer a case if it believes: '(a) that a miscarriage of justice may have occurred; and (b) that it is in the interests of justice that a reference should be made' (s. 194C, Criminal Procedure (Scotland) Act 1995). This has led some to suggest that the SCCRC does not need to second-guess the appeal court (see Duff, 2001: 341), that the test is more ethically based (Salter, 2006) and that the Scottish approach should be adopted by the CCRC (Green, 2006: para. 3.53).

However, on closer inspection the Scottish test is in reality more of a reflection of the Scottish appeal court test than at first appears. Section 106(3) of the Criminal Procedure (Scotland) Act 1995 (as amended by the Crime and Punishment (Scotland) Act 1997) permits a person to appeal 'against any alleged miscarriage of justice in which he was convicted', including any miscarriage on the basis of evidence not heard at the original trial, provided there is a reasonable explanation of why it was not heard or on the basis that the jury's verdict was one that no reasonable jury, properly directed, could have returned. Thus, the language of miscarriage of justice is not a general invitation to the SCCRC to refer cases irrespective of the likely approach of the Scottish High Court. Rather, it is expressly prevented from referring unless it considers the appeal test may be met.

Nevertheless, there is some indication that the SCCRC is willing to push at the boundaries of the appeal test somewhat. In *Harper* v. *H.M. Advocate*, the SCCRC, in referring a conviction for murder, acknowledged that the referral did not identify any ground previously recognized by the Court as amounting to a miscarriage of justice, but that in view of the material discovered during the investigation the SCCRC had an unease about the conviction. It is submitted that if there is a greater willingness to refer cases in Scotland (the referral rate is somewhat higher at around 10 per cent of applications) it is not so much due to the wording of the referral test but more to do with the nature of cases that come before it and the constructive relationship that has been nurtured between the SCCRC and the High Court.[15]

Are the number of referrals determined by the threshold test?

It has been assumed, thus far, that the statutory language may have a significant impact on the willingness of the CCRC to make referrals to the CACD. However, it should be recalled that the Criminal Appeal Act 1995 does not impose any obligation on the CCRC to make a referral. It does not follow that a relaxation of the test would necessarily produce an increase in referrals. It should also be recalled that the Home Office formerly had an unfettered power to refer convictions to the CACD. Nevertheless, following transfer of its powers to the CCRC, the number of referrals increased threefold (see Nobles and Schiff, 2001: 283). Clearly, there are dramatic differences between the CCRC and the old Home Office's Criminal Cases Unit, but the point is that the wording of the test alone does not dictate the level of referral.[16]

Are criticisms aimed at the wrong target?

Questions about whether the current threshold test is adequate and whether the CCRC's approach to the current test is appropriate are not easy to resolve. The notion that an aggrieved applicant's claim of miscarriage of justice should be measured against the approach of the very court that has already failed to recognize the potential injustice seems at first bizarre. However, the elephant in the room is the CACD. It is the body charged with deciding whether convictions should be upheld or quashed. It does so on the basis of the statutory safety test. No amount of changes to the CCRC referral test or creative interpretation of the existing test is likely to change this. Accusations that the CCRC is deferential or subordinate to the CACD are truisms.[17] That is the way that the system has been designed by Parliament.

While we have a Commission with a power to refer post-appeal grievances back to the same appellate structures, to apply the same test for receiving fresh evidence and to quash convictions, then such a Commission is bound to be deferential. If the Commission did not predict and respond to the likely approach of the appeal court then cases would just be rejected. Hopes would have been unjustifiably raised, time and resources would have been wasted and cases that might succeed would have been denied justice.

It is beyond the confines of this chapter to provide a thorough analysis of the role of the CACD but it is submitted that here, rather than in the concept of real possibility, lies the answer to why so few applications are referred and so many 'prisoners maintaining innocence' remain convicted (see Naughton, 2005a, 2008a):

> It may be that what really lies at the root of the problem is not the test we apply but the test that the Court of Appeal applies, the test of safety, because, of course, any change to that test would have corresponding implications for us; we would have to adjust our approach accordingly. (Zellick, 2006)[18]

In the third Birmingham Six appeal the CACD felt the need, when finally quashing the convictions, to explain its function and purpose. The comments reveal the limited nature of an appeal following conviction on indictment:

> The Court of Appeal (Criminal Division) is the creature of statute ... we have no power to conduct an open-ended investigation into an alleged

miscarriage of justice, even if we were equipped to do so. Our function is to hear criminal appeals, neither more nor less ... By section 2(1) of the 1968 Act we are directed to allow an appeal against conviction if, but only if, [we think that the conviction is unsafe]. In all other cases we are obliged to dismiss the appeal. Nothing in section 2 of the Act, or anywhere else obliges or entitles us to say whether we think that the appellant is innocent. This is a point of great constitutional importance. The task of deciding whether a man is guilty falls on the jury. We are concerned solely with the question whether the verdict of the jury can stand ... Rightly or wrongly (we think rightly) trial by jury is the foundation of our criminal justice system ... The primacy of the jury in the English criminal justice system explains why, historically, the Court of Appeal had so limited a function ... Since justice is as much concerned with the conviction of the guilty as the acquittal of the innocent, and the task of convicting the guilty belongs constitutionally to the jury, not to us, the role of the Criminal Division of the Court of Appeal is necessarily limited. Hence it is true to say that whereas the Civil Division of the Court of Appeal has appellate jurisdiction in the full sense, the Criminal Division is perhaps more accurately described as a court of review. (*R* v. *McIlkenny and others*)

These propositions help to explain why it is so difficult, once a defendant has been convicted by a jury, to persuade the CACD to quash the conviction.[19] The CACD shows great deference to the jury decision and does not seek to second-guess the jury decision on the guilt or innocence of the appellant. Instead, it is motivated by a desire to check the legal direction by the trial judge and to ensure fairness and due process at the trial.[20] The appeal is limited to those grounds of appeal which have been accepted at the leave stage or, if the case is referred by the CCRC, to those matters identified in the Statement of Reasons as leading to the referral (s. 14(4)(a) and (b), Criminal Appeal Act 1995).[21] The CACD does not consider the case or the evidence as a whole, there is no presumption of innocence and there is no question of the prosecution having the burden of proving guilt at the appeal.

Conclusion

I have attempted to reveal the real possibility debate as something of a red herring. The referral powers of the CCRC are in fact perfectly adequate given our current system. The key obstacle to success for alleged victims of wrongful conviction and/or imprisonment is the restrictive culture within the appellate system for addressing potential error. This is underpinned by statute, embraced by the CACD and merely reflected by the CCRC.

Notes

1. In rare cases the appellant may appeal to the House of Lords but only where there is a point of law of general public importance and again only with leave of the CACD or the House of Lords.
2. The 'Code for Crown Prosecutors' also permits a charge to be temporarily based only on reasonable suspicion where there is insufficient information to justify a charge on the full code test but it is thought inappropriate to release the suspect on bail (ibid.: para. 6).
3. Different considerations apply when the applicant is seeking to appeal against a summary conviction, as an appeal following referral takes the form of a retrial, so the test is whether the prosecution can prove guilt beyond reasonable doubt (see Kerrigan, 2006: 124–39).
4. Although accepting the reality of the deferential role, Duff (2001) suggested that it does not mean the CCRC is prevented from taking its own view of the evidence and acting 'out with and independent of the criminal justice process, not as further rungs on the ladder of the formal legal process' (2001: 362).
5. However, see Chapters 7 and 8, which analyse successful first appeals at the CACD against refusals to refer by the CCRC to show that, in practice, the CACD and CCRC's tests differ with the CACD test being much broader and operating more in the interests of justice as popularly understood.
6. These alternatives assume that the CCRC will retain its statutory function of referring cases to the CACD. It is acknowledged that this role has been criticized. A further alternative would be to remove the CACD's filter altogether, permitting an automatic right to a second appeal.
7. This formulation was proposed by the organisation JUSTICE to the Royal Commission on Criminal Justice (RCCJ) (see Pattenden, 1996: 402).
8. This is the test set out in s. 194C, Criminal Procedure (Scotland) Act 1995 (as amended by s. 25 of the Crime and Punishment (Scotland) Act 1997). The SCCRC must also find that it is in the interests of justice to refer the case (discussed further below).
9. This approach or something similar is implicit in the critique of Naughton (2006).
10. As Lord Bingham CJ put it in *ex parte Pearson*: 'its function would be mechanical rather than judgmental'.
11. This would be consistent with the formulation in *ex parte Pearson*, which includes 'less than a probability'.
12. See for example *R v. Gerald*, a case relating to the identification of exceptional circumstances. See also, the 'old' and 'law change' cases discussed by Nobles and Schiff (2005: 173).
13. This is not explicitly required in the Criminal Appeal Act 1995, but given that the CCRC must apply the Real Possibility Test to the question of whether an appeal will succeed it is inevitable that it will anchor its reasoning in the concept of unsafety.
14. It should be recalled that the CACD is itself a creature of statute and the test for quashing a conviction is laid down in the Criminal Appeal Act 1968.
15. Gerard Sinclair, the chief executive of the SCCRC, considered its interpretation of the statutory test to be similar but not identical to that adopted by the Court: 'the relationship in Scotland has demonstrated a clear wish on the part of the appeal court to accommodate the changes necessarily enforced upon it by the creation of a Scottish Commission. Likewise, the Commission eagerly awaits each and every decision issued by the [Scottish] High Court, in both successful and unsuccessful

referrals, to see what guidance or assistance, if any, the court is able to give it, in the ongoing interpretation of the "miscarriage of justice" test' (Sinclair, 2005: 28).

16. See, also, the analysis in Chapter 2 of the need for caution when trying to compare the CCRC and C3, as they are distinctly different.

17. 'It is difficult to construct a workable relationship between the Commission and the Court of Appeal that does not routinely subordinate the former to the latter' (Nobles and Schiff, 2001: 292).

18. Despite determined efforts on the part of the Government to change the safety test to prevent the CACD quashing a conviction where it was convinced of the appellant's guilt (see Office for Criminal Justice Reform, 2007), at the time of writing the clause seeking to achieve this has been removed from the Criminal Justice and Immigration Bill 2007 (which received Royal Assent on 8 May 2008).

19. In 2003, the CACD dealt with 1,685 applications for leave to appeal against conviction (approximately 3 per cent of those convicted in the Crown Court). Of these, 178 led to the conviction being quashed (10.56 per cent) (Home Office Research Development Statistics, 2004).

20. 'This court is not concerned with the guilt or innocence of the appellants; but only with the safety of the convictions. This may, at first sight, appear an unsatisfactory state of affairs, until it is remembered that the integrity of the criminal process is the most important consideration for courts which have to hear appeals against conviction. Both the innocent and the guilty are entitled to fair trials. If the trial process is not fair, if it is distorted by deceit or by material breaches of the rules of evidence or procedure, then the liberties of all are threatened' (*R* v. *Hickey and others*; quoted in *R* v. *Davies, Rowe and Johnson*).

21. Inserted by s. 315, Criminal Justice Act 2003.

22. Although it is not specified in the statute, it does seem that the appellant has the burden in respect of satisfying the court as to the grounds of appeal.

13
Press and Release: UK News Coverage of the CCRC since 1996

Paul Mason

Introduction

The media are central to public comprehension of criminal justice. Although we may have some direct contact with, say, the police, a courtroom or visiting a prisoner, for the most part we have limited direct contact or experience with these matters. Consequently, we rely on media representations of them for our knowledge. Indeed, in a much quoted statistic from the British Crime Survey, 75 per cent of the public reported that the media were their principal source of information about the criminal justice system (Kershaw *et al.*, 2001). More significantly, only 6 per cent of those surveyed considered that media coverage to be inaccurate. If most of the public believe what they consume about crime and law enforcement, then considerations of media representations of crime are crucial. The potential influence over public opinion on crime and justice, and potentially, over subsequent government policy, must take into account constructions of crime in the public sphere.

Questions have been asked about the reporting of crime since the seminal criminological studies of the 1970s (Chibnall, 1977; Cohen, 1971, 1972; Cohen and Young, 1973; Hall *et al.*, 1978; Young, 1971). These writers demonstrated that crime news was *constructed* rather than reported objectively. As well as concerns about the pernicious effect of over-representing violent and sexual crime (Roberts, 2001; Sparks, 1992; Wykes, 2001), studies have suggested that such reporting creates support for more draconian criminal justice measures (Mason, 2003; Reiner, 2007; Reiner *et al.*, 2003). Thus, as Reiner states, 'while news may be a competitive arena of conflicting viewpoints, it is culturally and structurally loaded. The news media ... reproduce order in the process of representing it' (Reiner, 2007: 236). This (re)presenting of crime and criminal justice in the media is driven by news values: a framework of concepts and ideas which produce a particular version of the world which becomes taken for granted by its audience: for example, that prison works or that celebrities matter. In his study of crime news, Steve Chibnall (1977: 23) explained these news values as 'professional imperatives which act as implicit guides to the construction of news stories'. His eight news values, recently updated by Jewkes (2003) to 12, help to explain how and why certain crime stories reach the press and others do not. Celebrity, novelty, simplification, sex and death all sell newspapers, and are key considerations in how a crime story is written, who is quoted and what perspective the story is told from.

Coverage of the Criminal Cases Review Commission (CCRC) is not immune to these news values. Print media focuses upon people and crimes, with mystery and speculation accounting for the tone of much of the coverage since 1996. But while the glamour of Ruth Ellis and the grisly exhumation of James Hanratty's body took precedence over an examination of the CCRC's workings and practice, news reportage over ten years offers some interesting insights, worthy of discussion.

Press coverage in numbers

This chapter is concerned with print media coverage of the CCRC between 1 January 1996 and 31 December 2006. Newspaper reports were collected using Nexis (LexisNexis, 2008), an online, searchable database containing all local and national print media, as well as international publications. The sample was collected using the terms 'Criminal Cases Review Commission' and 'CCRC'. This generated a total of 396 articles over the time frame. Stories were distributed across the years fairly consistently, with a peak of 72 stories in 2001, a year in which several well-known cases were being considered for appeal: Ronnie Biggs,[1] the Guinness fraud[2] and the so-called 'Ice Cream Wars'[3] case. The lowest year was 1996, which is as one would expect, since the CCRC did not start handling cases until the end of May 1997.

The distribution of stories concerning the CCRC in UK newspapers, predictably, given the subject matter, was that the broadsheets carried twice as many stories as the tabloids, with *The Guardian* (19 per cent), *The Times* (17 per cent) and *The Independent* (16 per cent) the heaviest contributors. Indeed, these three papers contributed more than half of all the stories about the CCRC between 1996 and 2006; while *The Guardian* and *The Times* carried more stories than all the tabloids put together. That said, *The Daily Mail* (10 per cent) and *The Mirror* (5 per cent) both reported on the CCRC at least as often as *The Daily Telegraph* (5 per cent).

Who says what about whom? Key themes in news coverage of the CCRC

People, rather than process, dominate news coverage of the CCRC since 1996. A sizeable majority of stories do not primarily concern the CCRC itself, but rather particular cases. This was true in both tabloid and broadsheet newspapers. If I were to concentrate purely on those news reports which discuss the CCRC itself – its process, workings and efficacy – I would be discussing merely a quarter of all the articles which mention it. Therefore, alongside these reports, I have included an examination of news reports concerned with, what I term, 'notorious/celebrity' cases. News reports on these cases made up a significant proportion of the total news coverage. Of the 397 cases concerning the CCRC from 1996–2006, 190 of them fell into this category, which represents just under half of all reports (48 per cent). Although the majority of these articles came from the broadsheets (63 per cent), the *proportion* of stories concerned with notorious cases was more equally divided between the two categories of newspaper. Reports on notorious cases made up 52 per cent of all CCRC articles in the tabloids, while it comprised only 42 per cent of all stories in the broadsheets. Within this theme I have identified two kinds of report: historical and celebrity stories, which will be dealt with individually further below.

There was a further identifiable group of articles which dealt principally with the appeal process. These reported on cases which had been referred to the CCRC, or which had reached the Court of Appeal (Criminal Division) (CACD). The stories were broadly descriptive, headlined as 'DOUBLE MURDERER WINS FRESH APPEAL' (*The Guardian*, 29 January 1998); 'SELBY RAIL CRASH PLEA REJECTED' (*The Daily Express*, 1 February 2004) and 'BABY MURDERS MUM WINS RIGHT TO APPEAL' (*The Mirror*, 3 February 2005). Such reports mentioned the role of the CCRC, but briefly. For example, 'the Criminal Cases Review Commission referred the case to the Court of Appeal' (*The Times*, 13 March 2001) or 'the body set up to investigate miscarriages of justice has indicated that a ruling on whether to put the case before the Court of Appeal is likely to be this month' (*The Independent*, 1 January 1999). These, primarily descriptive, cases offer little opportunity for analysis, and consequently I do not discuss them here.

Before I move on to discuss the broader themes of the news coverage of the CCRC, it is worth noting how the CCRC is referred to in newspaper reports. The labels journalists assign to people and institutions has a significant impact on how they are viewed (Blommaert, 2005; Dijk, 1993; van Dijk, 1991; Fairclough, 1992, 1995; Richardson, 2007). As Reisigl and Wodak (2001) have noted, these 'referential strategies' can have social and political purposes. For example, on 9 February 2001 the CCRC announced that the case of George Kelly, convicted and hanged for two murders in February 1950, would be considered by the CACD. The headline in *The Daily Telegraph* read 'HANGED MAN'S CASE GOES TO APPEAL' (9 February 2001), whereas, in *The Times*, the headline was 'APPEAL FOR KILLER WHO WAS HANGED' (9 February 2001). Notice here how Kelly is described. *The Times's* headline refers to Kelly by the crime he committed: Kelly is a murderer, who died on the gallows. In the *Telegraph* there is no mention of Kelly's crime in the headline; instead, he is 'a hanged man'. The latter evokes more sympathy than the former. It suggests innocence – Kelly was an ordinary man rather than a criminal, someone perhaps not deserving of his punishment.

Let us return to the print media's referential strategies in reporting the CCRC. How is the CCRC described, in what are often, brief, factual reports? In almost all the broadsheet coverage, the CCRC was described either using the full name, 'Criminal Cases Review Commission', or simply 'the Commission'. Indeed, it was rare across the whole sample that any report just used the initials 'CCRC'. This occurred in just 11 reports out of the 397 (0.8 per cent); and six of these were in *The Guardian*. In tabloid reports, however, there was a tendency to describe the CCRC as a 'legal watchdog', this terminology appeared in 27 reports in the tabloid press, nearly 20 per cent of all its coverage of the CCRC.

What should we make of these findings? Certainly the decision of most reports not to refer to the CCRC as simply 'the CCRC' is one based on specialist knowledge. The public, broadly conceived, are simply unaware of the CCRC or its work; and thus journalists use the longer terminology often with an explanation, such as 'the independent body set up to investigate miscarriages of justice' (*The Guardian*, 30 May 2003). The use of the term 'legal watchdog' by the tabloid press strikes me as significant. It implies a broader remit than the CCRC actually has, with connotations of powers usually reserved for the Home Office, Bar Council or Law Society. To refer to the CCRC as 'a watchdog' imbues the CCRC with a scrutinizing function it does not possess. An institution of review of alleged miscarriages of justice that failed first time at appeal it may be, but ombudsman for the legal profession it is not. This (inaccurate) shorthand is part of what Conboy terms 'the rhetorical patterns of tabloid language' where 'familiar names and nicknames are used in the tabloids as a bridge of familiarity, connecting readers to a world outside the confines of their lived experience' (Conboy, 2006: 22). Thus, the Financial Services Authority becomes 'city watchdog' (*Sunday Express*, 24 December 2000); Her Majesty's Prison Inspectorate is the 'prisons watchdog' (*The Express*, 27 October 2005); and the independent regulator for the UK communications industries, Ofcom, becomes 'TV watchdog' (*The Mirror*, 31 October 2006). In their investigation into how 'mugging' in mid-1970s Britain was reported by the press, Hall *et al.* (1978) discussed this process as the transformation of statements into a 'public idiom'. Although they were more interested in how those in power were quoted in the press, this process – (re)presenting the 'Criminal Cases Review Commission' as a 'legal watchdog' – gives the CCRC 'a popular force and resonance, naturalizing [it] with the horizon of understandings of the various publics' (cf. ibid.: 67).

Grave concerns and dishing the dirt

As I have previously noted, there are two kinds of notorious/celebrity miscarriage of justice cases which newspapers reported on in my sample. Celebrity cases were relatively few: news that the CCRC were reviewing the work of a Home Office pathologist in nine cases on 1 November 2006 was car-ried by three papers. *The Daily Mail* framed the story by noting that the pathologist in question had worked on the inquiry into the death of Terry Lubbock at Michael Barrymore's house in 2001 ('BARRYMORE DEATH CASE PATHOLOGIST FACES INVESTIGATION', 1 November 2006). This was a little surprising given that the CCRC mentioned nine other cases that they would re-examine, including the prominent[4] case of Michael Stone, convicted of the murder of six-year-old Megan Russell and her mother, Lin, in 1996. Along-side stories of Jeffrey Archer and Jonathan King, the case that received the most coverage was the CCRC's investigation of Barry George, convicted of the murder of TV presenter Jill Dando in 2001. The report had many of the news values for a high-profile crime story: celebrity, murder, mystery and specula-tion. News coverage of the case, and its path through to the CCRC, was awash with the latter: 'WAS JILL DANDO KILLED BY MISTAKE BY A HITMAN HIRED BY JEFFREY ARCHER?' asked *The Mirror*, somewhat improbably (11 July 2005). While *The Sunday Times* magazine ran a lengthy feature and interview with Barry George entitled 'WAS HIS FINGER ON THE TRIGGER?' (29 October 2006). And, tales of Serbian hitmen and constructions of George, which veered wildly from hapless, naive victim to celebrity-obsessed nut (*The Sun*, 12 December 2004), were commonplace. In amongst this coverage was overt criticism of the CCRC by the original investigating officer in the Dando case (*The Guardian*, 7 September 2006 and *The Sunday Express*, 15 October 2006). It was rare to find direct criticism of the CCRC by the original police officers involved in a case. In this instance, the officer in question was a very senior one. Detective Superintendent Hamish Campbell accused the CCRC of a 'con-tinued pursuit of certain issues in the case ... tantamount to calling him a liar' (*The Guardian*, 7 September 2006). It is, perhaps, surprising there are not more instances of media intervention by the police in high-profile appeals, given their policy of image management, as I note further below. It may be explained, in part, by the reinvestigative powers of the police themselves: for the police to question the process is tantamount to self-criticism.

News reports about historical, and in some cases posthumous, appeals were widespread in the sample. The ghosts of Ruth Ellis (see Hancock, 1963), James Hanratty[5] and Derek Bentley[6] loom large in the coverage, and reports of their appeals followed a similar pattern to celebrity cases, driven by the news val-ues of sex, death and intrigue. The Ruth Ellis case was regularly reported over four years, from the news that a Cardiff solicitor would lodge an appeal with the CCRC in 1999, to the CACD's dismissal and admonishment of the CCRC for referring the case in 2003. The style and tone of reporting in the Ellis appeal was similar to a contemporary murder trial. Indeed, it is interesting to compare the original coverage of the Ellis murder trial with the appeal to the CCRC. Back in 1955, Ellis was constructed as a film noir 'femme fatale': the news coverage consequently built on the twin pillars of glamour and sex. Nearly 50 years later, little appears to have changed. The CCRC's decision to refer the case to the CACD was reported in *The Independent* (9 February 2002) thus: 'The shooting dead of an upper-class playboy by a beautiful nightclub hostess caused a sensation in 1955. The trial of Ruth Ellis gripped the nation, and led to one of the most notorious cases in British criminal history'. News of the CCRC's review, and subsequent referral to the CACD, offered journalists the opportunity to revisit not only the facts of the original case, but the manner in which it was reported. Journalists reminded readers of the victim, David Blakely, a racing driver and Ellis's 'philandering lover' (*The Daily Mail*, 11 February 2002). Ellis was said to have been sexually abused, suffering depression and under the influence of another of her lovers, Desmond Cussen.

Similarly, the consideration of the James Hanratty case allowed newspapers to indulge in emotive narratives more usually witnessed in crime novels. *The Independent* (1 April 1997) wrote 'officers turned their attention from Alphon to Hanratty after a tip-off from William Nudds, an informer and habitual liar ... Two years later Alphon confessed in Paris to the rape and murder'. News coverage was punctuated with tales of 'illicit trysts', the movements of Soho nightclub owners and talk of exhumation of Hanratty's body: 'it is crucial his body is exhumed so that one of the most enduring mysteries can be solved', reported *The Daily Mail* (11 March 1998). The ingredients here – death, sex, violence, glamour and mystery – are all key drivers in contemporary crime narratives, which Steve Chibnall (1977: 32) summarized as 'the simultaneous portrayal and condemnation of the more exotic and lurid forms of deviance'.

These historic cases act as conduits between the past and present. In the reports on the Ellis case, newspapers made an overt association to the contemporary defence of diminished responsibility used by battered spouses such as Sarah Thornton[7]. *The Sunday Times* was one of several papers noting that the grounds for the Ellis appeal rested on the assaults by Blakely, leading to her losing her unborn child by a miscarriage. The Home Office's transfer of both the Hanratty and Bentley cases to the CCRC was discussed alongside the more recent M25 Three[8] appeal. The refusal of the then Conservative government to make decisions on such high-profile cases was seen as cynical politicking by *The Guardian* and *The Independent*. Both papers questioned the decision to pass the cases to the CCRC, rather than make a decision under the auspices of the Home Office. It was suggested by *The Guardian* (26 March 1997) that, in an election year, the Conservative government risked alienating its core supporters if it released the M25 Three. Its headline read 'ANGER AT FAILURE TO RESOLVE "UNFAIR" CONVICTIONS'.

Criticism was also evident in the reporting of the Ellis appeal. Over the four years of reports on the appeal, there was a palpable shift from the polarized discourses of Ellis as femme fatale/tragic victim, to overt criticism of the CCRC. On upholding the verdict of murder against Ellis, the CACD suggested that such historical appeals were wasting the Court's time. This led to headlines such as 'JUDGES THROW OUT TIME-WASTING ELLIS MURDER

APPEAL' (*The Independent*, 9 December 2003) and 'HANGING PLEA "HAS NO MERIT"' (*The Mirror*, 9 December 2003). All five newspapers that covered the case carried Lord Justice Kay's comments on the efficacy of the appeal. *The Daily Mail*, who had suggested previously that Ellis's conviction was 'expected to be quashed' (11 February 2002), was the most damning 'FAILED ELLIS APPEAL COSTS TAXPAYERS £200,000' (9 December 2003). In its report, *The Daily Mail* relied upon one of its central political frames, that of taxpayers' money being frittered away on seemingly pro-criminal, far flung, extremist schemes (Mason, 2007). A year earlier the paper offered a sympathetic construction of the Ellis appeal, in which it carried numerous quotes from Ellis's solicitor and sister. However, the paper's report of the CACD's dismissal was shaped by Lord Justice Kay's rebuke of the CCRC. *The Daily Mail* set the cost of the case to taxpayers against the utility of the institutions and actors involved: among the clutch of highly paid barristers who appeared was Michael Mansfield, QC, for Ellis's family. He is one of the top-paid silks in the country, commanding up to £7,000 for a day in court. Senior and junior barristers' fees, including Mr Mansfield's and David Perry's for the Crown, came to approximately £90,000.

The News of the World took a similar stance suggesting that the Ellis case 'has cost you and me £200,000, stopped genuine cases from getting a swift hearing and provided yet another gravy train for trendy lawyers'. This personalization, what Jewkes refers to as 'individualism' in her discussion of crime news values, results in 'events being viewed as the actions and reactions of people' (Jewkes, 2003: 43). *The Daily Mail* used the same technique when discussing the role of the CCRC. It pointed out that the CCRC received '£7 million a year in funds from the Home Office', but then noted that 'just 4% (of cases) are sent back directly on appeal'. Notice here how the paper intimates that the low referral rate of the CCRC is in some way suggestive of inefficiency or incompetence. The paper asks the reader to draw inferences from its preferred discourse: public money wasted on overpaid lawyers and inefficient institutions. Thus, £7million *of our money* could be put to better use, rather than squandered on such an organization. The whiff of 'political correctness gone mad' hangs in the air here, which 'forms part of a self-lubricating linguistic rationale whenever interventions in equality affairs are raised' (Conboy, 2006: 119). The CCRC's consideration of historic cases proved controversial. In dealing with the *causes célèbres* of Ruth Ellis, Derek Bentley and James Hanratty, the CCRC faced some strong criticism in the British press, and this forms my third theme.

Intervention, composition and capacity

There has been little sustained attempt by the CCRC to manage its image over the last ten years or so, at least overtly. In their work on the news reporting of HIV/AIDS (Human Immunodeficiency Virus/Acquired Immune Deficiency

Syndrome), Miller and Williams (1998) have argued that the ability of some groups to influence public debate could not be judged purely by their media profile. They point out, for example, that charitable organizations receiving government funding may be constrained in what they are able to communicate publicly. Terrence Higgins Trust worker, Nick Partridge, suggested:

> We have to be the responsible party, that's our role. One: it protects our charitable status, secondly our combative up-front campaigning has to be in the context of charity and ... I want this organisation to remain a trusted source of information. (Miller and Williams, 1998: 128)

In addition to this responsibility, the CCRC is bound by the statutory authority which regulates it. Section 23 of the Criminal Appeal Act (1995) prevents the CCRC from disclosing any information found in 'the course of its duties', and, as I have noted, much of the press coverage concerning the CCRC is primarily driven by such individual cases. It is also true that the CCRC issues a press release whenever it refers a case to the CACD,[9] evidence 'that the Commission understands the need to respond to the media, and to political pressure' (Nobles and Schiff, 2001: 298). Nonetheless, it is surprising that there were only a handful of occasions when the CCRC directly intervened in press debates about criminal justice or where its press releases were used by journalists. For example, of all its ten Annual Reports and accompanying press releases published since 1997, only nine news reports in total reported on them, four in *The Guardian* and three in *The Times*. This runs counter to recent developments in the communication strategies of New Labour and its criminal justice agencies. The police, prison and probation service, lawyers and judges, have all professionalized their media management strategies, borrowed from the corporate sphere (Mason, 2008; Schlesinger and Tumber, 1994). In policing, for example, image making and news management has been a central priority (Boyle, 1999a, 1999b; Leishman and Mason, 2003; Mawby, 2002). Legal professionals and the court system, too, have engaged in forms of media management. The Department for Constitutional Affairs undertook a lengthy consultative process with media professionals and journalists in planning the televising of appeal courts in 2005.

The only direct press intervention by the CCRC appeared when Professor Graham Zellick became its new Chairman in 2003. The 'outspoken professor' (*Financial Times*, 4 July 2003) made explicit comments about the use of expert witnesses at the launch of the CCRC's 2004 Annual Report (CCRC, 2004). His comments followed the overturning, on appeal, of three cases based on the expert testimony of Roy Meadow.[10] The (albeit brief) coverage of Zellick's appointment as Chairman was part of an ongoing commentary on the CCRC's composition since 1996. Before it had begun its work, journalists were critical of who had been appointed and who had been omitted.

Patricia Wynn Davies in *The Independent* noted that 'several candidates with knowledge of miscarriages of justice failed to make any headway' (17 December 1996). Along with several other papers in 1996, Davies was critical of the appointment of Sir Frederick Crawford as Chairman, given his membership of the Freemasons. *The Times*, too, were disapproving, and carried Labour MP Chris Mullin's call for Crawford to resign. The scepticism expressed by the press in the early stages of the CCRC was grounded in the decision by the then Home Secretary, Michael Howard, to allow the reinvestigation of cases to be carried out by police officers. *The Independent* was once again the principal voice of doubt: 'NEW BODY KEEPS POLICE IN CHARGE' (6 August 1996) it noted, while the next day it claimed the CCRC represented 'COLD COMFORT FOR VICTIMS OF INJUSTICE' (7 August 1996). Its most damning critique came in its coverage of the hunger strike by prisoners protesting against the slow progress of their cases through the CCRC. It carried several quotes by the head of Action Against Injustice, Chris Moore, including his description of the CCRC as being 'headed by a mason. It is a non-elected body and it is heavily-biased with people with prosecution experience'. Even by 2000, the paper was still unhappy with the use of police officers for reinvestigations. In reporting on the appointment of TV journalist David Jessel to the CCRC, *The Independent* noted, with some irony, that his former production company had undertaken independent investigations of cases of miscarriage of justice, but that in joining the CCRC he would no longer be able to do so: 'I certainly was of the opinion that the CCRC should have its own investigative arm but I'm told that it's not an option'.

The question of resources, of how the CCRC would cope, was also noticeable in the early reports on the CCRC. The question of its capacity to cope with the volume of appeals coming its way was an early and constant theme in news coverage of the CCRC. Before it had even begun its work, there were concerns about the number of cases it would receive; *The Independent* speculated that 'a flood of applications ... up to 1600' (*The Independent*, 6 August 1996) could be sent. The paper had reduced its prediction to 'between 500 and 750' by April of 1997 (*The Independent*, 9 April 1997). By this time, a string of reports had appeared concerning the under-resourcing of the CCRC, triggered by comments made by its then chairman, Sir Frederick Crawford. These reports all shared a particular lexical framework in which water references were used frequently. 'CRIMINAL REVIEW BODY DELUGED WITH CASES', reported *The Independent* (9 April 1997), a workload which the *Financial Times* suggested 'threatens to submerge' (9 April 1997) the Commission. Cases 'flooded' in (*The Guardian*, 31 May 1997) and Crawford himself described the first raft of applications as 'the initial wave' (*Daily Mail*, 9 April 1997). The CCRC's ability to deal with cases was constantly expressed in numbers. Cases were said to be coming in at a rate of 'five a day' (*The Independent*, 5 November 1997), 'six a day' for readers of *The Times* (9 April 1997) or even 'seven a day' in *The Guardian* (31 May 1997). This last figure is somewhat of a mystery, however, as the paper quoted a spokeswoman for the CCRC, who said they were receiving '35 fresh cases a week'. Crawford expressed these figures differently, as 'up to three million pages of material annually' (*The Times*, 9 April 1997). This theme of an overloaded CCRC remained throughout the reporting in my sample, albeit sporadically, with reports noting high numbers of applications in *The Times* (26 July 2005) and *The Sunday Mirror* (12 February 2006). Capacity was further emphasized in comparing case numbers to staff numbers. Yet here, too, there was confusion. Were there 13 full-time Commissioners (*The Guardian*, 9 April 1997)? Or was it 14 (*The Independent*, 9 April 1997)? By 1998, reports had shifted to a discussion of funding. *The Mirror* reported on the Commission's request for more money – 'LEGAL WATCHDOGS IN PLEA FOR £1.25 MILLION' (30 May 1998), a story also carried by *The Guardian* seven months later (16 December 1998). In 2000, the underfunding of the CCRC was reported in *The Times* (6 June 2000).

Reports on the under-resourcing of the CCRC offer it support. Broadly sympathetic, the UK press laid the blame at the Government's door, either in its refusal to offer more funds or provide more staff. However, the backlog of cases and failure to address patent miscarriages of justice – at least as the press saw it – was focused more on the CCRC. I have alluded to the criticism concerning how the CCRC was perceived for its work on historic and notorious cases: the drain on taxpayers' money, for example. This was further exacerbated by Decca Aitkenhead's piece in *The Guardian*, headlined 'LEAVE THE DEAD ALONE. THERE ARE ENOUGH LIVING VICTIMS WHO NEED HELP' (14 August 1998). She argued that posthumous appeals were clogging up the system, a position supported by one of the M25 Three, Raphael Rowe, in a letter to *The Guardian* several days later (19 August 1998). In keeping with their position on the Ruth Ellis appeal, *The Mail on Sunday* revelled in quoting the original trial judge in the Jeremy Bamber case.[11] Following the CACD's rejection of the case on 12 December 2002, the paper quoted Sir Maurice Drake in its headline 'YOU WOULD EVEN FIND SOMETHING GOOD TO SAY ABOUT GUY FAWKES'. Here, the paper reverts to its agenda of cost versus efficacy, which it would repeat the following year in its coverage of the Ruth Ellis appeal, as noted above:

> The CCRC started work in 1997 after a series of high-profile miscarriages of justice. With a £7 million annual budget, it has about 700 cases referred to it each year, only four per cent of which are sent back for appeal. In five years, 79 people have had their convictions quashed and 38 have been upheld. (*The Mail on Sunday*, 15 December 2002)

It is interesting that no other newspaper picked up on Drake's comments. This suggests that the *Mail on Sunday* sought out the judge after the CACD decision. The paper, and its sister publication, *The Daily Mail*, had made a similar argument about the public cost of the CCRC in 2001. On 9 July 2001 it ran a story about Derek Borrows, who had been fined £50 over a parking dispute, and had taken the case to the CCRC. Predictably, the paper used the case to make broader points about the CCRC: '£10,000 LEGAL AID BILL FOR £50 PARKING CASE: BATTLE OVER "MISCARRIAGE OF JUSTICE"' it cried. The news hook for the story was the launch of the CCRC's Annual Report (CCRC, 2001). At the launch, Chairman Sir Frederick Crawford outlined a reduction in its backlog of cases from 1,208 in 1999 to 580 cases in 2001. The story was only reported in *The Times* and *The Morning Star* (both on 10 July 2001). However, a Press Association report briefly mentioned Mr Borrows's appeal, which *The Mail on Sunday* clearly followed up on. Leaving the readers in little doubt where it stood on funding allocation, it quoted the Chairman of the Metropolitan Police Federation, Glen Smyth: 'This money would have been better spent on victims of crime rather than on a person who has admitted committing one. The end doesn't justify the cost' (*The Mail on Sunday*, 15 July 2001).

Conclusion

I have noted how stories about the CCRC are subjected to the same news values as other crime stories. Derek Borrows's £50 fine appeal works on novelty – the constant search for new angles on an existing story (Chibnall, 1977; Leishman and Mason, 2003). While the Borrows story was only picked up in *The Mail on Sunday*, the story of Dino the Dog was widely reported. In October 2001, Northampton Crown Court rescinded an order to destroy a German shepherd called Dino, after it had bitten a woman in Hyde Park in July 2001. The story was reported in six national newspapers, including *The Independent, The Guardian, The Times* and *The Daily Telegraph*. Criticism of the case was limited to Marcel Berlins in *The Guardian* (19 October 2004) who echoed both Decca Aitkenhead's argument about the CCRC's choice of cases, and *The Daily Mail's* criticism on the use of taxpayers' money:

> the CCRC is a good thing. But does it not have stronger and more urgent miscarriages of justice to investigate than the fate of dogs who bite? Are there not people at this moment languishing in our prisons, guiltless of the crimes of which they were convicted? To put it crudely, has the CCRC not got better things to do with its time and taxpayers' money?

The perceived clogging up of the CCRC with novelty, celebrity and posthumous cases was regularly used as a point of attack in press criticism of the CCRC. Bob Woffinden, a regular commentator on miscarriage of justice cases, wrote several pieces criticizing the slow progress of appeal cases (*The Guardian*, 6 October 1998; *The Times*, 30 March 1999). It is an interesting point whether the speed a case progresses through the CCRC is a factor in public confidence in the CCRC. In their assessment of the CCRC in 2001, Nobles and Schiff argue that the CCRC should be judged against 'the range of attitudes and ambitions that led to its creation, as well as the ambitions that it claims for itself' (2001: 281). In considering the unsatisfactory progress of many cases sent to the CCRC, they note the trade off in public confidence between speed and diligence. Indeed, for the most part, this confidence is not a public one but a media constructed one. It would seem, from the press coverage since 1996, that criticism of the CCRC itself is more closely associated with delay than carelessness. This is largely delimited by the need for newspapers to simplify, polarize and personalize: it is far easier to report on the length of time the M25 Three waited to be released than to explain the flaws in the CCRC's procedure.

Notes

1. Ronnie Biggs was one of 15 men involved in the Great Train Robbery: a gang who stole £2.6m from the Glasgow to London mail train in August 1963. He was sentenced to 30 years, and his case was reviewed by the CCRC in 2001. It was rejected in January 2002 (see Hattenstone, 2004).
2. Ernest Saunders, Gerald Ronson, Sir Jack Lyons and Anthony Parnes were convicted in August 1990 for their involvement in a conspiracy to drive up the price of shares in Guinness, during a takeover battle in 1986. The case was sent to the CCRC in February 2001 (see *R* v. *Lyons and others*).
3. Thomas 'TC' Campbell and Joe Steele were convicted for the murders of six people by starting a fire in a tenement flat in Ruchazie, Glasgow, in April 1984, in a turf war over areas served by ice-cream vans. They were released in April 2004, after the Court of Appeal quashed their conviction. They had both served 17 years in prison (see Seenan, 2001).
4. Coverage of this case reached more than 900 articles since Stone's arrest for the murders was reported in 1997.
5. James Hanratty was hanged in 1962 after being convicted of murdering government scientist, Michael Gregsten, and raping his mistress, Valerie Storie, on 22 August 1961. The case became known as the 'A6 Murder' named after the road on which the murder took place (Woffinden, 1997).
6. Derek Bentley was hanged on 28 January 1953 for his part in the murder of PC Sidney Miles during a bungled break-in at a warehouse in Croydon, Surrey. He was 19. Christopher Craig, Bentley's co-defendant, fired the fatal shot, but, because he was still a juvenile, he received an indeterminate life sentence. The case was made into a film, *Let Him Have It* (directed by Peter Medak, 1991), named after the words Bentley is alleged to have shouted to Craig moments before the shots were fired (see Trow, 1990).
7. Sara Thornton had her conviction for murder reduced to manslaughter on 30 May 1996 after the CACD ordered a retrial. She was released from prison after she was sentenced to five years, which she had already spent in prison. It was not clear, however, whether the jury reached their decision based on grounds of provocation, diminished responsibility or a combination of both (*R* v. *Thornton* (No. 2)).
8. Three men, Raphael Rowe, Michael Davis and Randolph Johnson, jailed for a series of brutal robberies close to the M25 motorway, had their convictions quashed by

the CACD in July 2000 after they had each served ten years in prison (see *R v. Davies, Rowe, and Johnson*).

9. For an outline of the CCRC's media policy, see CCRC (2008i).
10. These were the cases of Sally Clark (see Batt, 2005), Angela Cannings (see Cannings and Davies, 2006) and Donna Anthony (see Verkaik, 2005).
11. In October 1986 Jeremy Bamber was convicted of the murders of five members of his family at White House Farm in Essex. He was sentenced to life imprisonment with a minimum term of 25 years. His appeal was rejected by the CACD in 2002 (see BBC News, 1986).

14
The CCRC as an Option for Canada: Forwards or Backwards?

Clive Walker and Kathryn Campbell

Introduction

It may appear to strike a discordant note in a book about 'critical perspectives' even to posit that the Criminal Cases Review Commission (CCRC) could perform as any kind of role model. However, the CCRC has long vaunted its attractiveness as an original and effective device. Though no longer unique, following the establishment of the Norwegian Criminal Cases Review Commission (NCCRC) (NCCRC, 2008), it has attracted interest from jurisdictions as diverse as Holland and Japan (CCRC, 2006a). As might be expected, common law jurisdictions have also cast curious glances. In particular, Canadian interest has been expressed on several occasions, most recently through the work of the Inquiry into Pediatric Forensic Pathology under Justice Stephen T. Goudge in Ontario, which has embarked upon a systemic examination of the lessons to be learnt from other jurisdictions (Goudge, 2007).

This chapter will, firstly, examine the situation in Canada and seek to show how, following all appeals, the conviction review process allows for individuals who believe they have been wrongly convicted to apply for a review of their case to the (Federal) Minister of Justice. While ostensibly developed to address miscarriages of justice, it will be argued that this conviction review process is cumbersome, onerous and lengthy, rendering it inaccessible and ultimately ineffective for most wrongly convicted individuals. Secondly, it will address the feasibility of the establishment of an independent review, modelled on the precedents from the United Kingdom but taking into account the many existing criticisms that speak of its deficiencies and problems. Arguments will be made for a more holistic approach that works in conjunction with lobby groups and the court system, as a more equitable and accessible means for addressing miscarriages of justice in Canada.

Process overview

The application of existing processes

Once convicted of a criminal offence, Canadians have the opportunity for their convictions to be revisited through the conviction or ministerial review process. However, the road to review is long and arduous. The power to appeal against criminal convictions has existed since 1923, and there are Courts of Appeal or appellate divisions of Superior Courts in every province and territory in Canada (or a total of 12 in ten provinces and two territories). In those cases where leave to appeal to provincial Courts of Appeal and the Supreme Court of Canada has been refused, the last avenue for redress is through conviction or ministerial review. This option has been available since the enactment of the first Criminal Code in 1892 (Criminal Code, 1985), in which the former section 1022 allowed the Minister of Justice to order new trials and refer cases or points to the appropriate Court of Appeal for its opinion (Department of Justice, 1998). In 1968, section 690 of the Criminal Code formalized this process and in 1993 the Criminal Conviction Review Group (CCRG) was formed to facilitate the conviction review process. A further change took place in 2002 establishing the present CCRG, comprised of a group of six lawyers and a special advisor, who examine cases and make recommendations to the Minister of Justice as to whether a miscarriage of justice has likely occurred. This body functions in a similar fashion to the former C3 Division of the Home Office (Taylor and Mansfield, 1999).

This conviction review process is available to any person who has been convicted of summary or indictable offences through either the Criminal Code or under any federal legislation or regulation, including the Controlled Drugs and Substances Act 1996 and the Income Tax Act 1985. It is also available to those convicted persons who have been designated as either long-term or dangerous offenders. These latter designations are usually requested by the Crown Attorney at sentencing in cases where it has been demonstrated that the individual is at risk of committing future violent or sexual offences. Given that the CCRG has no legislative authority to revisit sentences, its only capacity is to review whether there is a reasonable basis to conclude that a dangerous or long-term offender designation is a likely miscarriage of justice. The CCRG receives very few of these requests.

The criteria to be met for a conviction review require that all avenues of appeal have been exhausted and that new and significant information (often referred to as fresh evidence) related to the conviction has come to light since the original trial and appeals. Following a preliminary assessment to ascertain that all the information is included in the application, and that a conclusion has been reached that there may be a reasonable basis to conclude that a miscarriage of justice has likely occurred, a case will be advanced to the investigation stage. According to the Department of Justice, this 'new and significant' information must be reasonably capable of belief, relevant to the issue of guilt and could have affected the verdict if presented at trial. These criteria could be met by new information related to alibi, confession or identification evidence, scientific evidence pointing to innocence or another person's guilt, proof of non-disclosure of important evidence, false witness testimony, or other evidence that substantially contradicts trial testimony (Department of Justice, 2003a).

The investigation process can take several months, sometimes even years. Essentially, the investigative lawyers who work for the CCRG have the power to subpoena documents and witnesses, undertake scientific testing at government expense, request previous forensic and scientific testing of evidence, consult with police, prosecutors and defence counsel involved in the original trial and appeal(s), and request any other relevant information and documentation (Department of Justice, 2008). Although the results of the investigation (the investigation brief) are shared with the applicant and his or her counsel, the final report (Advice to the Minister) which contains the recommendations on the merits of the application is not shared with the applicant as this report is considered to be advice to the Minister and protected by solicitor–client privilege.

There have been a few exceptions when the Minister has waived privilege and allowed this information to be shared publicly, most recently in the case of Steven Truscott, to be discussed below. It is then the Minister's decision whether to dismiss or allow the application. Applications are allowed in those cases where the Minister is 'satisfied by the application that there is a reasonable basis to conclude that a miscarriage of justice likely occurred' (Criminal Code, s. 696.3). Ultimately, an applicant for conviction review is not required to establish innocence, *per se*, and factual innocence is not a prerequisite to the Minister granting a remedy. Rather, the standard is whether there is a reasonable basis to conclude that a miscarriage of justice has 'likely occurred', and the deliberation centres around questions of the strength of new evidence and the overall safety of the conviction. In allowing an application, the Minister can order a new trial, order a new hearing (in the case of a dangerous or long-term offender) or refer the matter to the appropriate provincial Court of Appeal, as if it were an appeal by the convicted person. The Minister can also seek the assistance of the Court of Appeal before rendering a decision by referring a question or questions to a Court of Appeal for its opinion.

A recent example of an infamous Canadian case illustrates this process. In 1959, when he was 14 years old, Steven Truscott was convicted of murdering 12-year-old Lynne Harper in Goderich, Ontario. Truscott was initially sentenced to death, but this was commuted to life imprisonment, and he served ten years before being released on parole. During that time, he appealed against his conviction to the Ontario Court of Appeal and the Supreme Court of Canada and was refused by both courts (*Re Truscott*). He lived in relative obscurity until 2001, when he attempted to have his conviction reviewed. He filed a conviction review application with the CCRG in 2001, and, given the high profile nature of his case and conviction, the Minister appointed an agent to conduct the review: retired Justice Fred Kaufman. Kaufman finished his 700-page investigative report in 2004 (Kaufman, 2004), whereupon the Minister of Justice, at that time Irwin Cotler, referred the case back to the Ontario Court of Appeal to be treated as a straight appeal. The Court of Appeal began to hear the case in June 2006 and, in August 2007, acquitted Truscott but fell short of declaring him innocent, with the conclusion 'that, while it cannot be said that no jury acting judicially could reasonably convict, we are satisfied that if a new trial were possible, an acquittal would clearly be the more likely result' (*R v Truscott*, para. 787).

While not necessarily typical of the cases that normally request ministerial review, Truscott's case illustrates two important features. One is the involvement of a political actor whose sympathy, or lack of it, can be crucial to the outcome. In this case, it should be noted that Irwin Cotler is a highly notable ex-professor of law at McGill University, whose liberality is pronounced even for a Minister of Justice and Attorney General of Canada in a Liberal Party government (a position he held from 2003 until 2006). Not all government ministers can be guaranteed to place the interests of the individual so highly above the reputation of the administration of the criminal justice system. The second feature concerns the slow pace of the process, as it took six years from the time his application was received by the CCRG for the Court of Appeal to reach a decision. The CCRC certainly entails advantages in addressing the first feature, though the combination of painstaking reinvestigation and the need to refer back to the courts means that the second feature remains equally troubling in the UK.

The options in the hands of the Minister afford different opportunities to applicants. When the Minister of Justice asks the (provincial) Court of Appeal a particular question, or asks it to treat an applicant's request as an appeal, it is the applicant's responsibility to establish, on a balance of probabilities, that a miscarriage of justice has occurred. Courts of Appeal will treat these types of cases as they would any fresh evidence case, which may include hearing examinations and cross-examinations of witnesses, as well as legal arguments. The Supreme Court of Canada can also hear cases on fresh evidence. Moreover, conviction review can come about as the result of a reference to the Supreme Court of Canada under s. 53 of the Supreme Court Act 1985, although that occurs quite infrequently. In these cases, it is usually the result of a reference from the Minister of Justice on a particular matter, as was the case in the *Reference re Milgaard*. David Milgaard had served 22 years in jail for a murder he did not commit, and the Supreme Court reference resulted in a recommendation to the Minister that a new trial take place. The Minister at that time followed the advice of the Court.

However, the Attorney General of Saskatchewan chose not to prosecute Milgaard a second time (*Milgaard* v. *Mitchell*), and he was ultimately exonerated through DNA evidence in 1997. Another person (Larry Fisher) was arrested for the murder and rape shortly afterwards. Milgaard received $10 million in compensation for his ordeal, the largest amount awarded in Canada to date for a wrongful conviction. Another official inquiry, chaired by Justice MacCallum, was established in 2004 but is yet to report (MacCallum, 2004).

References by the Minister to a Court of Appeal or the Supreme Court of Canada in cases of alleged miscarriages of justice, while not unique, are often outside the norm of cases heard by these courts. These courts are more accustomed to hearing appeals on strict legal arguments from decisions of superior courts and provincial/territorial courts, as well as addressing constitutional questions. While it is not normally their role, Courts of Appeal become fact-finding courts in these instances, hearing evidence and making findings on credibility. Irrespective of the province or territory, all the Courts of Appeal are bound by the *Palmer* rules (*R* v. *Palmer*), which dictate the principles for considering fresh evidence on appeal. First, the evidence should generally not be admitted if, by due diligence, it could have been adduced at trial provided that this general principle will not be applied as strictly in a criminal case as in civil cases (*McMartin* v. *The Queen*). Second, the evidence must be relevant in the sense that it bears upon a decisive or potentially decisive issue in the trial. Third, the evidence must be credible in the sense that it is reasonably capable of belief. Fourth, it must be such that if believed it could reasonably, when taken with the other evidence adduced at trial, be expected to have affected the result.

When the Minister of Justice orders a new trial the issues are markedly different. In such cases, the Minister is essentially quashing the original conviction and ordering a new trial requiring that the courts treat the person as innocent, until proven guilty. The onus is then on the prosecution to prove its case beyond a reasonable doubt. This remedy appears to be used less frequently than referrals to Appeals Courts by the Minister in cases of ministerial review. Most likely, this choice may be due to the fact that a new conviction is unlikely in many cases as a result of the amount of time passed since the original trial, the difficulty with witness memory and the degradation of physical evidence. What tends to result from orders for a new trial is that Attorneys General are reticent to reopen and retry these cases. Often, proceedings are stayed or charges are dropped, as was the case with David Milgaard. Another illustration is the case of Steven Kaminski. Kaminski served seven years in prison for the alleged sexual assault of a co-worker in 1992 and was labelled a dangerous offender. Following his conviction review, the Minister ordered a new trial, but the Alberta Attorney General declined to reprosecute the offence, due in part to the unreliability of the complainant.

Kaminski was later awarded $2.2 million in compensation (Harris, 2006). No inquiry has ensued in this case.

Criticisms

In practice, very few cases reach the point where they are assessed for ministerial review. Recent statistics reveal that over a two-year period, from April 2005 to March 2007, the CCRG received 57 applications, completed five investigations and made three decisions: one case was dismissed and two cases were referred to the Courts of Appeal (Campbell, 2009). Certainly, these low numbers do not represent the actual incidence of wrongful conviction in Canada. However, there are a number of reasons why this remedy is not relied on more frequently by those who believe they have been wrongly convicted. Long held criticisms of the ministerial review process centre around its lack of expediency, lack of accountability and costly nature (Campbell, 2008). Clearly, the process is lengthy and expensive and is only available once an individual has exhausted all other levels of appeal, which can take many years and at considerable costs. Moreover, the criteria for ascertaining whether or not a miscarriage of justice has occurred are rather vague. Recent guidelines (which emerged from W. Colin Thatcher's application for a review of his conviction (*R* v. *Thatcher*), which was dismissed by the Minister of Justice in 1994) have attempted to clarify the process. They establish that conviction review, in and of itself, is considered to be an extraordinary measure and, far from being a 'fourth' level of appeal, the Minister's role is not to substitute his or her decision for that of the judiciary or jury. Furthermore, these guidelines provide no new real information but attempt to codify existing practices, thus fundamentally defining the role of conviction review by the process of elimination.

In Canada, the Minister of Justice is also the Attorney General of Canada and the Chief Prosecutor. It would appear on the face of it that, by requiring the Justice Minister to oversee the conviction review process and make ultimate decisions to dismiss or allow applications, a conflict of interests is created (Braiden and Brockman, 1999). It seems contradictory to require a member of the executive branch of government to overrule the judiciary in those instances where a case is referred back to the Court of Appeal; this conflict may be a large reason as to why so few cases are actually reviewed. Rosen (1992: 15–16) believed there is a prosecutorial bias on the part of the Department of Justice, which is manifest in 'deference to judicial determinations of guilt and an insufficiently rigorous questioning of the foundations of criminal convictions'. As a result, it is quite possible that the CCRG and, by extension, the Minister of Justice and Courts of Appeal have a difficult time in disturbing or questioning the finality of criminal convictions emanating from the lower courts (Braiden and Brockman, 1994: 21; Kaiser, 1989: 133).

Future review

The concept of an independent review commission for Canada

The idea of an independent commission for Canada is not novel. It has already been noted that a number of investigations of high-profile wrongful convictions have triggered commissions of inquiry, and some of them have in turn addressed the importance of a more permanent review body. Thus, a recurrent response of the Canadian government to wrongful convictions has been to set up Royal Commissions or Commissions of Inquiry to examine what mistakes were made in individual cases. Since 1986, there have been six Commissions of Inquiry, examining the circumstances of the wrongful conviction of eight individuals in Canada (Donald Marshall Jr, Guy Paul Morin, Thomas Sophonow, James Driskell, Ronald Dalton, Randy Druken, Gregory Parsons and David Milgaard). Those which took up the issue of review processes will now be outlined.

In 1986, in the province of Nova Scotia, a Royal Commission was established to investigate the wrongful conviction of Donald Marshall Jr, a case involving racism, coercion of youthful witnesses and lack of police and Crown disclosure of evidence. Marshall was 17 years old when he was wrongly convicted of the murder of Sandy Seale in 1971 and served 11 years prior to his release on appeal. The subsequent Royal Commission had a wide ranging mandate to examine all aspects of the administration of criminal justice in this instance. One of its recommendations in 1989 was that the power of conviction review should not rest solely with the government but should be vested in an independent body. More specifically, the Inquiry advocated that:

> the provincial Attorney General commence discussions with the federal Minister of Justice and other provincial Attorneys General with a view to constituting an independent review mechanism – an individual or a body – to facilitate the reinvestigation of alleged cases of wrongful conviction ... that this review body have investigative power so it may have complete and full access to any and all documents and material required in any particular case, and that it have coercive power so witnesses can be compelled to provide information (Royal Commission on the Donald Marshall Jr. Prosecution 1989).

A second Commission of Inquiry, which took place in Ontario in 1998, studied the wrongful conviction of Guy Paul Morin, also advocated for the establishment of a similarly independent commission. Morin was initially acquitted of murdering nine-year-old Christine Jessop in 1985, but was later found guilty in 1992 and sentenced to life imprisonment. He was finally acquitted in 1995, due to DNA evidence that proved he could not have committed the crime. The Report of the Kaufman Commission on

Proceedings Involving Guy Paul Morin found that contaminated forensic scientific evidence helped to convict Morin, as well as unsubstantiated confession evidence from two jailhouse informants. Amongst its many cogent recommendations was one which called for the creation of a Criminal Case Review Board, requiring that the:

> government of Canada should study the advisability of the creation, by statute, of a criminal case review board to replace or supplement those powers currently exercised by the federal Minister of Justice pursuant to section 690 of the Criminal Code. (Kaufman, 1998: 1237)

Next, in 2001, a Commission of Inquiry (Cory, 2002) was established in Winnipeg, Manitoba to examine factors that had contributed to the wrongful conviction of Thomas Sophonow. Sophonow had undergone three trials, two appeals and had spent almost four years in prison for the murder of Barbara Stoppel in 1981. The Manitoba Court of Appeal had eventually acquitted him in 1985. Following his thorough review of the investigative and trial proceedings, former Supreme Court Justice Cory found much evidence pointing to unscrupulous Crown and police practices, as well as an over-reliance on jailhouse informants, which all had an impact on Sophonow's wrongful conviction. In his numerous recommendations, Justice Cory pointed to the need for an independent commission:

> I recommend that, in the future, there should be a completely independent entity established which can effectively, efficiently and quickly review cases in which wrongful conviction is alleged. In the United Kingdom, an excellent model exists for such an institution. I hope that steps are taken to consider the establishment of a similar institution in Canada. (Ibid.)

The final inquiry of relevance concerned James Driskell, who was wrongfully convicted for the murder of Perry Harder in 1991. Driskell was released on bail in 2003. In 2005, Minister of Justice and Attorney General of Canada, Irwin Cotler, quashed the conviction, stayed the charges and ordered a new trial for Driskell, but the Manitoba authorities decided not to proceed and instead established a public inquiry. In 2007, former Ontario Chief Justice Patrick LeSage, writing in his Report of the Commission of Inquiry into Certain Aspects of the Trial and Conviction of James Driskell, concurred with Justice Cory's recommendation for an independent commission. While enumerating the problems James Driskell had encountered in the post-conviction review process, Justice LeSage underscored the difficulties inherent to the 'adversarial nature of the present process'. His belief was that an independent commission would have to meet a lower threshold prior to commencing a review and that commissioners would have access to information through disclosure rules that may be more difficult for applicants to obtain.

These commissions have been very costly and often time-consuming, but they often provide appropriate direction for police and Crown Attorneys in order to prevent similar miscarriages of justice from occurring in the future. Unfortunately, their recommendations are not binding, and it is up to individual provinces to institute them at their discretion.

In 2002, some of the forgoing calls for the increased legitimacy and effectiveness of the conviction review process through the establishment of an independent commission were addressed in the most recent amendments to the Criminal Code, ss. 696.1–696.6. The Department of Justice, in response to increasing criticisms from lobby groups for the wrongly convicted and from the Canadian Bar Association, and following widespread consultations with provincial governments, rejected the idea of an independent commission and developed what they termed the 'Reform Model' (Department of Justice, 2003a). While this model was described as a 'compromise between a separate review body similar to the English model and the status quo [at that time] of s. 690 of the Criminal Code' (ibid.: 4), it is difficult to see how it differs significantly from the existing processes, aside from a few specific legislative changes. Essentially, the Minister of Justice continues to maintain the power to revisit convictions, but there are now guidelines as to when a person is eligible for review, as well as criteria for when a remedy can be granted and the inclusion of summary convictions in the types of convictions eligible for review. Under these amendments, the members of the CCRG and other agents investigating on behalf of the minister were granted the power to compel the production of documents and appearances of witnesses. Other non-legislative changes were also included to increase the appearance of distance from the Department of Justice, including moving the CCRG to a separate facility and the appointment of a special advisor to oversee the review process and advise the Minister. The current special advisor is Bernard Grenier, a retired Quebec provincial court judge. In enumerating why the UK model was not appropriate in this jurisdiction, it was stated that 'the Canadian experience with cases of wrongful convictions bears little resemblance to that of the United Kingdom' (Regulations Respecting Applications for Ministerial Review, 2002). While this statement may have been a tenable reference to the different prosecutorial systems in the two countries, any alleged differences in the causes, forms and consequences of miscarriages of justice appear rather less tenable, and the failure to construct a less Ministerial-based system remains inconsistent with the federal government's aim to increase 'transparency and accountability' around the process.

The CCRC as a model for Canada

The CCRC can be criticized in many aspects (Naughton, 2007b; Walker and Starmer, 1999b; Walker and McCartney, 2008). Nevertheless, given the many deficiencies of the current Canadian conviction review process, there are several advantages to be derived from an independent commission, along the lines of the CCRC.

First, separation from the Department of Justice would secure great symbolic significance to the public at large and to prisoners who depict themselves as victims of miscarriages of justice in particular. Outside of the offices of government, there seems to be support for the development of a commission that is truly independent. The constitutional independence of the CCRC is provided for in the Criminal Appeal Act 1995, s. 8(2), whereby it 'shall not be regarded as the servant or agent of the Crown or as enjoying any status, immunity or privilege of the Crown'. The government is not involved with the selection procedure, does not decide the ways in which the CCRC should do its work and, most crucially of all, is not involved in its decision-making role (cf. Scullion, 2004). At least one-third of the CCRC's membership must be legally qualified, and under s. 8(6) at least two-thirds 'shall be persons who appear to the Prime Minister to have knowledge or experience of any aspect of the criminal justice system'. However, there are criticisms that the current CCRC membership derives too heavily from prosecution interests and that it also largely reflects the white, male, middle-class background that is so often a feature of judicial institutions in the UK.

Of course, independence from the executive is not the whole picture for the CCRC, and there remain the limits imposed by the rules and practices of the appeal courts, which place restraints on what it may accomplish. In order to refer a case to the Court of Appeal (Criminal Division) (CACD) in England, Wales and Northern Ireland, the CCRC under s. 13(1) must 'consider that there is a real possibility that the conviction ... would not be upheld were a reference to be made'. This 'real possibility' can be realized through 'an argument, or evidence, not raised in the proceedings'. There is no longer a need to provide 'new evidence', as interpreted by the Home Office. Yet, the Act leaves much to be determined through the interpretations and also the receptivity of the CACD, which have to be second-guessed by the CCRC.

More radical solutions would have been to give the CCRC the power to determine applications or at least to make recommendations to the CACD either to acquit or to order a retrial, placing the onus on the judges to find reasons to disagree. In some respects, the Canadian system adopts the latter solution. While the two bodies (CCRG and CCRC) function similarly with respect to the steps involved in investigating claims of miscarriages of justice, the questions that the two commissions ultimately ask of the courts are manifestly different. In reviewing an applicant's file for conviction review, the Minister of Justice for Canada must consider whether a miscarriage of justice has 'likely occurred'. If decided affirmatively, then the applicant's case can either be referred back to the Court of Appeal or be sent to the Attorney General of that province for a new trial. While with both options the fate of the applicant rests with the courts, by ordering a new trial the Minister is effectively quashing the conviction and acquitting the applicant, and it is then up to the Attorney General to decide whether or not to reprosecute the offence.

For its part, the CCRC cannot quash a conviction but at best must consider if there is 'a real possibility that the conviction, verdict, finding or sentence would not be upheld were the reference to be made'. Many criticisms of the CCRC have centred around the fact that it must rely on the CACD and cannot decide cases on their own merit (Duff, 2001; Malleson, 1995; Nobles and Schiff, 2001). A Report by the Home Affairs Select Committee in 2004 expressed concern that out of cases processed by the CCRC up until 31 December 2003, only 4 per cent had been referred to an appropriate appeal court, with around half that number resulting in an overturned conviction (House of Commons Home Affairs Select Committee, 2004: q. 34). The Home Affairs Select Committee also echoes the suggestion that the CCRC is too dependent upon the CACD in determining the outcome of its reviews and in decisions to refer or reject cases (ibid.: q. 5 and q. 8). An earlier review likewise called for a relaxation in the CCRC's standards. The Select Committee (1999: paras. 26 and 44) had previously argued that the CCRC could take a changed approach to its investigation of cases in that it could 'prune the amount of detailed work done' with no loss of effectiveness, describing its investigative processes as 'highly technical and formulaic'.

However, there are problems with a more cursory review. The risks arise that less obvious grounds for referral will be overlooked so that cases are not referred or referred on weaker grounds than necessary, with no certainty that the necessary investigative work will be undertaken in time by defence lawyers, prosecutors or appellate judges. If the quality of preliminary investigation is reduced, honed down to a mechanical filtration and rejection process with eligibility thresholds being effectively increased, the CCRC will quickly become as discredited as the previous system (see Chapter 12). In the view of the CCRC itself, it might 'perpetuate the very miscarriages of justice that the Commission was set up to review' (CCRC, 2001: 26). There is also the danger of incurring the wrath of the CACD if a sizeable proportion of referrals fails. The CCRC Chairman, Professor Graham Zellick, has argued that the test is satisfactory and that the CCRC reaches its own conclusion on whether the conviction is 'unsafe' and without second-guessing the Court of Appeal (House of Commons Home Affairs Committee, 2006: q. 32). More directive powers for the CCRC, including the power to quash a verdict, could be seen as interfering too much with judicial independence and the finality of verdicts. Out of respect to victims, and also to ensure that justice is decided in public rather than in dossiers, there is still much to be said for returning the case to court.

Interim solutions to smooth the relationship between commissions and appeal courts seek to ensure that the appeal courts have sufficient resources to keep pace with the referring commission, understand and appreciate its role as a force for justice, and are prepared to interpret their judicial review powers in ways which do not negate its efforts. In reality, the picture is mixed. The leading case on the interpretation of s. 13 has been *R v. Criminal Cases Review Commission, ex parte Pearson* (para. 149) in which it was held that the meaning of 'real possibility' 'plainly denotes a contingency which in the Commission's judgment is more than an outside chance or a bare possibility but which may be less than a probability or likelihood or a racing certainty'. Those standards were applied both to the admission of fresh evidence (where relevant) and also to the assessment of the evidence by the CACD. The 'assessment' for these purposes means, ultimately, whether there would be an impact on a jury and not what the appeal judges themselves would conclude concerning the strength of the case. Whether this formula provides a sufficiently clear signal of society's determination to avoid miscarriages remains to be seen. It still leaves a lot of discretion – some defendants might be lucky to be heard by receptive judges, others might not.

Moving from powers to the resources necessary to secure them, whilst both the CCRC and the CCRG are plagued by fiscal restraints, the CCRC appears to have access to much greater resources. The CCRG's small office of six lawyers and one special advisor pales in comparison to the CCRC's eleven Commissioners and 43 Case Review Managers (CRMs), albeit that account must also be taken of divergent population size (Canada's being around half of the United Kingdom's), federal complexity and crime rates. Although apparently in a stronger position, financial restraints have affected the CCRC from time to time, including the present (CCRC, 2007a: 5). Nevertheless, the output of the CCRC far exceeds the CCRG. Since its inception in 1997, the CCRC has completed work on 8,951 applications of which 356 were referred to the CACD, a referral rate of 4 per cent. In turn, the appeal courts have determined 313 referrals, of which 187 have had their conviction quashed and 33 sentences have been varied, which translates into a 'success' rate of 70 per cent (ibid.: 19). In the previous five years up to the end of 2007, the CCRG has received 132 applications, and decisions were made in 15 cases. Of those cases, four were sent back to the Court of Appeal and in four cases a new trial was ordered. Unfortunately, the CCRG does not keep public records on the outcome of referrals to provincial appellate courts, so a truly comparable 'success rate' with the CCRC is not possible. It can be established that the actual number of applicants who achieve some sort of 'success' is rather low in both jurisdictions. However, the greater resources in the UK allow for a greater rate of throughput of cases and this inevitably results in more referrals and court interventions. Account would also have to be taken of the attitudes of appellate courts, though there is no starkly obvious difference in approach, and so one might argue that the abiding concern for finality in criminal justice and hostility to outside intervention is universal amongst senior judges (Nobles and Schiff, 2000).

So far, the comparisons have tended to show the CCRC in a more favourable light than the CCRG. However, the unified nature of the

CCRG – the fact that it applies throughout Canada – may be one aspect where the CCRC could be improved. In reality, there is more than one UK based CCRC, for account must also be taken of the separate Scottish Criminal Cases Review Commission (SCCRC) which was established in 1999 under the Criminal Procedure (Scotland) Act 1995, s. 194A-L.[1] It has eight Commissioners plus nine legal officers (SCCRC, 2008a). From 1 April 1999 until 31 March 2008, it concluded 939 applications, of which 75 were referred; 44 have been determined by the High Court, out of which 39 were 'successful'. It is arguable that valuable resources and time could be better spent on a unified United Kingdom Commission, which would better secure the dissemination of practices and experiences. Though Scotland has a distinct criminal process (as do some Canadian provinces), the differences should not be reflected in expensive offices and equipment or the reinvention of working systems, and the separation is explained by a pandering to historical symbolism, rather than a determination to combat miscarriages of justice.

Though an independent CCRC, modelled on the precedents from the UK, would be an improvement on the current arrangements for Canada, any reforms in Canada should seize the opportunity of a clean break and seek to improve on the CCRC in several respects. First, the body should take a more holistic view of miscarriages of justice. The concentration on individual post-appeal disputes is certainly valuable and arguably involves the most acute and intransigent problems in the criminal justice system (see Naughton, 2007b: 79–90). After all, the system has successively applied its best efforts to produce justice but has clearly not satisfied everyone. Yet, it is arguable that many policy lessons could be derived from an analysis of the thousands of cases which the CCRC has dealt with and the referrals made so far, in order to discern patterns and to give advice to criminal justice stakeholders. In this way, the CCRC could act as a form of criminal justice inspectorate. One example it has given is the repetition of applications where there is little corroborative evidence in sex-related convictions (CCRC, 2001: 25).

Next, it has stood on the sidelines of many recent important debates about miscarriages of justice. It was not involved in the joint working group of the Royal Colleges for Paediatricians and Pathologists, chaired by Helena Kennedy QC, which, responding to cases such as Sally Clark (see Batt, 2005) and Angela Cannings (see Cannings and Davies, 2006), recommended a national protocol to ensure that all sudden infant deaths in England and Wales were investigated thoroughly, quickly and consistently (The Royal College of Pathologists, 2004). The SCCRC was sidelined in debates about fingerprint standards in the light of the case of Shirley McKie (Scottish Parliament Justice 1 Committee, 2007). Again, controversy over the use of Low Template DNA Analysis was settled by a report from Professor Brian Caddy, who is a member of the SCCRC, but he did not see fit to discuss his brief report with either Commission and instead reported to the Home Office's Forensic

Regulator, a process reminiscent of pre-CCRC failings (Caddy, 2008). The only CCRC policy paper to be issued to date has been a response to the Home Office's now abandoned policy on 'quashing convictions' (CCRC, 2006b).

Finally, a more holistic approach should take account of the 'routine' and 'mundane' miscarriages of justice that are overturned through the normal appeals process, as well as the 'exceptional' miscarriages of justice that are dealt with by post-appeal bodies such as the CCRC, and should thereby seek to learn lessons from appeals within the system, as well as exceptional complaints and referrals after the system assumes that it has concluded (Naughton, 2007b: ch. 2). These wider views would also affect the modes of operation of the CCRC and would require closer working on the development of policy with lobby groups, the courts and prisons inspectorates, and Parliamentary select committees. In some respects, the Canadian penchant for commissions of inquiry does at least occasionally address these wider issues, and there is a danger that the permanent CCRC will deflect attention from systemic problems.

Conclusion

Neither the Canadian nor the UK model for revisiting convictions is ideal. Both have relatively low 'success' rates and neither has an exemplary track record for policy change to prevent future miscarriages of justice. The CCRG and CCRC both function to review convictions and to refer to other bodies for decision-making. Perhaps it is unreasonable to expect more of them, but, on that basis alone, the establishment of the CCRC has secured gains over executive-based review such as still applies in the CCRG, though the failure to resource it generously or to reform the CACD undermine its delivery.

Note

1. As amended by the Crime and Punishment (Scotland) Act 1997, s. 25.

15

A View from the United States

Robert Schehr

Introduction

In the US there is something of a palpable aversion to the consideration and adoption of the jurisprudential practices of our 'foreign friends'. Whether it is Canada to the north, Latin America to the south or our dear friends across the sea in the UK, the plain fact is, no matter how intelligently planned, decided and implemented, there simply seems to be no appetite for external influence. Perhaps we are missing an important culturally transmitted gene that allows for an open-minded assessment of the activities of transnational courts and legislatures as each pertain to advancing due process to correct and avoid error. It is, quite frankly, not something that we think much about. After all, jurisprudence in the US is exceptional – our Supreme Court justices have said so (Schehr, 2008). That American legal scholars and practitioners would prudishly ignore procedural and institutional innovations originating beyond domestic boundaries should come as little surprise to anyone who has studied twentieth and twenty-first century American jurisprudence.

Now to the questions that are the focal point of this chapter: are we in the US aware that the Criminal Cases Review Commission (CCRC) exists? And, has the CCRC had an influence on us, and if so, what has it been? I suppose it is those of us who toil in the trenches to repair unsafe verdicts and the lives devastated by wrongful convictions who are the most likely to be aware that the CCRC exists. But even among these select few I doubt very much whether they know anything more about the CCRC than that it exists. This should not be viewed as a lack of interest on the part of legal scholars and practitioners in the US but, rather, an indication of the pragmatic need to focus on their work, and a more prolific cultural and disciplinary aversion to institutional remedies sought in transnational jurisdictions (ibid.).

How is it that we in the US came to learn about the CCRC at all? It appears that the conversation about the activities of the CCRC and their possible adaptability for US purposes began at the start of the new millennium. Early in 2001, Peter Neufeld, one of the co-founders, along with Barry Scheck of

The Innocence Project in New York, cited the activities of the CCRC and the Canadian Royal Commissions as possible sources of inspiration in the US. The following year, Scheck and Neufeld (2002) co-authored an article in *Judicature*, wherein they recognized the potential benefit accruing from the creation of a CCRC-type body in the US, but for political reasons they decided to propose a divergent path to institutional review of domestic wrongful and unlawful conviction cases. It is important to note that the US has a long tradition of establishing investigatory commissions to deconstruct some of the nation's most compelling moments of historical crisis. For example, two years prior to publication of the *Judicature* article, the state of Illinois had already established its commission to study the death penalty.

It is also the case that many due process and investigation reforms have appeared without the presence of either federal or state investigatory commissions. The existence of innocence projects in 41 states, a national innocence network, a national innocence policy group and widely publicized exposure of exoneration cases has generated the momentum for changes in jurisdictions across the US. Thus, the US federalist system of state-based legislative and judicial independence, as well as a deeply ingrained suspicion of federal-level bureaucracy, serves as a cultural filter through which responses to any proposal for federal oversight must be interpreted.

This chapter has four objectives. First, to acknowledge the problem of wrongful conviction in the US and the many reforms taking place at both the federal and state levels to address the matter. Second, to discuss the long-standing US reliance on investigatory commissions as a way to counter executive and legislative authority. Third, to address the ways in which innocence commissions have been organized in many of the states in the US. Fourth, to propose a federal-level model of an innocence commission that is suited to the US tradition of investigatory commissions as information gathering and recommendation issuing, and where the guiding principle of *parrhesia* is predominant.

What is parrhesia, and what does it have to do with innocence commissions?

To speak freely, candidly and with a great degree of risk is to engage in a form of speech known as 'parrhesia'. Foucault (1984) has suggested that the origins of parrhesia can be found in Athenian culture, beginning around the fifth century BC and continuing until the fifth century AD. Why is parrhesia important? Parrhesia signifies both the spirit and procedural impetus for investigatory commissions. In a series of lectures delivered at the University of California at Berkeley, Foucault sought to explore the meaning and relevance of parrhesia as a crucial ingredient of democracy. According to him, the term is constituted by five criteria: (a) frankness; (b) truth; (c) danger; (d) criticism; and (e) duty. For a person to speak *frankly* through parrhesia means to avoid rhetoric. The parrhesiastes (the one practising parrhesia through speech) implores his or her interlocutor to know precisely what he or she means and believes. To speak *truthfully* through parrhesia was referred to by the Greeks as 'parrhesiazesthai', 'to tell the truth' (ibid.: 2). Unlike more contemporary epistemological notions of truth, the Greek parrhesiazesthai was believed to be in possession of the truth because he (and it was a he) was someone who was constituted by moral qualities that enabled him to both know the truth and be able to convey the truth. In short, 'what I say is true, because I know it is true. And I know it is true because it is true' (ibid.). The third component of parrhesia is *danger*. In order to be speaking parrhesia the parrhesiastes must be facing some kind of danger as a result of his or her truth telling. To the extent that one is directly confronting a powerful person with some kind of typically unwelcome truth, one is engaged in a state of parrhesia. Related to the experience of danger is the fact that parrhesia is a form of *criticism* that is focused at an interlocutor. The news delivered by the parrhesiastes to the interlocutor may include direct criticism of the interlocutor and his or her behaviour. This criticism is always delivered by a parrhesiastes who is of a status inferior to the interlocutor. That is, the parrhesiastes is typically power-less. Finally, to speak with parrhesia is to engage a *duty* to tell the truth. Even though he or she may face punishment for speaking frankly to those in power, he or she must do so.

Investigatory commissions created for the purpose of understanding systematic problems associated with criminal due process operate in ways consistent with parrhesiastic speech. According to Simon (2005: 1422), crime victims have emerged as exemplaries of parrhesiastes because they 'can destabilize political and legal authority'. I contend that wrongful-conviction exonerees are victims who possess the same righteous fortitude and moral imperative necessary to destabilize political and legal authority through their parrhesiastic speech. When combined with our Cartesian emphasis on empirically based fact claims, parrhesiastic speech situations, based on the five criteria established above, form the foundation for contemporary US innocence commissions, a point I will return to in the final part of this chapter.

The issue

It is by now no secret to scholars of transnational criminal law and procedure that the US lays claim to the highest number of actual innocence exonerations among states with adversarial justice systems. Innocence Network data suggests that since the mid-1990s there have been 217 DNA exonerations (The Innocence Project, 2008a). An analysis of national exoneration data in both DNA and non-DNA cases indicates that there have been 389 exonerations between 1989 and 2004 (Gross *et al.*, 2005). Through postmortem case review (primarily DNA), wrongful-conviction scholarship has identified six primary causes: police and prosecutorial misconduct; false eyewitness identification; false confessions; prison informant testimony; defective science; and inadequate indigent defence.

Despite the absence of a federal-level commission to review wrongful convictions, widely publicized exposure of exoneration cases has led to significant due process and crime scene investigation reforms at both the federal and state levels. For example, in 2004, the Congress of the United States passed the Justice For All Act. The Act grants any federal inmate the right to petition a federal court for DNA testing to support a claim of innocence, and it encourages states to adopt adequate measures to preserve evidence and make post-conviction DNA testing available to inmates seeking to prove their innocence. Other key provisions include helping states that have the death penalty to create effective systems for the appointment and performance of qualified counsel, together with better training and monitoring for both the defence and prosecution. It provides substantial funding to the states for increased reliance on DNA testing in new criminal investigations, increases the amount of compensation available to wrongfully convicted federal prisoners and expresses the sense of Congress that all wrongfully convicted persons should be reasonably compensated. Importantly, the law also requires states seeking funding under many of its provisions to certify the existence of governmental entities capable of conducting independent external investigations of state and local crime laboratories where there are serious allegations of misconduct or negligence (see The Innocence Project, 2008b). Nationally, as 2007 came to a close:

> 42 states had passed laws granting post-conviction DNA testing, 22 states had laws on the books regarding preservation of evidence, seven states and dozens of jurisdictions adopted better eyewitness identification procedures, nine states and 500 cities, towns or counties enacted policies to record interrogations, six states had statewide commissions to develop comprehensive reform to prevent wrongful convictions, and 22 states and the District of Columbia have laws to compensate the wrongly convicted. (Scheck and Neufeld, 2008: 10)

The policy arm of the Innocence Network tracked 200 bills in 39 states in 2007 alone, and testified in nine states. Among the reforms of most pressing interest here is the establishment of innocence commissions. Innocence commissions now exist in seven states: California, Connecticut, Illinois, North Carolina, Pennsylvania, Virginia and Wisconsin. In addition to these seven states, Arizona, Maryland, Massachusetts, Nevada, Texas and Mississippi have each established an oversight body to investigate specific aspects of their state's administration of justice. I will speak more specifically about US innocence commissions in the next section, but for now I wish to only mention them as a crucial component of the national innocence movement's efforts to ferret out the problems of wrongful convictions.

History of commission work in the US

Sometimes metaphor is the best way to convey an idea. I am particularly fond of the way Simon (2005) describes investigatory commissions. He refers to them as 'political stem cells'. What he means is that commissions appear in government agencies as a by-product of that agency's mission, but are used as a way to improve upon it. Commissions are generally created to address a problem by thoroughly investigating it. This has been the case since at least the sixteenth century when, in 1576, reference is made to the 'Commyssyon of Sewers' in Oxford, England (ibid.: 1427).

In the US, commissions have been a long-standing mechanism for problem solving and accountability. For example, in 1794 President George Washington established an investigatory commission to deconstruct the problems that gave rise to the Whiskey Rebellion, and to recommend punishment for those who participated in it. But, it was not until the late nineteenth and early twentieth centuries that investigatory commissions came in to wide use for understanding the mounting problems associated with industrialization (ibid.: 1419). It was also believed that commissions could serve as an independent check on bureaucratic authority. It appears that in this regard the US followed the lead of France, 'one of the first countries to recognize that legislative investigatory bodies could serve as essential checks on domestic political actors' (ibid.: 1429). In 1857, Congress passed a law making it illegal to refuse to provide information to either the House of Representatives or the Senate. In 1881, the United States Supreme Court argued in *Kilbourne* v. *Thompson* that it was legal for Congress to subpoena testimony from US citizens, but that 'investigations had to be in subject areas over which Congress had authority, their purpose had to be related to the passage of legislation, and they could not simply probe into the private affairs of citizens' (cited in *McGrain* v. *Daugherty*). These standards were eased in *re Chapman*, where the Court argued that Congress could probe any aspect of a witness's life and did not have to state clearly the purpose of its investigations.

Despite its popularity as a counterweight to government authority, investigatory commissions did not receive their full legal imprimatur until January of 1927 when the Supreme Court ruled on their constitutionality in the landmark case of *McGrain* v. *Daugherty*. The *McGrain* decision was the first to uphold the authority of Congress to establish investigatory commissions with full subpoena powers that would provide Congress with the authority to probe the lives of ordinary citizens. In addition, *McGrain* served as a legal precedent for compelling the appearance and testimony before the House UnAmerican Activities Commission of those who were suspected communists during the 1950s' 'Red Scare'. Over the past 40 years *McGrain* has been relied upon many times, including during the Watergate hearings (1973), the Iran-Contra hearings (1987), the Clinton impeachment hearings (1998) and the 9/11 investigations (2004). In addition, *McGrain* has been used as a check on claims of executive privilege through assertion of Congressional subpoena authority used to question presidential aides.

Investigatory commissions have existed at the state and federal level since the founding of the US. They have been viewed as a key counterweight to entrenched political power when it was considered important for the American people to understand events of political, economic and cultural significance. However, *there has been no such federal level commission established to investigate the known problems associated with wrongful and unlawful convictions.* Commissions have been established to assess police corruption and torture that sometimes led to wrongful and unlawful convictions (for example, the Wickersham Commission, 1929; the Knapp Commission, 1970; the Mollen Commission, 1992; the Christopher Commission, 1991; and the Chicago Goldston Commission, 2002), but there have been no federal commissions to investigate systematic due-process and investigation errors.

Lacking a federal-level systematic review process, actors in the states moved on their own to discern the nature of problems associated with exoneration cases. Over time, and with the creation of the national Innocence Network and the Innocence Policy Network, the insights generated as a result of case-specific analysis have been culled, analysed and distributed back to the states in the form of policy initiatives. Because of their mutually accepted finality, analyses typically concentrate on DNA exonerations. By adopting a case-method approach to deconstructing exoneration cases – working backwards from the exoneration to the commencement of case review – scholars are able to discern key moments in each case that led to faulty verdicts. With case-specific data in hand, the national network of innocence projects agreed to accumulate post-mortem case assessments in one location so that scholars, journalists and legislators could begin discerning patterns. Among the cases most frequently culled for analysis are the 217 DNA exonerations documented on The Innocence Project website (The Innocence Project, 2008a).

So, while recognition of the need for more systematic review of exoneration data was apparent to US scholars and practitioners, there were no institutionally created commissions to conduct such a review. However, Scheck and Neufeld (2002) commenced their missionary work to convince legislators and practitioners about the need to create an investigatory commission that focused solely on criminal due-process reform by evoking an institution that was known to virtually every American – the National Transportation and Safety Administration (NTSA).

The National Transportation and Safety Administration (NTSA)

In an interview with the Institute of International Studies at the University of California at Berkeley in 2001, Peter Neufeld laid out the basic argument in favour of a federal-level innocence commission (see Kreisler, 2001). Following a description of the wrongful conviction of California native, Herman

Atkins, which included faulty eyewitness testimony and defective science, Neufeld explained that in most other professions errors leading to erroneous outcomes, particularly those involving matters of life and safety, would lead to audits for determining the cause of the faulty conclusion. However, in the criminal justice system these errors, if they are identified, are typically swept under the rug and ignored. So, unlike in the medical profession where audits will take place to determine why errors that were committed led to the infliction of undue pain and suffering, in the justice system there will be no such inquisition to determine those factors that led to the wrongful incarceration, and sometimes death, of an actually innocent man or woman. It is in this interview that Neufeld raises the example of the NTSA.

In addition to investigatory commissions, the NTSA signified, at least for some in the US innocence community, a model that should be replicated with regard to investigation of due-process error. Among government agencies the NTSA enjoys significant freedom with regard to investigations of accidents involving air, rail, marine and car travel. In the paragraphs that follow, if the reader would substitute references to 'air, auto, rail, and marine accidents' with 'wrongful convictions', it will be clear how a federal-level commission established like the NTSA would capture the imagination of US legal scholars and practitioners.

Established as part of the Independent Safety Board Act of 1974, the NTSA responsibilities assigned to the National Transportation and Safety Board (NTSB) include:

1. Vigorous investigation of accidents.
2. Demands continuous review, appraisal, and assessment of the operating practices and regulations of all transportation agencies.
3. Calls for the making of conclusions and recommendations that may be critical of or adverse to any such agency or its officials.
4. Most important is the statute's emphasis on independent review. Specifically, no Federal agency can properly perform such functions unless it is totally separate and independent from any other department, bureau, commission, or agency of the United States. (United States Statutes At Large, 1976: 2166–7)

Among the many investigatory privileges granted to the NTSB it is its responsibility to initiate investigations of any air, car, rail, pipeline, marine and 'other accident which occurs in connection with the transportation of people or property which, in the judgment of the Board, is catastrophic, *involves problems of a recurring character*, or would otherwise carry out the policy of this title' (ibid.: 2168; my emphasis). The NTSB has the authority to charge the Secretary of Transportation with determining the 'facts, conditions, and circumstances' of accidents and will use subsequent reports to determine probable cause for further investigation, filing of charges and the like. Reports pertaining to accident investigations will be made public through publication in the Federal Register. Among the more appealing aspects of the NTSB's responsibilities is its mandate to issue periodic reports stipulating ways of avoiding the likelihood of a recurrence of transportation accidents and by 'proposing corrective steps to make the transportation of persons as safe and free from risk of injury as is possible' (ibid.: 2169). Related to this responsibility is the mandate to 'initiate and conduct special studies and special investigations on matters pertaining to safety in transportation; and assess and reassess techniques and methods of accident investigation and to publish recommended procedures' (ibid.). Finally, the NTSB has broad investigatory powers that include holding hearings; requiring testimony by subpoena; issuing oaths; entering any property upon disclosure of appropriate credentials and written notice of inspection; and inspecting any records, files, papers, processes, controls and facilities relevant to the accident in question. Failure to comply with NTSB subpoenas, orders or inspection notices will, upon District Court review, lead to contempt of court charges.

Scheck and Neufeld (2002) made direct reference to the NTSB as a model of investigatory review that should be adopted for assessment of due-process error leading to wrongful and unlawful convictions. They underscored the significance of an investigatory commission charged with post-mortem 'accident' reconstruction as a way to improve due process. Such a commission would be able to answer questions like: 'What went wrong? Was it system error or an individual's mistake? Was there any official misconduct? And, most important of all, what can be done to correct the problem and prevent it from happening again?' (ibid.: 98). Inspired by the NTSB's familiar mandate that has long served the nation's public interest, Scheck and Neufeld (ibid.: 99) argued for the creation of innocence commissions to 'investigate and monitor errors in the criminal justice system just as the NTSB investigates and monitors airplane and other major transportation accidents in the United States'. The purpose of innocence commissions would be to investigate immediately the causes of wrongful convictions regardless of whether exonerations were the result of DNA. Like the NTSB, innocence commissions should have subpoena authority, access to investigative resources and political independence (ibid.). While making reference to both the Canadian Royal Commissions, or Commissions of Inquiry, and the CCRC, Scheck and Neufeld (ibid.: 100) were clear about their disinclination to adopt either. Specifically, they proclaimed 'our reluctance to advocate this model arises from practical and political concerns. Proposals based on a CCRC model could be too easily, albeit unfairly, attacked as requiring large government bureaucracies based on un-American notions of an inquisitional justice system that would squander precious law enforcement funds on prisoners making frivolous claims'. I have articulated similar, but substantively different, concerns about adoption of a CCRC-type model in the US (Schehr, 2005; Schehr and Weathered, 2004).

US innocence commissions

Returning to Simon's (2005) reference to commissions being similar to political stem cells, innocence commissions in the US have emerged in various states and appear to be breeding new life and interest in their creation in still others. There are seven recognized innocence/justice commissions that have either commenced and concluded their operations (Arizona, Illinois and Virginia) or continue to operate in the US (California Commission on the Fair Administration of Justice; Connecticut Innocence Commission; North Carolina Actual Innocence Commission; Pennsylvania Innocence Commission; and Wisconsin Justice Commission). Additional states have convened commissions to assess the state's death penalty procedures (Maryland); have established a commission by statute that would provide for investigation of cases where claims of actual innocence are alleged (North Carolina); have investigated the efficacy of indigent defence (Nevada, Massachusetts); have evaluated the state's medical examiner's office (Mississippi); and have conducted an evaluation of criminal procedures leading to wrongful convictions (Texas). My discussion here will focus solely on the seven well-established commissions and their activities.

Typically, US innocence commissions have been established at the behest of powerful and uniquely situated men and women, often with some connection to state legislatures and the state's highest court of appeal, attorney general and law enforcement offices. Commissions have emerged, due in part to the exposure of exonerations occurring within respective states. While variations exist, successful commissions are typically constituted by members of the judiciary, law enforcement administration, state and local prosecutors, criminal defence attorneys, state legislators and crime victims. Each of the seven commissions listed above share two common characteristics. First, innocence commissions are principally charged with post-mortem exoneration-case deconstruction leading to identification of systematic errors occurring during case investigations and due-process violations. Second, each commission is charged with making recommendations for systematic reforms. So, unlike the CCRC, whose mandate is to evaluate miscarriage of justice claims on post-conviction review and make referrals to the appeal courts, US innocence commissions have been structured to operate like the NTSB, where their primary purpose is to investigate exoneration cases for determining what led to the wrongful and/or unlawful conviction and for making recommendations for improvements. With the exception of North Carolina's Innocence Inquiry Commission (NCIIC), however, US innocence commissions are not typically put in the service of post-conviction case review.

State-based innocence commissions have issued reports and made recommendations for changes to investigation strategies and due process to state legislatures concerning mistaken eyewitness identification, false confessions, evidence preservation, improved forensic analysis, the use of prison inform-ant testimony and enhanced indigent defence funding and training. In 2002, for instance, the state of North Carolina commenced a review of the state's criminal justice system with 'regard to the prevention and rectification of wrongful convictions' (NCIIC, 2008a). From those deliberations sprung three commissions: the North Carolina Actual Innocence Commission, the North Carolina Center on Actual Innocence (an innocence project) and the NCIIC. These three commissions have different mandates. For example, the North Carolina Actual Innocence Commission reviews post-conviction exoneration cases to determine their causes and make recommendations for reform. The Center on Actual Innocence is an innocence project charged with investi-gating post-conviction review cases of actual innocence. Finally, the NCIIC was established by state statute in 2006 and is 'charged with providing an independent and balanced truth-seeking forum for credible claims of actual innocence' (ibid.). The commission is comprised of members from the judi-ciary, law enforcement, the defence bar, prosecutors, victim's advocates and the public. Only claims that include both 'credible and verifiable' evidence of actual innocence, and that have not been raised during trial or on post-conviction appeal will be considered. To date, the NCIIC is reviewing 149 cases, has rejected 90, has three cases under investigation and one case remanded for a hearing. All told, the Commission has received 243 cases (NCIIC, 2008b).

It is possible that the NCIIC, with its mandate to review post-conviction cases to provide a balanced assessment of actual innocence claims, could generate additional stem cells across the US. Yet, the unit of analysis remains the administration of justice in the respective state. This is an important dis-tinction to make. Because most law in America is experienced locally, that is, within the states, it makes sense that state-based innocence commissions are the norm. What has been questionable is whether a federal-level inves-tigatory body would benefit the US. I have argued against this for many reasons and will only briefly mention them here (Schehr, 2005; Schehr and Weathered, 2004).

At the time of writing, the US has a population of 304,155,035, living in 3,141 counties, parishes and non-governmental geographic divisions. A 2004 Bureau of Justice Statistics assessment of criminal cases processed in just the month of May in the 75 largest counties in the US indicated that 57,497 felony cases were filed. Run out over the course of one year that amounts to 689,964 felony cases filed. The US is an enormous country covering 3.79 million square miles. While we have one Supreme Court, the United States is broken into 11 federal circuits, and the District of Columbia, that allow for the easing of the Supreme Court's caseload. By 2005, the 12 regional courts of appeal saw their caseload rise to an all-time high of 68,473 (United States Courts, 2005).

An accurate projection of the magnitude of cases that a federal-level innocence commission is likely to confront can be determined by assessing appellate caseloads by state. According to the National Center for State Courts, during 2005 (the most recent year for data reported) there were a total of 282,298 reported cases/petitions submitted to all US appellate courts (National Center for State Courts, 2008). Consider just seven states with regard to the sum of mandatory and discretionary petitions filed to both the state Court of Appeals and the state Supreme Court in 2005. In the state of California the sum was 30,891. In Florida, the sum was 28,680. In Texas, the sum was 20,025. The state of Ohio produced 14,120 petitions, Illinois generated 11,478 and Louisiana produced 10,465. The state of New York, which has two intermediate appellate courts, generated 16,531 petitions.

In his 2007 Year-End Report on the Federal Judiciary, Chief Justice of the United States Supreme Court, John Roberts, announced that the Court's caseload increased from 8,521 filings in 2005 to 8,857 filings in the 2006 term – a 4 per cent increase. During the 2006 term, '78 cases were argued and 74 were disposed of in 67 signed opinions, compared to 87 cases argued and 82 disposed of in 69 signed opinions in the 2005 term' (Roberts, 2007).

In short, there are simply too many cases for one federal-level innocence commission to review with the quality necessary to assess their merit. The cases that have moved to the point of appellate review in the state courts of appeal are not being thoroughly researched and evaluated for the efficacy of innocence claims. In fact, there is no free standing claim of actual innocence allowable in the US. Rather, the appellate courts review cases for instances of constitutional error.

In addition to what I believe are serious concerns with efficiency (something that I believe the CCRC is also struggling to address as it pertains to the increasing magnitude of case review), my more nuanced structural concern with regard to the implementation of a federal-level innocence commission is that it becomes a state strategic selection mechanism, an institution of bureaucratic crime control that would, for many reasons that I have argued elsewhere, serve to stifle the investigative efforts of state-based innocence projects (Schehr, 2005).

The future of investigatory innocence commissions in the US

There are two tiers to consider with regard to investigatory commission mandates – the federal level and the state level. At the federal level, what I believe would be beneficial is a statutorily created investigatory commission fashioned like the NTSB. Lets call this commission the National Safe Conviction Board (NSCB). The NSCB will manifest all the virtues of parrhesia in that it will be predicated on truth-seeking through creation of an institutional body that will create the framework for frankness, truth, danger (for those who testify), criticism (of criminal justice institutions, its practices and its staff) and duty (to the pursuit of justice). By privileging the voices of exonerees, the NSCB makes a commitment to institutional change because as parrhesiastes the exonerees have the ability to destabilize political and legal authority. They are victims of a kind of juridic malpractice that has subjected them to loss of liberty, unimaginably inhumane living conditions, loss of family and friends, loss of livelihood, loss of psycho-emotional stability and loss of human dignity. Much like those who are called to testify before Truth and Reconciliation Boards, their stories constitute the narrative deconstruction of institutional corruption, ineptitude and a callous disregard for human life. They are the speakers of truth who are saying what is true because they know it is true. They will speak out, as will those institutional actors who know problems exist, because they feel it is their duty to tell the truth. To induce structurally parrhesiastic speech, along with a commitment to empirical data collection and analysis, the NSCB will be mandated to perform the following tasks:

1. The NSCB will be mandated to carry out vigorous investigations of all exoneration cases across the US to determine precisely what went wrong.
2. It will demand continuous review, appraisal and assessment of the operating practices and regulations of all criminal justice agencies.
3. From its analysis of criminal justice agencies, the NSCB will draw conclusions and make recommendations that may be critical of or adverse to law enforcement, forensic analysts, prosecutors, judges, defence attorneys, juries and the like.
4. The NSCB will be an independent investigatory commission with full subpoena authority, the authority to hold hearings, issue oaths, freely investigate any records, files, papers, processes, controls and facilities relevant to the accident in question.
5. Basing its decision on the facts, conditions and circumstances of the wrongful and unlawful convictions it analyses, the NSCB has the authority to instigate further investigation and file charges.
6. The NSCB will be especially sensitive to problems of a recurring character, such as police and prosecutorial misconduct, false eyewitness identification, false confession, defective science, prison informant testimony and indigent defence.
7. It can, on its own, commission studies to assess and reassess techniques and methods of crime scene investigation and due process, and will publish recommended changes.
8. A federal commitment to rigorous investigation, analysis and recommendations for changes to crime scene investigation and due process will serve the US far better than a federal-level case investigation body.

Recall that American jurisprudence is based on a federalist emphasis on shared power between the federal government and the 50 states. And, while the application of the Fourteenth Amendment's due process guarantee to the states, as part of incorporation of the Bill of Rights into state law, has meant that there is quite a bit of overlap between federal and state law, American citizens experience the law locally within their respective municipal, county and state jurisdictions. Thus, any significant changes affecting crime scene investigation, evidence preservation and analysis, witness and suspect interviewing, informer procuring, and indigent defence must be focused on problem identification and analysis and recommendations for changes to, principally, the state-based administration of justice.

At the level of the state, North Carolina exemplifies the most promising holistic approach to the problem of wrongful and unlawful convictions. As previously discussed, North Carolina has statutorily created three separate commissions, each with a unique but overlapping mandate. The tripartite system involving two levels of case review to determine actual innocence (North Carolina Center on Actual Innocence and Innocence Inquiry Commission) and the North Carolina Actual Innocence Commission's commitment to post-mortem case review and recommendations for systemic changes signify a thoughtful local response to improving crime scene investigation and due process. In the schematic generated below, the Actual Innocence *Commission* would manifest the same characteristics as the NSCB described above. Actual Innocence *Projects* would continue to operate as they currently do in a relatively autonomous way to investigate cases of alleged actual innocence. I do not support statutorily mandated creation of innocence projects because they are often too limiting with regard to the kind of cases that can be investigated (typically DNA only). While operating an innocence project can be fiscally challenging, and procedural hurdles exist to limit some of what they are able to accomplish by way of case processing, their autonomy is an important aspect of their overall effectiveness. One way to balance the resource deprivation experienced by innocence projects, and to make certain that cases that otherwise may fall through the cracks but for a more thorough review with access to expert analyses of evidence, case investigators, and the like, is to formally establish an Innocence Inquiry Commission that serves to review cases where actual innocence has been alleged. The Commission members would be diverse and typically represent a broad spectrum of criminal justice officials, lay people and victims. Here, the status of 'victim' would include both crime victims and the wrongfully convicted. This kind of institutional response replicated across the 50 states in the US would no doubt generate considerable improvements in due process. The proposal would look something like this:

State Wrongful and Unlawful Conviction Review Schematic:

1. Actual Innocence Commission: post-mortem exoneration case reviews and systemic recommendations.

2. Actual Innocence Project: Innocence Project case investigation.
3. Innocence Inquiry Commission: actual innocence case review panel.

Conclusion

In this chapter I have attempted to demonstrate the problems facing the United States with regard to the prevalence of wrongful and unlawful conviction, and I have identified some of the federal- and state-level measures instituted to remedy the problem. I have argued that the US is positioned to approach the problem of wrongful and unlawful conviction through application of parrhesia, a different model than the one implemented by the CCRC. The history of US investigatory commissions and their role as significant institutional checks on political authority was discussed as the context for the larger discussion of US-based innocence commissions. While in the US there was limited awareness of the CCRC and its activities, US innocence activists, Barry Scheck and Peter Neufeld, turned to a more familiar American narrative to explicate the need for a federal-level wrongful and unlawful conviction review board. They introduced the idea of an oversight board based on the model of the NTSB. Having established the efficacy of the NTSB with regard to case investigation, I have spoken about state-based US innocence commissions and their purpose. I have argued that because of the federalist nature of jurisprudence in the US, a state-based model makes more sense. Finally, I have proposed a two-tiered model of institutional review: (1) a federal-level investigatory body modelled after the NTSB and called the NSCB; and (2) a state-based tripartite institutional model that operates at both the level of post-conviction case investigation and analysis, and at a state-based policy level, much like the federal NSCB.

Part V
Conclusion

16
Conclusion

Michael Naughton

The Royal Commission on Criminal Justice (RCCJ) (1993) and JUSTICE (1994) were in harmony about the key problem to be resolved and the characteristics of the new body to deal with alleged miscarriages of justice that was required to replace the discredited system under C3 Division of the Home Office:

1. It would understand miscarriages of justice in terms of the possible wrongful conviction of an innocent person.
2. It would conduct thorough investigations that sought to get to the bottom of allegations of miscarriages of justice, that is, it would seek the truth of claims of innocence.
3. It would be independent of both government and the courts.

Against this background, the following is a critical summary of the key findings of the Criminal Cases Review Commission's (CCRC) most significant deficiencies, gleaned from the forgoing chapters, and the conclusions that may be drawn. Finally, I will outline the sociological processes by which existing organizations come to be reformed and/or replaced, and by which the CCRC is likely to come to be reformed or replaced itself as more and more evidence of its failings is exposed.

Key findings and conclusions

The overwhelming finding to be drawn from this book is that the CCRC should not be regarded as corresponding in any way with the body that was recommended by the RCCJ, nor as tallying with JUSTICE's subsequent blueprint for the same recommended body. Put simply, despite the CCRC, the criminal justice system remains unable to guarantee that innocent victims of wrongful conviction will have their convictions referred back to the appeal courts and that the problem that was identified by the RCCJ and JUSTICE (1994) remains unresolved.

More specifically, the CCRC is not the appropriate body to deal with the possible wrongful conviction of the innocent for the following specific and interrelated reasons:

1. The CCRC does not work on miscarriages of justice as understood by the RCCJ and JUSTICE in terms of the wrongful conviction of the innocent, operating, instead, within a legal notion of a miscarriage of justice based on the correctness of criminal conviction in law (Chapters 2 and 3).
2. Virtually every chapter in this book has noted how the CCRC is curtailed by the requirement to refer only those cases where it is believed that there is 'a real possibility that the case will not be upheld' (Chapters 4, 7, 8 and 12).
3. This means that the CCRC does not act 'entirely' and 'completely independently' of the courts as it declares on its website and in its annual reports. On the contrary, the CCRC is always in the realm of trying to second-guess how the appeal courts may view referred cases (Chapter 1, 2 and 7). Moreover, the research by Maddocks and Tan (Chapter 9) shows that the CCRC not only fails to see that working under the criteria set by the appeal courts limits its much proclaimed independence and is contrary to the reason for its existence, it sees itself in a positive role as the 'gatekeeper' for the Court of Appeal (Criminal Division) (CACD), playing its part in the criminal justice process in this way.
4. As such, an appropriate way to describe the CCRC is as a 'legal watchdog' body, striving to ensure that convictions are correct in law, referring only those cases that are deemed to contain a possibility that the CACD will see the conviction as unsafe (Chapters 1 and 13). There is nothing wrong with this *per se*, but it is contrary to what the CCRC is widely thought to do and what was anticipated by the RCCJ and JUSTICE (1994).
5. The CCRC is further shackled to the appeal courts by the more limited powers of referral at its disposal than were permitted under the C3 system: whereas previously all referrals by the Home Secretary were received as first appeals, the CCRC has to bear in mind the decisions of the appeal courts in first appeals and cannot send cases back on the same grounds (Chapter 2). The result, as Malone (Chapter 8) has noted, is that the CCRC deals, in practice, not with fresh evidence as required by the CACD in first appeals, but with fresh, fresh evidence when thinking about whether a case should be referred back to the CACD for a second time, and fresh, fresh, fresh evidence if it is deciding whether it should refer a case for a second time, and so on. In consequence, although there is no limit in theory to the number of applications that alleged victims of miscarriages of justice can make to the CCRC, each application will be considered through a narrower lens with a diminishing chance of referral.
6. The CCRC's dependence on the criteria of the appeal courts has the knock-on effect that its reviews are mere safety checks on the lawfulness

or otherwise of criminal convictions, as opposed to the kind of in-depth inquisitorial investigations, that were presented by Green (Chapter 4) and Eady (Chapter 5) and called for by Sekar (Chapter 6), that seek the truth of claims of innocence by alleged victims of miscarriages of justice in the way that was expected by the RCCJ and previously conducted by JUSTICE. As a result, guilty offenders who fulfil the Real Possibility Test will have their cases sent back to the CACD, whilst cases may not be referred by the CCRC even when it turns up evidence that indicates an applicant's factual innocence – if it does not satisfy the test, for example, when the evidence was available at the original trial (Chapters 1 and 11). This further pitches the CCRC at perverse odds with what was proposed by the RCCJ and drafted by JUSTICE (1994).

7. The CCRC's restricted referral powers have also produced a patent lack of consistency between the tests of the CACD and the CCRC. This is aptly illustrated by practitioners Newby (Chapter 7) and Malone (Chapter 8) who note that cases abound where the CACD has quashed appeals 'in the interests of justice' and on a 'lurking doubt', for instance (see also Chapter 11). Yet, their experiences indicate that the CCRC would not consider even referring such cases to the CACD, opting instead to cite legal rulings in its Statements of Reasons that seem to justify not referring cases when they could just as easily cite legal authorities that would support referral. As a result, the cautious approach to referring cases back to the CACD that was identified as a key problem with the C3 system by the RCCJ and JUSTICE (1994) has been formalized in the statute that governs how the CCRC operates (Chapter 2): the CCRC is more cautious in its approach to possible miscarriages of justice than the CACD, which is presented as willing to find ways of overturning cases where appellants are believed to be innocent in the overall interests of justice.

8. By binding the CCRC to the criminal appeals system, then, we have transferred a political constitutional problem under C3 to a constitutional problem with the legal system, which cannot ensure that potentially innocent victims of wrongful conviction will have their cases referred back to the appeal courts, which was the reason for the public crisis of confidence that led to the setting up of the RCCJ and, subsequently, the CCRC in the first place.

9. The CCRC is not only dependent on the courts, it is dependent upon the government in terms of its funding, which determines all aspects of its work, and the proposed reductions to its funding will, inevitably, have adverse impacts upon its applicants (Chapter 3). Moreover, as Bird (Chapter 10) has emphasized, government in a wider sense is also implicated in the reduced ability of defence lawyers to provide the quality defence work required at the post-appeal stage of the CCRC, inasmuch as the funds provided are inadequate, which was seen as crucial by the

RCCJ and JUSTICE (1994) for assisting innocent victims to overturn their wrongful convictions (Chapter 9).

10. Although the primary object of this book is the limits of the CCRC that governs England, Wales and Northern Ireland, the two chapters on how allegations that innocent people have been wrongly convicted are dealt with in Canada (Chapter 14) and the US (Chapter 15) demonstrate the true extent of the loss of the concept of innocence in the UK, whether miscarriages of justice are dealt with by the CCRC or the SCCRC (Chapters 3 and 12). And, although a CCRC-style body was considered by Walker and Campbell (Chapter 14) as a potential way forward for Canada to resolve the existing constitutional problem with its own post-appeal procedures, which resemble the C3 method, the extent of the CCRC's deficiencies, also noted by Walker and Campbell, suggest that such a move would be folly. To be sure, sight must be retained of the central importance of the concept of the wrongful conviction of the innocent, as opposed to a legal notion of miscarriages of justice, and the important constitutional role that it plays in effecting changes to the criminal justice system to prevent and overturn them (Chapters 2 and 15; see also Naughton, 2007b: 26–36).

From the forgoing findings, it is not surprising that there is a general disillusionment among the contributors of this book who are engaged in trying to overturn the convictions of potentially innocent people about the CCRC's (lack of) ability to investigate and help to correct possible wrongful convictions of the innocent. In Part II, for instance, Green (Chapter 4), Eady, (Chapter 5) and Sekar (Chapter 6), who undertake voluntary sector investigations in the pursuit of the truth of claims of innocence, are disappointed by the CCRC for its evident unwillingness to accept the findings from investigations that point to the possibility that factually innocent people may have been wrongly convicted.

This frustration is shared by the leading criminal appeal practitioners in Part III, Newby (Chapter 7) and Malone (Chapter 8), who are at a loss to understand why, even from a legal perspective, the CCRC is not referring cases that they see as potentially meritorious. Bird (Chapter 10) echoed this frustration, noting the exodus of criminal appeal firms and individual practitioners willing to take on CCRC work due to a general disenchantment with the meagre remuneration available, which is seen as a message from those that hold the legal-aid purse strings of a lack of interest in the wrongful conviction of the innocent and commitment to correct them. Maddocks and Tan (Chapter 9) show that Commissioners and Case Review Managers (CRMs) at the CCRC not only do not see the relevance of working with applicant solicitors, they are often hostile towards them, seeing them as a hindrance.

Yet, the academic contributions by Nobles and Schiff (Chapter 11) and Kerrigan (Chapter 12) look at the CCRC from a different angle to account for why it operates against the expectations of the voluntary sector and practitioners, pointing out that it actually performs its tasks as it is mandated to by its governing statute – the Criminal Appeal Act 1995 – and that it would be failing its statutory duty if it did otherwise. This not only confirms the extent to which the CCRC is not able to deal with the problem of the wrongful conviction of the innocent, it shows just how far it is from the body that was recommended by the RCCJ and JUSTICE (1994).

In this context, it is apparent that there is still a need for a specific body to help alleged innocent victims of wrongful conviction that, unlike the CCRC, is not bound to the criteria of the appeal courts and is sufficiently resourced and empowered so that it is not dependent on government. Only then will such a body be able to function in the interests of justice as popularly understood and as was articulated by the RCCJ and JUSTICE (1994).

This is not the place to outline the precise details as to how such a body would operate; this requires a specific project of its own to determine, and possibly a further Royal Commission on the continuing failings of the appeals system, despite the setting up of the CCRC. However, it is obvious that a new body to deal with alleged innocent victims of wrongful conviction would be aided by a specific Act of Parliament that would serve as a beacon to show that the government takes seriously the inherent flaws of the criminal justice system, the perennial problem of the wrongful conviction of the innocent, and the restrictions to overturning wrongful convictions by the CCRC and the CACD that have been identified in this book.

From the aforementioned findings, however, another criminal appeal act to repair the existing system would not seem appropriate as it may, even inadvertently, bind any new body for assisting alleged innocent victims of wrongful conviction, who may be innocent, to the courts. Instead, I believe that we need an Innocence Act, similar to the US, so that, once and for all, alleged wrongful convictions – that show compelling evidence of innocence upon a full reinvestigation that is completely independent, even if it was available at trial but not used, and/or the jury have already heard it and decided against it, for example – can be guaranteed to be overturned (see Naughton, 2008c).

INUK and its member innocence projects have, effectively, resurrected JUSTICE's practical work with alleged innocent victims of wrongful conviction who may be innocent, purifying the concept of miscarriages of justice that had been contaminated by the process of legalification, when the CCRC was set up, by making clear the distinction from the wrongful conviction of the innocent. Drawing from the example of the focus on innocence in the US and Scheck and Neufeld's apparent decision not to entertain the CCRC route (Chapter 15), the INUK and its member innocence projects, likewise, present a possible model for any new body that may be established (Chapter 2).

Perhaps most significantly, though, a major conclusion to be drawn from this book is that until a new independent body is established, alleged wrongful conviction cases, where there is evidence of innocence but which are deemed legally inadmissible by the CCRC or the CACD, need to be directed away from the CCRC and towards the Secretary of State, to be considered for the Royal Prerogative of Mercy and a Free Pardon (Chapter 2). To be sure, prior to the CCRC, Free Pardons were not uncommon, with seven granted against criminal convictions over the period 1987–97 for a variety of offences, including theft, possession of a firearm, drug offences and a couple of assault offences. However, it is revealing that no Free Pardons have been granted since the establishment of the CCRC and the CCRC has not sought a Free Pardon for any of its 11,000 plus applicants to date.[1] This route needs to be reopened, especially by innocence projects that find evidence of innocence that does not meet the CCRC's Real Possibility Test. Applications to the Secretary of State for a Free Pardon will, also, serve to reinstate alleged wrongful convictions back into public discourse, further highlighting the inappropriateness of the CCRC in helping potentially innocent victims to overturn wrongful convictions.

Final thought

As a final thought, and picking up on the last point, it seems appropriate to note that organizations like the CCRC do not fall from the sky ready formed. On the contrary, they are the products of on-going historical processes that bring them to life as they are established to replace the failed organizations that went before them. For instance, just as the CCRC replaced C3 Division, as it became abundantly clear that it was not an adequate solution to assisting potentially innocent people to overturn their wrongful convictions, the Police Complaints Authority (PCA) was replaced by the Independent Police Complaints Commission (IPCC) in recognition of its failings (see Macpherson, 1999; Liberty, 2008).

In this process of transformation and transition from the existing to the new, critique of the limitations of the existing is vital: it is how the deficiencies of the existing are made known. To stay with the same comparators, just as the organization JUSTICE provided the blueprint for the CCRC in its report 'Remedying Miscarriages of Justice', closing its decades of calls for such a body (see JUSTICE, 1994),[2] it was the organization Liberty that was at the forefront of deploying criticisms on the PCA for almost 20 years and providing the overall design and scope for what would become the IPCC in the findings of its study 'An Independent Police Complaints Commission' (see Harrison and Cunneen, 2000).

Bodies like the CCRC and the IPCC, then, are not final solutions, and must, themselves, be subjected to a systematic and on-going critical interrogation to unearth their own flaws so that they, too, may be replaced with improved ways of dealing with the problems that they have been set up to address. However, when new bodies such as the CCRC and the IPCC are set up, there are often criticisms that they will not do what they are set up to do or what they claim they will be able to do. At the time, though, such condemnations are resisted by those speaking in support of such new bodies. This is especially so if like JUSTICE and Liberty in the examples being discussed, they contributed to, or fought so long and hard for the creation of the new body. In defence of new bodies it is argued that critiques that claim that they will fail are merely theoretical, speculative and/or unsubstantiated and that it is premature to write off the new body which must be given more time to prove itself before rushing to negative judgement about its inability to deal with the problem that it has been set up to address (see Naughton, 2007b: 95–114).

To be sure, the process to replace the existing with the new takes time whilst real cases that give evidence to the failings of the new body are exposed. As outlined in Chapter 2 above, an historical analysis of changes to the criminal justice system reveals a link between public awareness of real cases that exemplify the need for such changes to protect us from apparent injustices or mechanisms to address those injustices when they occur, i.e. evidence that real people are affected in harmful ways that the new body is believed to be able to protect against.

As this relates to the IPCC, a motion at Liberty's 2008 Annual General Meeting provides evidence that, despite the part that it played in replacing the failed PCA with the IPCC in 2004, it has already commenced its work that may eventually see its demise and replacement with another police complaints body:

> This AGM notes with great concern the failure of the IPCC to deliver an adequate service to complainants that is robust, impartial and fair, but instead has made decisions that are too often of poor quality. This AGM is therefore concerned that the IPCC is not fulfilling its general functions under section 10 of the Police Reform Act 2002 (PRA). Particularly in view of Liberty's historical support for the establishment of the IPCC and Part 2 of PRA, this AGM is gravely disappointed that the IPCC has failed to address the concerns of complainants via its Advisory Board and this AGM resolves that Liberty will draw those concerns to the attention of the IPCC and the Home Office, with a view to obtaining a formal independent review of the quality of IPCC decision making. (Liberty, 2008b: 3)

At the root of Liberty's apparent dissatisfaction with the operations of the IPCC are cases that give evidence to its weaknesses, in particular the fatal shooting of Jean Charles de Menezes by the Metropolitan police in July 2005 (see, for instance, Liberty, 2007a, 2007b).

As indicated above, the CCRC has been more difficult to penetrate with critiques of the inadequacies of its operations as its establishment encouraged an erosion of media interest in the wrongful conviction of the innocent in the widespread belief that the CCRC was the appropriate body to deal with them. This stemmed from what I have termed above as the legalification of miscarriages of justice (Chapter 2; see also Naughton, 2006), which blurred lay concerns with miscarriages of justice as understood by the wrongful conviction of the factually innocent with miscarriages of justice in the legal sense – a conflation of fact and law or legal technicalities. In consequence, alleged miscarriages of justice, understood as the wrongful conviction of the innocent, have been rendered largely invisible as the CCRC works on them away from public view.

Further exacerbating the problem, media reportage on the CCRC has increasingly moved away from analyses of the inherent deficiencies of the post-appeal system for alleged victims of miscarriages of justice (understood in the lay sense as potentially innocent victims) to reports of cases referred back to the CACD by the CCRC, or the part it played when such cases are overturned (Chapter 13), which gives the idea that the CCRC is dealing with alleged miscarriages of justice in an appropriate way and we no longer need to worry about them.

It is clear from this book, however, that the CCRC is not the solution to the wrongful conviction of the innocent, and that the problem that caused the public crisis of confidence in the criminal justice system that led to the RCCJ and the CCRC remains: the flaws of the criminal justice system mean that innocent people can be wrongly convicted and the system (still) does *not* contain the appropriate means of ensuring that wrongful convictions will be overturned when they occur.

In this light, the CCRC's ability to engender public confidence in its operations is thoroughly undermined. To be sure, the overwhelming conclusion to be drawn from the contributions of this book, whether they derive from the voluntary/campaigning sector, criminal practitioner or academic sphere, and whatever the particular political or ideological persuasion of the contributor, is that the CCRC is so deeply problematic that its perception as the hope for the innocent can no longer be sustained.

Notes

1. Thank you to Paul Jackson and Mary Boshell, Ministry of Justice, Miscarriages of Justice Unit, for providing these statistics in an email of 5 January 2009.
2. However, as demonstrated, the CCRC is not to be equated with what was proposed in JUSTICE's (1994) report.

References

Auld, Lord Justice (2001) 'A Review of the Criminal Courts of England and Wales by The Right Honourable Lord Justice Auld' <http://www.criminal-courts-review.org.uk> Accessed 4 November 2008.

Batt, J. (2005) *Stolen Innocence: The Sally Clark Story – A Mother's Fight for Justice* London: Ebury Press.

BBC News (1986) ' "Evil" Bamber Jailed for Family Murders', 28 October.

BBC News (1999) 'UK "Clear leads" to Dando's killer', 23 October.

BBC News (2000) ' "Concrete Coffin" Couple Released', 8 June.

BBC News (2002a) 'Medical Flaws Hit Barrymore Inquiry', 30 September.

BBC News (2002b) 'Sex Shop Murder Case Reopened', 31 October.

BBC News (2003) 'The Michael Stone Verdict', 6 January.

BBC News (2004) 'Man Re-convicted of Same Murder', 25 October.

BBC News (2006) ' "Adam Torso" Remains Are Buried', 12 December.

BBC News, (2007) 'Murder Conviction Doubts Raised', 11 April.

Bennetto, J. and Nunes, C. (2005) 'TV Campaigner Celebrates Eighth Victory out of Nine in Battle against Rough Justice' *The Independent*, 11 June.

Blommaert, J. (2005) *Discourse: A Critical Introduction*, Cambridge: Cambridge University Press.

Bowcott, O. (2003) 'Pair Win Appeal against Murder Conviction after 14 years in Jail' *The Guardian*, 18 June.

Boyle, R. (1999a) 'Spotlight Strathclyde: Police and Media Strategies' *Corporate Communications* 4(2): 93–7.

Boyle, R. (1999b) 'Spotlighting the Police: Changing UK Police-Media Relations in the 1990s' *International Journal of the Sociology of Law* 27: 229–50.

Braiden, P. and Brockman, J. (1999) 'Remedying Wrongful Conviction through Applications to the Minister of Justice under Section 690 of the Criminal Code' *Windsor Yearbook of Access to Justice* 17: 3–34.

Caddy, B. (2008) 'A Review of the Science of Low Template DNA Analysis' <http://police.homeoffice.gov.uk/news-and-publications/publication/operational-policing/ Review_of_Low_Template_DNA_1.pdf> Accessed 19 April 2008.

Callaghan, H. and Mulready, S. (1995) *Cruel Fate: One Man's Triumph over Injustice*, Amhurst: University of Massachusetts Press.

Campbell, K. M. (2008) 'The Fallibility of Justice in Canada: A Critical Examination of Conviction Review' in Kilias, M. and Huff, R. (2008) (eds) *Wrongful Conviction: International Perspectives on Miscarriages of Justice*, Philadelphia, PA: Temple University Press.

Campbell, K. M. (2009) *Miscarriages of Justice in Canada: Causes, Response and Prevention*, Toronto: University of Toronto Press.

Cannings, A. and Davies, M. L. (2006) *Against All Odds The Angela Cannings Story: A Mother's Fight to Prove her Innocence*, London: Time Warner Books.

Carroll, S. (2007) 'Man Jailed for Murder of Girl, 16, Wins Appeal', *The Guardian*, 31 August.

Carter, H. and Bowers, S. (2000) 'Verdict Quashed after 19 Years' *The Guardian*, 31 March.

Cathcart, B. (2004) 'The Strange Case of Adolf Beck', *The Independent*, 17 October.

CCRC (Criminal Cases Review Commission) (1998) 'Annual Report: 1997–98' Birmingham: Criminal Cases Review Commission: ISBN 1-84082-302-X.

CCRC (Criminal Cases Review Commission) (1999) 'Annual Report: 1998–99' <http://www.ccrc.gov.uk/CCRC_Uploads/report1998_1999.pdf> Accessed 12 November 2008.

CCRC (Criminal Cases Review Commission) (2000) 'Annual Report: 1999–2000' <http://www.ccrc.gov.uk/CCRC_Uploads/report1999_2000.pdf> Accessed 14 November 2008.

CCRC (Criminal Cases Review Commission) (2001) 'Fourth Annual Report: 2000–01' <http://www.ccrc.gov.uk/CCRC_Uploads/report2000_2001.pdf> Accessed 20 December 2008.

CCRC (Criminal Cases Review Commission) (2002) 'Annual Report: 2001–02' <http://www.ccrc.gov.uk/CCRC_Uploads/report2001_2002.pdf> Accessed 3 November 2008.

CCRC (Criminal Cases Review Commission) (2003) 'Annual Report: 2002–03' <http://www.ccrc.gov.uk/CCRC_Uploads/2003%20-%202004_AnnualReport.pdf> Accessed 3 November 2008.

CCRC (Criminal Cases Review Commission) (2004) 'Annual Report: 2003–04' <http://www.ccrc.gov.uk/CCRC_Uploads/report2003_2004.pdf> Accessed 14 November 2008.

CCRC (Criminal Cases Review Commission) (2005a) 'Annual Report: 2004–05' <http://www.ccrc.gov.uk/CCRC_Uploads/420165_CCRC_AR_V9lo.pdf> Accessed 6 November 2008.

CCRC (Criminal Cases Review Commission) (2005b) 'Murder Convictions of Michael Byrne, Malcolm Byrne and Victor Boreman Referred to the Court of Appeal' <http://www.ccrc.gov.uk/NewsArchive/news_384.htm> Accessed 30 December 2008.

CCRC (Criminal Cases Review Commission) (2006a) 'Annual Report: 2005–06' <http:// www.ccrc.gov.uk/CCRC_Uploads/Annual%20Report%202005%20-%202006.pdf> Accessed 6 November 2008.

CCRC (Criminal Cases Review Commission) (2006b) 'Quashing Convictions' <http://www.ccrc.gov.uk/CCRC_Uploads/QUASHING_CONVICTIONS_RESPONSE_FOR_WEBSITE.pdf> Accessed 15 April 2008.

CCRC (Criminal Cases Review Commission) (2007a) 'Annual Report: 2006–07' <http://www.ccrc.gov.uk/CCRC_Uploads/CCRC%20Annual%20Report%202006-07.pdf> Accessed 6 November 2008.

CCRC (Criminal Cases Review Commission) (2007b) 'News 20 June – Commission Refers Murder Conviction of Barry George to the Court of Appeal' <http://www.ccrc.gov.uk/NewsArchive/news_452.htm> Accessed 8 November 2008.

CCRC (Criminal Cases Review Commission) (2008a) 'Annual Report: 2007–08' <http://www.ccrc.gov.uk/CCRC_Uploads/Annual%20Report%202007%20-%202008.PDF> Accessed 6 November 2008.

CCRC (Criminal Cases Review Commission) (2008b) 'Our History' <http://www.ccrc.gov.uk/about/about_28.htm> Accessed 3 November 2008.

CCRC (Criminal Cases Review Commission) (2008c) 'Deciding the Outcome of your Case' <http://www.ccrc.gov.uk/canwe/canwe_34.htm> Accessed 4 November 2008.

CCRC (Criminal Cases Review Commission) (2008d) 'Can We Help' <http://www.ccrc.gov.uk/canwe.htm> Accessed 4 November 2008.

CCRC (Criminal Cases Review Commission) (2008e) 'Our Role (Overview)' <http://www.ccrc.gov.uk/about/about_27.htm> Accessed 15 December 2008.

CCRC (Criminal Cases Review Commission) (2008f) 'News' <http://www.ccrc.gov.uk/ NewsArchive/news_473.htm> Accessed 20 December 2008.

CCRC (Criminal Cases Review Commission) (2008g) 'About Us' <http://www.ccrc.gov. uk/about.htm> Accessed 24 June 2008.

CCRC (Criminal Cases Review Commission) (2008h) 'FAQ' <www.ccrc.gov.uk/about/ about_faq.asp#45> Accessed 10 November 2008.

CCRC (Criminal Cases Review Commission) (2008i) 'News and Press Releases' <http://www.ccrc.gov.uk/news.asp> Accessed 12 December 2008.

CCRC (Criminal Cases Review Commission) (2008j) 'Case Library' <http://www.ccrc. gov.uk/cases/case_44.htm> Accessed 24 June 2008.

CCRC (Criminal Cases Review Commission) (2008k) 'Notes for Legal Representatives provided by the Legal Service Commission' <http://www.ccrc.gov.uk/documents/ LegalRepresentation.pdf> Accessed 24 June 2008.

Cheston, P. (2000) 'Noye Stabbed his M25 Victim up to the Hilt' *London Evening Standard*, 6 April.

Chibnall, S. (1977) *Law and Order News: An Analysis of Crime Reporting in the British Press*, London: Tavistock Press.

Cohen, S. (1971) (ed.) *Images of Deviance*, Harmondsworth: Penguin.

Cohen, S. (1972) *Folk Devils and Moral Panics*, Harmondsworth: Penguin.

Cohen, S. and Young, J. (1973) (eds) *The Manufacture of News: Social Problems Deviance and Mass Media*, London: Constable.

Colvin, M. (1994) 'Miscarriages of Justice: The Appeal Process' in McConville, M. and Bridges, L. (eds) *Criminal Justice in Crisis*, Aldershot: Edward Elgar.

Conboy, M. (2006) *Tabloid Britain: Constructing A Community Through Language*, London: Routledge.

Conlon, G. (1990) *Proved Innocent*, London: Hamish Hamilton.

Cook T. (2007) 'The Wrong Side of Law' *The Guardian*, 21 February.

Cory, P. (2002) *The Inquiry Regarding Thomas Sophonow* <http://www.gov.mb.ca/justice/ publications/sophonow/toc.html> Accessed 15 April 2008.

CPS (Crown Prosecution Service) (2004) 'The Code for Crown Prosecutors' <http://www.cps.gov.uk/publications/docs/code2004english.pdf> Accessed 5 November 2008.

Crawford, F. (2000) 'The work of the Criminal Cases Review Commission' [oral evidence] House of Commons Select Committee on Home Affairs, HC 429, 11 April 2000, HMSO: London.

Department for Constitutional Affairs (2006a) 'Judicial Statistics: England and Wales for the year 2005' London: The Stationery Office: Cm 6799.

Department for Constitutional Affairs (2006b) 'Judicial Statistics (Revised): England and Wales for the year 2005' London: The Stationery Office: Cm 6903.

Department of Justice (1998) *Addressing Miscarriages of Justice: Reform Possibilities for Section 690 of the Criminal Code: A Consultation Paper* <http://canada.justice.gc.ca/en/ cons/amj/coverre.html> Accessed 15 April 2008.

Department of Justice (2003a) *Applications for Ministerial Review: Miscarriages of Justice, Annual Report* <http://canada.justice.gc.ca/eng/pi/ccr-rc/rep03-rap03/rep03-rap03.pdf> Accessed 17 April 2008.

Department of Justice (2003b) *Applying for a Conviction Review* Minister of Justice, Communication Branch, Department of Justice. Ottawa, Canada.

Department of Justice (2008) *Addressing Possible Miscarriages of Justice* <http://www. justice.gc.ca/eng/pi/ccr-rc/rep07-rap07/02.html> Accessed 15 April 2008.

Devlin, A. and Devlin, T. (1998) *Anybody's Nightmare* Norfolk: Taverner Publications.

Devlin, P. (1981) *The Judge*, Oxford: Oxford University Press.

Dijk, V. (1993) *Elite Discourse and Racism*, Newbury Park: Sage.

Dijk, T.van (1991) *Racism and the Press*, London: Routledge.

Dodd V. and Wintour P. (2007) 'No One Faces Charges in Cash for Honours Inquiry', *The Guardian*, 20 July.

Driscoll M. (1992) 'Queue Forming at the Appeal Court's Door', *The Sunday Times*, 17 May.

Duce, R. (1997) 'Murder Nightmare Ends after 25 Years', *The Times*, 4 December.

Duff P. (2001) 'Criminal Cases Review Commissions and "Deference" to the Courts: The Evaluation of Evidence and Evidentiary Rules', *Criminal Law Review* (May): 341–62.

Dyer, C. (1999) 'Appeal Quashes Murder Conviction' *The Guardian*, 11 December.

Dyer, C. (2005) 'Murder Cases may be Reopened after Criticism of Pathologist' *The Guardian*, 25 November.

Ede, R. and Shepherd, E. (2000) *Active Defence*, 2nd edn, London: Law Society.

Elks, L. (2008) *Righting Miscarriages of Justice? Ten years of the Criminal Cases Review Commission*, London: JUSTICE.

Ellis, P. (2007) 'Criminal Cases Review Commission' <http://www.peterellis.org.nz/MediaReleases/2007-0514_peterellis_CriminalCases.htm> Accessed 29 December 2008.

Ericson, R. (1994) 'The Royal Commission on Criminal Justice System Surveillance' in McConville, M and Bridges, L. (1994) (eds) *Criminal Justice in Crisis*, Aldershot: Edward Elgar.

Fairclough, N. (1992) *Discourse and Social Change*, Cambridge: Polity Press.

Fairclough, N. (1995) *Critical Discourse Analysis: The Critical Study of Language*, London: Longman.

Fisher, H. (1977) Report of an Inquiry by the Honourable Sir Henry Fisher into the Circumstances Leading to the Trial of Three Persons on Charges Arising out of the Death of Maxwell Confait and the Fire at 27 Doggett Road, London SE6, London: HMSO.

Foot, P. (1986) *Murder at the Farm: Who Killed Carl Bridgewater?* London: Sidgewick & Jackson.

Foucault, M. (1984) 'Discourse and Truth', Fearless Speech Lectures, University of California at Berkeley <http://foucault.info/documents/parrhesia/foucault.DT1.wordParrhesia.en.html> Accessed 4 November 2009.

Gibb A. (1997) 'Focus Groups' *Social Research Update* 19 (Winter 1997), University of Surrey.

Goudge, S. (2007) *Inquiry into Pediatric Forensic Pathology* <http://www.goudgeinquiry> Accessed 15 April 2008.

Goulden, B. (2008) 'Warehouse Fire Probe Cost Reaches Pounds 3.6m; BLAZE: Inquiry into Blaze which Claimed Four Lives Likely to Take another Six Months', *Coventry Evening Telegraph*, 23 April.

Green, A. (1997) 'How the Criminal Justice System Knows' *Social and Legal Studies* 6(1): 5–22.

Green, A. (2006) 'Joint Memorandum Submitted by United Against Injustice, Innocence Network UK and INNOCENT to Select Committee on Home Affairs' [written evidence] 4 September, London: HMSO.

Green, A. (2008) *Power, Resistance, Knowledge*, Sheffield: Midwinter and Oliphant.

Gross, S., Jacoby, K., Matheson, D., Montgomery, N. and Patil, S. (2005) 'Exonerations in the United States 1989 through 2003' *Journal of Criminal Law and Criminology* 95(2): 523–60.

Hall, S., Critcher, C., Jefferson, C., Clarke, T., and Roberts, B. (1978) *Policing the Crisis: Mugging, the State and Law and Order*, London: Macmillan.

Hancock, R. (1963) *Ruth Ellis: The Last Woman to be Hanged*, London: Weidenfeld & Nicolson.

Harris, K. (2006) 'Innocent Albertan Got $2.2M Payout' *Calgary Sun*, 4 October <http://www.injusticebusters.com/2003/Kaminski_Steven.htm> Accessed 15 April 2008.

Harrison, J. and Cunneen, M. (2000) 'An Independent Police Complaints Commission' London: Liberty <http://www.liberty-human-rights.org.uk/publications/6-reports/police.pdf> Accessed 23 December 2008.

Hattenstone, S. (2004) 'My Beloved Dad, the Train Robber, Part II' *The Guardian*, 17 January.

Hill, P. J. and Hunt, G. (1995) *Forever Lost, Forever Gone*, London: Bloomsbury.

Hill, P., Young, M. and Sargant, T. (1985) *More Rough Justice*, Harmondsworth: Penguin.

Home Office Research Development Statistics (2004) 'Crime Statistics: England and Wales 2003' <http://www.homeoffice.gov.uk/rds/crimstats03.html> Accessed 7 November 2008.

House of Commons (Hansard) (2008) 'Written Answers', 25 April <www.publications.parliamentuk/pa/cm200708/cmhansrd/cm080425/text/80425w0013.htm> Accessed 20 December 2008.

House of Commons Home Affairs Committee (1998) 'The Work of the Criminal Cases Review Commission' (1998–99 HC 106).

House of Commons Home Affairs Committee (2006) 'The Criminal Cases Review Commission' (2005–06 HC 1635-i).

House of Commons Home Affairs Select Committee (2004) 'The Work of the Criminal Cases Review Commission' (2003–04 HC 289-i).

House of Commons Select Committee on Home Affairs (1999) 'First Report: The Work of the Criminal Cases Review Commission', HC 106, published on 23 March 1999, London: HMSO.

Howie, M. (2006) 'Miscarriage of Justice Inquiries Soar' *The Scotsman*, 4 July <http://news.scotsman.com/miscarriagesofjustice/Miscarriage-of-justice-inquiries-soar.2789390.jp> Accessed 24 December 2008.

Innocence Project, The (2008a) 'Facts on Post-Conviction DNA Exonerations' [Online] <http://www.innocenceproject.org> Accessed May 29 2008.

Innocence Project, The (2008b) 'Reforms by State' [Online] <http://www.innocenceproject.org/news/LawView.php> Accessed May 7 2008.

INQUEST (1997) 'Death in Police Custody Report on the Death of Ibrahima Sey 1997' London: INQUEST.

INUK (Innocence Network UK) (2008a) 'The 10th Anniversary of the CCRC' Inaugural Innocence Network UK Symposium, 31 March 2007 <http://www.innocencenetwork. org.uk/events_past.htm> Accessed 22 December 2008.

INUK (Innocence Network UK) (2008b) <http://www.innocencenetwork.org.uk/membership.htm> Accessed 20 December 2008.

INUK (Innocence Network UK) (2008c) <http://www.innocencenetwork.org.uk> Accessed 18 December 2008.

James, E. (2003) *A Life Inside: A Prisoner's Notebook*, London: Atlantic Books.

Jessel, D. (1994) *Trial and Error*, London: Headline.

Jewkes, Y. (2003) *Media and Crime*, London: Sage.

Johnson, B. and Cross, M. (2005) 'Technology to the Rescue' *The Guardian*, 14 July.

JUSTICE (1989) *Miscarriages of Justice*, London: JUSTICE.

JUSTICE (1994) *Remedying Miscarriages of Justice*, London: JUSTICE.

JUSTICE (2008a) 'Miscarriages of Justice' <http://www.justice.org.uk/ourwork/criminaljustice/index.html> Accessed 17 December 2008.

JUSTICE (2008b) 'JUSTICE Telephone Voice Message on 020 7329 5100 – Option 4' Called on 18 December 2008.

Kaiser, P. (1989) 'Wrongful Conviction and Imprisonment: Towards an End to the Compensatory Obstacle Course' *Windsor Yearbook of Access to Justice* 9: 96–153.

Kaufman, F. (1998) Commission on Proceedings Involving Guy Paul Morin <http://www.attorneygeneral.jus.gov.on.ca/english/about/pubs/morin> Accessed 15 April 2008.

Kaufman, F. (2004) 'Report to the Minister of Justice' <http://canada.justice.gc.ca/eng/pi/ccr-rc/sec690-art690/exec.html> Accessed 15 April 2008.

Kee, R. (1986) *Trial and Error: The Maguires, the Guildford Pub Bombings and British Justice*, London: Hamish Hamilton.

Kelbie, P. (2001) ' "Ice-cream War" Case Murderers Freed by Court' *The Independent*, 12 December.

Kennedy, L. (2002) *Thirty-Six Murders & Two Immoral Earnings*, London: Profile Books.

Keogh, A. (2008) 'Abuse of Process' <http://www.wikicrimeline.co.uk/index.php?title=Abuse_of_process_page_4> Accessed 3 January 2009.

Kerrigan, K. (2006) 'Miscarriage of Justice in the Magistrates Court – The Forgotten Power of the Criminal Cases Review Commission', *Criminal Law Review* (February): 124–39.

Kershaw, C., Chivite-Matthews, N., Thomas, C., and Aust, R. (2001) *The 2001 British Crime Survey*, London: HMSO.

Kreisler, H. (2001) 'A Passion for Justice: Conversation with Peter Neufeld' 27 April <http://globetrotter.berkeley.edu/people/Neufeld/neufeld-con5.html> Accessed 21 December 2008.

Kyle D. (2003) 'Correcting Miscarriages of Justice: The Role of the Criminal Cases Review Commission' *Drake Law Review* 52: 657–76.

Lahiri, S. (2000) 'Uncovering Britain's South Asian past: the case of George Edalji' *Violence and Abuse*, 6(1), January.

Leigh L. (2000) 'Correcting Miscarriages of Justice: The Role of the Criminal Cases Review Commission' The Bower Lecture, 28 September 1999, *Alberta Law Review* 38(2): 365–77.

Leigh, L. H. (2006) 'Lurking Doubt and the Safety of Convictions', *Criminal Law Review* (September): 809–16.

Leishman, F. and Mason, P. (2003) *Policing and the Media: Facts, Fictions and Factions* Cullompton: Willan Publishing.

LeSage, P. (2007) *Report of the Commission of Inquiry into Certain Aspects of the Trial and Conviction of James Driskell* <http://www.driskellinquiry.ca> Accessed 15 April 2008.

Lewis, G. (2004) 'Counting the Cost of Injustice' *Wales on Sunday*, 19 September.

Lewis, P. (2006) 'Flawed Evidence Clears Three of Murder' *The Guardian*, 20 June.

LexisNexis (2008) 'Nexis' <http://w3.nexis.com/new> Accessed 12 December 2008.

Liberty (2007a) 'Liberty Accuses IPCC of "Delaying Justice" with Belated Stockwell Shooting Report' <http://www.liberty-human-rights.org.uk/news-and-events/1-press-releases/2007/ipcc-stockwell-shooting-report.shtml> Accessed 24 December 2008.

Liberty (2007b) 'Liberty Responds to Independent Police Complaints Commission Announcement on Stockwell Shooting Investigation' <http://www.liberty-human-rights.org.uk/news-and-events/1-press-releases/2007/stockwell-response.shtml> Accessed 24 December 2008.

Liberty (2008a) 'The Police' <http://www.yourrights.org.uk/yourrights/how-to-enforce-your-rights/the-police/index.html> Accessed 24 December 2008.

Liberty (2008b) Annual General Meeting 2008', 7 June 2008 at City University <http://www.liberty-human-rights.org.uk/news-and-events/2-agm/report-on-the-2008-agm.pdf> Accessed 5 December 2008.

LSC (Legal Services Commission) (2008) 'Criminal Defence Service' <http://www.legalservices.gov.uk/criminal/crime_contracts.asp> Accessed 11 June 2008.

Macpherson, W. (1999) The Stephen Lawrence Inquiry: Report of an Inquiry by Sir William Macpherson of Cluny, Presented to Parliament by the Secretary of State for the Home Department by Command of Her Majesty, February 1999: Cm 4262-I.

Maguire, A. (1994) *Miscarriage of Justice*, Niwot, CO: Roberts Rinehart Publishers.

Malleson, K. (1995) 'The Criminal Cases Review Commission: How will it work?' *Criminal Law Review* 16(2): 929–37.

Mason, P. (2003) (ed.) *Criminal Visions: Media Representations of Crime and Justice*, Cullompton: Willan Publishing.

Mason, P. (2006) (ed.) *Captured by the Media: Prison Discourse in Media Culture*, Cullompton: Willan Publishing.

Mason, P. (2007) 'Misinformation, Myth and Distortion: How the Press Construct Imprisonment in Britain' *Journalism Studies* 8(3): 481–96.

Mason, P. (2008) 'Crime, Media and the State' in Sim, J., Tombs, S. and Whyte, D. (eds) *State, Power, Crime: Critical Readings in Criminology*, London: Sage.

Mawby, R. C. (2002) *Policing Images: Policing, Communication and Legitimacy*, Cullompton: Willan Publishing.

May J. (1990) 'Report of the Inquiry into the Circumstances Surrounding the Convictions Arising out of the Bomb Attacks in Guildford and Woolwich in 1974' HC 556, 1989–90, London: HMSO.

May J. (1992) 'Second Report on the Maguire Case' HC 296, 1992–93, London: HMSO.

May J. (1994) 'Report of the Inquiry into the Circumstances Surrounding the Convictions Arising out of the Bomb Attacks in Guildford and Woolwich in 1974, Final Report' HC 449, 1993–94, London: HMSO.

McCallum, E. P. (2004) *Commission of Inquiry into the Wrongful Conviction of David Milgaard* <http://www.milgaardinquiry.ca> Accessed 15 April 2008.

McCartney, C., Quirk, H., Roberts, S. and Walker, C. (2008) 'Weighed in the Balance' *Guardian Unlimited*, 29 November <http://www.guardian.co.uk/commentisfree/2008/nov/29/ukcrime-prisonsandprobation> Accessed 22 December 2008.

McConville M. and Hodgson J. (1993) 'Custodial Legal Advice and the Right to Silence' *Royal Commission on Criminal Justice Research Study* 16, London: HMSO.

McConville, M., Hodgson, J., Bridges, L. and Pavlovic, A. (1994) *Standing Accused: The Organisation and Practices of Criminal Defence Lawyers in Britain*, Oxford: Oxford University Press.

McConville, M., Sanders, A., Leng R. (1991) *The Case for Prosecution*, Routledge: London.

McCue A. (2005) 'Online Child Porn Investigation Costs Police £15m', 7 March <http://management.silicon.com/government/0,39024677,39128445,00.htm> Accessed 20 December 2008.

Miller, D. and Williams, K. (1998) 'Sourcing AIDS News' in Miller, D., Kitzinger, J., Williams, K. and Beharrell, P. (eds) *The Circuit of Mass Communication*, Glasgow: Glasgow Media Group.

Mullin, C. (1986) *Error Of Judgement: The Truth About The Birmingham Bombs*, London: Chatto & Windus Ltd.

National Center for State Courts (2008) 'Caseload Tables' <http://www.ncsconline.org/d_research/CSP/2006_files/StateCourtCaseloadTables-AppellateCourts.pdf> Accessed 22 December 2008.

Naughton, M. (2001) 'Wrongful Convictions: Towards a Zemiological Analysis of the Tradition of Criminal Justice System Reform' *Radical Statistics* 76: 50–65.

Naughton, M. (2003) 'How Big is the "Iceberg?": A Zemiological Approach to Quantifying Miscarriages of Justice' *Radical Statistics* 81: 5–17.

Naughton, M. (2005a) 'Why the Failure of the Prison Service and the Parole Board to Acknowledge Wrongful Imprisonment is Untenable' *The Howard Journal of Criminal Justice* 44(1): 1–11.

Naughton, M. (2005b) 'Redefining Miscarriages of Justice: A Revived Human Rights Approach to Unearth Subjugated Discourses of Wrongful Criminal Conviction' *British Journal of Criminology* 45(2): 165–82.

Naughton, M. (2006) 'Wrongful Convictions and Innocence Projects in the UK: Help, Hope and Education' *Web Journal of Current Legal Issues*, 3 <http://webjcli.ncl.ac.uk/2006/issue3/naughton3.html> Accessed 5 December 2008.

Naughton, M. (2007a) 'Confronting an Uncomfortable Truth: Not all Alleged Victims of False Accusations will be Innocent!', *FACTion* 3(10): 8–12.

Naughton, M. (2007b) *Rethinking Miscarriages of Justice: Beyond the Tip of the Iceberg*, Basingstoke: Palgrave Macmillan.

Naughton, M. (2008a) 'Factual Innocence versus Legal Guilt: The Need for a New Pair of Spectacles to View the Problem of Prisoners Maintaining Innocence' *Prison Service Journal*, May: 32–7.

Naughton, M. (2008b) 'Wrongful Convictions: How the Birmingham Six could Still be in Jail Today' *The Independent*, 13 October <http://www.independent.co.uk/opinion/letters/letters-wrongful-convictions-959403.html> Accessed 23 December 2008.

Naughton, M. (2008c) 'Justice Must Be Seen to be Done' *The Guardian*, 20 November <http://www.guardian.co.uk/commentisfree/2008/nov/20/justice-law> Accessed 24 December 2008.

Naylor, B. (2001) 'Reporting Violence in the British Print Media: Gendered Stories' *The Howard Journal of Criminal Justice* 40(2): 180–94.

Naylor, L. (2004) *Judge for Yourself How Many Are Innocent*, London: Roots Books.

NCCRC (Norwegian Criminal Cases Review Commission) (2008) 'Introduction' <http://www.gjenopptakelse.no/index.php?id=31> Accessed 29 December 2008.

NCIIC (North Carolina Innocence Inquiry Commission) (2008a) 'About us' <http://www.innocencecommission-nc.gov/ABOUTUS.htm> Accessed 23 December 2008.

NCIIC (North Carolina Innocence Inquiry Commission) (2008b) 'Statistics' <http://www.innocencecommission-nc.gov/statistics.htm> Accessed 23 December 2008.

Nobles, R. and Schiff, D. (2000) *Understanding Miscarriages of Justice: Law, the Media, and the Inevitability of Crisis*, Oxford: Oxford University Press.

Nobles, R. and Schiff, D. (2001) 'The Criminal Cases Review Commission: Reporting Success?' *Modern Law Review* 64: 280–99.

Nobles, R. and Schiff, D. (2002) 'The Right to Appeal and Workable Systems of Justice', *Modern Law Review* 65(5): 676–701.

Nobles, R. and Schiff, D. (2005) 'The Criminal Cases Review Commission: Establishing a Workable Relationship with the Court of Appeal', *Criminal Law Review* (March): 173–89.

Nobles, R. and Schiff, D. (2008) 'Absurd Asymmetry – A Comment on *R* v. *Cottrell and Fletcher* and BM, KK and DP (Petitioners) v. Scottish Criminal Cases Review Commission', *Modern Law Review* 71(3): 464–72.

Office for Criminal Justice Reform (2007) 'Quashing Convictions: A Report by the Lord Chancellor, the Home Secretary and the Attorney General', London: HMSO.

Pattenden R. (1996) *English Criminal Appeals: 1844–1994*, Oxford: Clarendon Press.

Price, C. (1985) 'Confession Evidence, the Police and Criminal Evidence Act and the Confait Case' in Baxter, J. and Koffman, L. (1985) (eds) *Police: The Constitution and the Community: A Collection of Original Essays on Issues Raised by The Police and Criminal Evidence Act 1984*, Abingdon: Professional Books.

Price, C. and Caplan, J. (1976) *The Confait Confessions*, London: Marion Boyars.

RCCJ (Royal Commission on Criminal Justice) (1993) 'Report', London: HMSO.

RCCP (Royal Commission on Criminal Procedure) (1981) 'Report', (Cmnd 8092), London: HMSO.

Regulations Respecting Applications for Ministerial Review – Miscarriages of Justice (2002) Can. Gaz. 136, part. 1, no. 39. <http://dsp-psd.pwgsc.gc.ca/Collection-R/LoPBdP/BP/bp285-e.htm> Accessed 15 April 2008.

Reiner, R. (2007) 'Media-Made Criminality: The Representation of Crime in the Mass Media' in Reiner, R., Maguire, M. and Morgan, R. (2007) (eds) *The Oxford Handbook of Criminology*, Oxford: Oxford University Press.

Reiner, R., Livingstone, S., and Allen, J. (2003) 'From Law and Order to Lynch Mobs: Crime News Since the Second World War' in Mason, P. (2003) (ed.) *Criminal Visions: Media Representations of Crime and Justice*, Cullompton: Willan Publishing.

Reisigl, M. and Wodak, R. (2001) *Discourse and Discrimination: Rhetorics of Racism and Anti-Semitism*, London: Routledge.

Richardson, J. E. (2007) *Analysing Newspapers: An Approach from Critical Discourse Analysis*, Basingstoke: Palgrave Macmillan.

Roberts, J. (2007) '2007 Year-End Report on the Federal Judiciary' <http://www.supremecourtus.gov/publicinfo/year-end/2007year-endreport.pdf> Accessed 22 December 2008.

Roberts, M. (2001) 'Just Noise? Newspaper Reporting and Fear of Crime' *Criminal Justice Matters* 43: 10–11.

Roberts, S. and Malleson, K. (2002) 'Streamlining and Clarifying the Appellate Process', *Criminal Law Review* (April): 272–82.

Rose D. (1996) *In the Name of the Law*, London: Vintage.

✱ Rose, J., Panter, S. and Wilkinson, T (1997) *Innocents: How Justice Failed Stefan Kiszko and Lesley Molseed*, London: Fourth Estate.

Rosen, P. (1992) 'Wrongful Convictions in the Criminal Justice System' Ottawa: Library of Parliament, Background Paper-285E.

Royal College of Pathologists and The Royal College of Paediatrics and Child Health [Report of a working group] 'Sudden Unexpected Death in Infancy' (2004) <http://www.rcpath.org/index.asp?PageID=455> Accessed 15 April 2008.

Royal Commission on the Donald Marshall Jr. Prosecution (1989) *Commissioner's Report: Findings and Recommendations*, Halifax: Nova Scotia <http://www.gov.ns.ca/nsarm/virtual/mikmaq/clsl9.asp> Accessed 15 April 2008.

Rozenberg, J. (2004) 'Dog on Death Row Given New Chance' *The Daily Telegraph*, 13 September.

Ryan, B. and Havers, M. (1977) *The Poisoned Life of Mrs Maybrick*, London: Kimber.

Salter M. (2006) [cited in oral evidence] 'House of Commons Select Committee on Home Affairs: The Work of the Criminal Cases Review Commission', HC 1635-i, 10 October.

SCCRC (Scottish Criminal Cases Review Commission) (2006) 'Annual Report and Accounts 2005–06' <http://www.sccrc.org.uk/viewfile.aspx?id=96> Accessed 24 December 2008.

SCCRC (Scottish Criminal Cases Review Commission) (2008a) <http://www.sccrc.org.uk> Accessed 15 April 2008.

SCCRC (Scottish Criminal Cases Review Commission) (2008b) 'About the Commission' <http://www.sccrc.org.uk/home.aspx> Accessed 29 December 2008.

Scheck, B. and Neufeld, P. (2002) 'Toward Formation of "Innocence Commissions" in America' *Judicature* 86(2): 98–105.

Scheck, B. and Neufeld, P. (2008) 'Changing Lives and Laws' The Innocence Project 2007 Annual Report <http://issuu.com/mattjkelley/docs/ 2007_ip_annual_report> Accessed 22 December 2008.

Scheck, B., Neufeld, P. and Dwyer, J. (2000) *Actual Innocence: Five Days to Execution and other Dispatches from the Wrongly Convicted*, New York: New American Library.

Schehr, R. (2005) 'The Criminal Cases Review Commission as State Strategic Selection Mechanism' *American Criminal Law Review* 42(4): 1289–302.

Schehr, R. (2008) 'Shedding the Burden of Sisyphus: International Law and Wrongful Convictions in the United States' *Boston College Third World Law Journal* 28(1): 129–65.

Schehr, R. and Weathered, L. (2004) 'Should the United States Establish a Criminal Cases Review Commission?' *Judicature* 88(3): 122–5.

Schiff, D. and Nobles, R. (1996) 'Criminal Appeal Act 1995: The Semantics of Jurisdiction' *Modern Law Review* 59: 573–81.

Schlesinger, P. and Tumber, H. (1994) *Reporting Crime: The Media Politics of Criminal Justice*, Oxford: Clarendon Press.

Scottish Parliament Justice 1 Committee (2007) *Inquiry into the Scottish Criminal Record Office and the Scottish Fingerprint Service*, vol. 1 <http://www.scottish.parliament.uk/nmCentre/news/news-comm-07/cj107-002.htm> Accessed 24 December 2008.

Scullion, K. (2004) 'Wrongful Convictions and the Criminal Conviction Review Process Pursuant to Section 696.1 of the Criminal Code of Canada' *Canadian Journal of Criminology and Criminal Justice* 46: 189–96.

Seenan, G. (2001) 'Ice Cream War Duo Freed for Appeal' *The Guardian*, 12 December.

Sekar, S. (1997) *Fitted in: Cardiff 3 and the Lynette White Inquiry*, London: The Fitted In Project.

Sengupta, K. (2000) 'Noye "Stabbed Cameron with Considerable Force"' *The Independent*, 7 April.

Simon, J. (2005) 'Parrhesiastic Accountability: Investigatory Commissions and Executive Power in an Age of Terror' *Yale Law Journal* 114: 1419–57.

Sinclair G. (2005) 'Miscarriages of Justice' *The Journal: Magazine of the Law Society of Scotland*, August.

Sparks, R. (1992) *Television and the Drama of Crime: Moral Tales and the Place of Crime in Public Life*, Milton Keynes: Open University Press.

Spencer, J. R. (2006) 'Does Our Present Criminal Appeal System Make Sense?' *Criminal Law Review*: 677–94.

Sutherland Committee (1996) 'Criminal Appeals and Alleged Miscarriages of Justice' Cmnd. 3425, Edinburgh: HMSO.

Taylor, P. (2000) *Taylor on Appeals*, London: Sweet & Maxwell.

Taylor, N. and Mansfield, M. (1999) 'Post-Conviction procedures' in C. Walker and K Starmer (1999) (eds) *Miscarriages of Justice*. London: Blackstone.

The Observer (1992) ' "Murderer" Waits 42 Months for Appeal after Evidence Withdrawn', 17 May.

Trow, M. J. (1990) *'Let Him Have it Chris': The Murder of Derek Bentley*, London: Constable.

United Against Injustice (UAI) (2008) 'Member Organisations' <http://www.unitedagainstinjustice.org.uk/index.html#members> Accessed 20 December 2008.

United States Courts (2005) 'Legal Decisions, Legislation and Forces of Nature Influence Federal Court Caseload in FY 2005' <http://www.uscourts.gov/Press_Releases/judbus031406.html> Accessed 23 December 2008.

United States Statutes At Large (1976) 'Law and Concurrent Resolutions Enacted During the Second Session of the Ninety-Third Congress of the United States of America 1974 and Proclamations', vol. 88, Washington: United States Government Printing Office.

Verkaik, R. (2003) 'Second Pathologist under Scrutiny after Clark Case' *The Independent*, 31 January.

Verkaik, R. (2005) 'Appeal Court Clears Mother of Killing Children' *The Independent*, 12 April.

Walker, C. (2002) *The Anti-Terrorism Legislation*, Oxford: Oxford University Press.

Walker, C. and Broderick, J. (2006) *The Civil Contingencies Act 2004: Risk, Resilience and the Law in the United Kingdom*, Oxford: Oxford University Press.

Walker, C. and McCartney, C. (2008) 'Criminal Justice and Miscarriages of Justice in England and Wales' in Kilias, M. and Huff, R. (2008) (eds) *Wrongful Conviction: International Perspectives on Miscarriages of Justice*, Philadelphia, PA: Temple University Press.

Walker, C. and Starmer, K. (eds) (1999a), *Justice in Error* London: Blackstone.

Walker, C. and Starmer, K. (1999b) *Miscarriages of Justice*, London: Blackstone.

Ward, J. (1993) *Ambushed: My Story*, London: Vermilion.

Weathered, L. (2007) 'Does Australia Need a Specific Institution to Correct Wrongful Convictions?', *Australian and New Zealand Journal of Criminology*, 40(2): 179–98.

Webster, R. (1998) *The Great Children's Home Panic*, Oxford: The Orwell Press.

Webster, R. (2003) 'Appeal Court Recognises Dangers of Police Trawling' <http://www.richardwebster.net/print/xmaybery.htm> Accessed 7 November 2008.

Weedon, J. (2006) [oral evidence] 'House of Commons Select Committee on Home Affairs: The Work of the Criminal Cases Review Commission', HC 1703- i and ii, 10 October.

Woffinden, B. (1987) *Miscarriages of Justice*, London, Toronto, Sydney: Hodder & Stoughton.

Woffinden, B. (1997) *Hanratty: The Final Verdict*, London: Pan Macmillan Publishers.

Woffinden, B. (1998) 'Wrong Again: Sion Jenkins is Innocent' *New Statesman*, 10 July: 28–9.

Woffinden, B. (1999a) 'No, You Can't See. It Might Help Your Client' *The Guardian*, 4 May.

Woffinden, B. (1999b) 'Thumbs Down' *The Guardian*, 12 January.

Woffinden, B. (2003) 'Child Abuse Verdicts Unsafe' *The Guardian*, 15 March.

Wykes, M. (2001) *News, Crime and Culture*, London: Pluto Press.

Young, J. (1971) *The Drug Takers*, London: Paladin.

Zellick, G. (2005) 'Facing up to Miscarriages of Justice', *Mannitoba Law Journal* 31: 555–64.

Zellick, G. (2006) [oral evidence] 'House of Commons Select Committee on Home Affairs: The Work of the Criminal Cases Review Commission', HC 1703- i and ii, 10 October.

Index